Building Microservices with Go

Develop seamless, efficient, and robust microservices with Go

Nic Jackson

BIRMINGHAM - MUMBAI

Building Microservices with Go

First published: July 2017

Production reference: 2100119

Published by Packt Publishing Ltd.
Livery Place
35 Livery Street
Birmingham
B3 2PB, UK.

ISBN 978-1-78646-866-6

www.packtpub.com

Credits

Author
Nic Jackson

Reviewers
Magnus Larsson
Erik Lupander

Commissioning Editor
Kunal Parikh

Acquisition Editor
Karan Sadawana

Content Development Editor
Zeeyan Pinheiro

Technical Editor
Vivek Pala

Copy Editor
Karuna Narayan

Project Coordinator
Vaidehi Sawant

Proofreader
Safis Editing

Indexer
Francy Puthiry

Graphics
Jason Monteiro

Production Coordinator
Nilesh Mohite

About the Author

Nic Jackson is a developer advocate working for HashiCorp.com; he has over 20 years, experience in software development and leading software development teams. A huge fan of mobile application and microservice architecture, he is constantly looking out for the most efficient way to reuse code and improve development flow.

In his spare time, Nic coaches and mentors at Coder Dojo teaches at Women Who Go and GoBridge, speaks and evangelizes good coding practice, process, and technique.

About the Reviewers

Magnus Larsson has been in the IT business since 1986. He is an experienced architect in areas such as distributed systems, systems integration, and SOA. He is currently engaged in exploring the benefits of modern technologies such as microservices, container technologies, reactive frameworks, and mobile solutions.

Magnus has a special dedication to the open source community for Java and has been active in various projects over the years. He enjoys exploring other languages and currently finds the Go language very interesting for building microservices. He is also a frequent speaker at conferences such as Cadec, Spring I/O, Jfokus, and jDays.

Magnus lives outside Gothenburg, Sweden, with his family. When time permits, he enjoys cross-country skiing, which must be done either on roller skis or indoors, in the Gothenburg area for most of the year.

He has worked for large corporations such as Digital Equipment Corporation, AstraZeneca, and Ericsson Hewlett Packard Telecom over the years. In 2000, Magnus co-founded Callista Enterprise AB, a Swedish-based consultancy company specialized in software architecture.

Erik Lupander is a software architect and developer with over 15 years of professional experience. A lifelong computer and software enthusiast, he wrote his first GW-BASIC programs at the age of 7 back in the mid-80s.

Erik holds an M.Sc. in applied informatics from the University of Gothenburg and has worked in a variety of roles in the software industry ever since. While JVM-based languages and architecture has been his bread and butter, he is a polyglot software craftsman at heart who, among other technologies, has embraced the Go programming language and microservice architecture.

Erik has spoken at software conferences such as Scandev (2012), dev:mobile (2014), and Cadec (2016, 2017) about topics ranging from OpenGL ES to Golang and microservices.

He lives just outside Gothenburg, Sweden, with his wife and two children. Aside from family, computers, and software, he enjoys alpine skiing, golf, and running, and he is an avid supporter of IFK Gothenburg.

Erik is currently employed by Callista Enterprise AB, a Swedish-based consultancy specialized in software architecture. His previous employers include Siemens Medical Solutions, Epsilon IT, University of Gothenburg, and Squeed AB.

www.PacktPub.com

For support files and downloads related to your book, please visit `www.PacktPub.com`.

Did you know that Packt offers eBook versions of every book published, with PDF and ePub files available? You can upgrade to the eBook version at `www.PacktPub.com`and as a print book customer, you are entitled to a discount on the eBook copy. Get in touch with us at `service@packtpub.com` for more details.

At `www.PacktPub.com`, you can also read a collection of free technical articles, sign up for a range of free newsletters and receive exclusive discounts and offers on Packt books and eBooks.

`https://www.packtpub.com/mapt`

Get the most in-demand software skills with Mapt. Mapt gives you full access to all Packt books and video courses, as well as industry-leading tools to help you plan your personal development and advance your career.

Why subscribe?

- Fully searchable across every book published by Packt
- Copy and paste, print, and bookmark content
- On demand and accessible via a web browser

Customer Feedback

Thanks for purchasing this Packt book. At Packt, quality is at the heart of our editorial process. To help us improve, please leave us an honest review on this book's Amazon page at `https://www.amazon.com/dp/1786468662`.

If you'd like to join our team of regular reviewers, you can e-mail us at `customerreviews@packtpub.com`. We award our regular reviewers with free eBooks and videos in exchange for their valuable feedback. Help us be relentless in improving our products!

Table of Contents

Preface

Microservice architecture is sweeping the world as the de facto pattern for building web-based applications. Golang is a language particularly well suited to building them. Its strong community, encouragement of idiomatic style, and statically-linked binary artifacts make integrating it with other technologies and managing microservices at scale consistent and intuitive. This book will teach you the common patterns and practices, and show you how to apply these using the Go programming language.

It will teach you the fundamental concepts of architectural design and RESTful communication, and introduce you to the patterns that provide manageable code that is supportable in development and at scale in production. We will provide you with examples of how to put these concepts and patterns into practice with Go.

Whether you are planning a new application or working in an existing monolith, this book will explain and illustrate with practical examples how teams of all sizes can start solving problems with microservices. It will help you understand Docker and Docker Compose, and how they can be used to isolate microservice dependencies and build environments. We will conclude by showing you various techniques to monitor, test, and secure your microservices.

By the end, you will know the benefits of the system resilience of a microservice and the advantages of the Go stack.

What this book covers

`Chapter 1`, *Introduction to Microservices*, looks at what makes the Go language suitable for building microservices and takes a look at the standard library that has all the components required to build a basic microservice. Looking at the standard elements first will give you a grounding and make you appreciate how some of the frameworks that we will discuss later can be incredibly useful.

`Chapter 2`, *Designing a Great API*, looks at what makes a good API. We will introduce both REST and RPC, explaining the differences between them. We will also examine the best practices for writing and versioning APIs.

`Chapter 3`, *Introducing Docker*, explains how you can wrap your application into a Docker image and how you can use Docker and Docker Compose as part of your development workflow. We will see how it is possible to build a small lightweight image for your application and some good practices for using Docker and writing Dockerfiles.

`Chapter 4`, *Testing*, will introduce the various techniques to ensure that your microservices are of the highest quality. We will look at unit testing, behavioral testing, and performance testing, providing you with practical advice and knowledge of the core testing frameworks.

`Chapter 5`, *Common Patterns*, introduces some of the standard patterns often employed in microservice architecture. We will take an in-depth look at load balancing, circuit breaking, service discovery, and the autopilot pattern to see what a Go-specific implementation for this would look like.

`Chapter 6`, *Microservice Frameworks*, builds on frameworks that implement many of the common features needed for a microservice. We will compare and contrast these through examples of their usage.

`Chapter 7`, *Logging and Monitoring*, examines essential techniques to ensure that your service is behaving correctly, and when it does not, ensures you have all the information at your disposal for successful diagnostics and debugging. We will look at using StatsD for simple metrics and timings, how to handle log file information, and approaches to logging more detailed data and platforms such as NewRelic, which provides a holistic overview of your service.

`Chapter 8`, *Security*, takes a look at authentication, authorization, and security for your microservice. We will look at JWT and how you can implement middleware for validating your requests and keeping things secure. We will also look at the bigger picture, looking at why you should implement TLS encryption and a principle of no trust between your services.

`Chapter 9`, *Event-Driven Architecture*, discusses that a common pattern to allow your microservices to collaborate using Events; you will learn about two of the most common eventing patterns and see how you can implement them in Go. We will also look at the introduction of Domain-Driven Design and how the use of a ubiquitous language can help your software development process.

`Chapter 10`, *Continuous Delivery*, discusses the concepts behind continuous delivery. We will then examine in detail a continuous delivery setup for one of the simple applications we created earlier in the book.

What you need for this book

Go compiler for running your Go codes successfully. You can find it on `https://golang.org`.
You also need Docker for container applications. Dockers are available on `https://www.docker.com/`.

Who this book is for

If you are looking to apply techniques to your own projects by taking your first steps into microservice architecture, this book is for you.

Conventions

In this book, you will find a number of text styles that distinguish between different kinds of information. Here are some examples of these styles and an explanation of their meaning.

Code words in text, database table names, folder names, filenames, file extensions, pathnames, dummy URLs, user input, and Twitter handles are shown as follows:

"The `@SpringBootApplication` annotation replaces the different annotation required in the Spring framework."

A block of code is set as follows:

```
@SpringBootApplication
@EnableZuulProxy
public class ApiGatewayExampleInSpring
{
  public static void main(String[] args)
  {
    SpringApplication.run(ApiGatewayExampleInSpring.class, args);
  }
}
```

Any command-line input or output is written as follows:

```
mvn spring-boot:run
```

New terms and **important words** are shown in bold.

Warnings or important notes appear like this.

Tips and tricks appear like this.

Reader feedback

Feedback from our readers is always welcome. Let us know what you think about this book-what you liked or disliked. Reader feedback is important for us as it helps us develop titles that you will really get the most out of. To send us general feedback, simply e-mail `feedback@packtpub.com`, and mention the book's title in the subject of your message. If there is a topic that you have expertise in and you are interested in either writing or contributing to a book, see our author guide at `www.packtpub.com/authors`.

Customer support

Now that you are the proud owner of a Packt book, we have a number of things to help you to get the most from your purchase.

Downloading the example code

You can download the example code files for this book from your account at `http://www.packtpub.com`. If you purchased this book elsewhere, you can visit `http://www.packtpub.com/support` and register to have the files e-mailed directly to you. You can download the code files by following these steps:

1. Log in or register to our website using your e-mail address and password.
2. Hover the mouse pointer on the **SUPPORT** tab at the top.
3. Click on **Code Downloads & Errata**.
4. Enter the name of the book in the **Search** box.

5. Select the book for which you're looking to download the code files.
6. Choose from the drop-down menu where you purchased this book from.
7. Click on **Code Download**.

Once the file is downloaded, please make sure that you unzip or extract the folder using the latest version of:

- WinRAR / 7-Zip for Windows
- Zipeg / iZip / UnRarX for Mac
- 7-Zip / PeaZip for Linux

The code bundle for the book is also hosted on GitHub at `https://github.com/PacktPublishing/Building-Microservices-with-Go`. We also have other code bundles from our rich catalog of books and videos available at `https://github.com/PacktPublishing/`. Check them out!

Errata

Although we have taken every care to ensure the accuracy of our content, mistakes do happen. If you find a mistake in one of our books-maybe a mistake in the text or the code-we would be grateful if you could report this to us. By doing so, you can save other readers from frustration and help us improve subsequent versions of this book. If you find any errata, please report them by visiting `http://www.packtpub.com/submit-errata`, selecting your book, clicking on the **Errata Submission Form** link, and entering the details of your errata. Once your errata are verified, your submission will be accepted and the errata will be uploaded to our website or added to any list of existing errata under the Errata section of that title. To view the previously submitted errata, go to `https://www.packtpub.com/books/content/support` and enter the name of the book in the search field. The required information will appear under the **Errata** section.

Piracy

Piracy of copyrighted material on the Internet is an ongoing problem across all media. At Packt, we take the protection of our copyright and licenses very seriously. If you come across any illegal copies of our works in any form on the Internet, please provide us with the location address or website name immediately so that we can pursue a remedy. Please contact us at `copyright@packtpub.com` with a link to the suspected pirated material. We appreciate your help in protecting our authors and our ability to bring you valuable content.

Questions

If you have a problem with any aspect of this book, you can contact us at `questions@packtpub.com`, and we will do our best to address the problem.

1
Introduction to Microservices

First, we are going to look at how easy it is to create a simple web server with a single endpoint using the `net/http` package. Then, we will move on to examine the `encoding/json` package to see just how easy Go makes it for us to use JSON objects for our requests and our responses. Finally, we will look at how routing and handlers work and how we can manage context between these handlers.

Building a simple web server with net/http

The `net/http` package provides all the features we need to write HTTP clients and servers. It gives us the capability to send requests to other servers communicating using the HTTP protocol as well as the ability to run a HTTP server that can route requests to separate Go funcs, serve static files, and much more.

To begin we should ask the question, *what technical book would be complete without a simple hello world example?* I say none and this is exactly where we will begin.

In this example, we are going to create an HTTP server with a single endpoint that returns static text represented by the JSON standard, this will introduce the basic functions of the HTTP server and handlers. We will then modify this endpoint to accept a request that is encoded in JSON and using the `encoding/json` package return a response to the client. We will also examine how the routing works by adding a second endpoint that returns a simple image.

By the end of this chapter, you will have a fundamental grasp of the basic packages and how you can use them to quickly and efficiently build a simple microservice.

Building a web server in Go is incredibly easy thanks to the HTTP package, which is distributed as part of the standard library.

It has everything you need to manage routing, dealing with **Transport Layer Security** (**TLS**), which we will cover in `Chapter 8`, *Security*, support for HTTP/2 out of the box, and the capability to run an incredibly efficient server that can deal with a huge number of requests.

The source code for this chapter can be found on GitHub at `http://github.com/building-microservices-with-go/chapter1.git`, all the examples in this and subsequent chapters will reference the source extensively so if you have not already done so, go and clone this repo before continuing.

Let's look at the syntax for creating a basic server then we can walk through the packages in more depth:

Example 1.0 `basic_http_example/basic_http_example.go`

```
09 func main() {
10  port := 8080
11
12  http.HandleFunc("/helloworld", helloWorldHandler)
13
14  log.Printf("Server starting on port %v\n", 8080)
15  log.Fatal(http.ListenAndServe(fmt.Sprintf(":%v", port), nil))
16 }
17
18 func helloWorldHandler(w http.ResponseWriter, r *http.Request) {
19   fmt.Fprint(w, "Hello World\n")
20 }
```

The first thing we are doing is calling the `HandleFunc` method on the `http` package. The `HandleFunc` method creates a `Handler` type on the `DefaultServeMux` handler, mapping the path passed in the first parameter to the function in the second parameter:

```
func HandleFunc(pattern string, handler func(ResponseWriter, *Request))
```

In line **15** we start the HTTP server, `ListenAndServe` takes two parameters, the TCP network address to bind the server to and the handler that will be used to route requests:

```
func ListenAndServe(addr string, handler Handler) error
```

In our example, we are passing the network address `:8080"` this means we would like to bind the server to all available IP addresses on port `8080`.

The second parameter we are passing is `nil`, this is because we are using the `DefaultServeMux` handler, which we are setting up with our call to `http.HandleFunc`. In `Chapter 3`, *Introducing Docker*, you will see the use of this second parameter when we introduce more sophisticated routers, but for now we can ignore it.

If the `ListenAndServe` function fails to start a server it will return an error, the most common reason for this is that you may be trying to bind to a port that is already in use on the server. In our example, we are passing the output of `ListenAndServe` straight to `log.Fatal(error)`, which is a convenience function equivalent to calling `fmt.Print(a ...interface{})` followed by a call to `os.Exit(1)`. Since `ListenAndServe` blocks if the server starts correctly we will never exit on a successful start.

Let's quickly run and test our new server:

```
$ go run ./basic_http_example.go
```

You should now see the application output:

```
2016/07/30 01:08:21 Server starting on port 8080
```

What if you do not see the preceding output and instead see something like the following?

```
2016/07/19 03:51:11 listen tcp :8080: bind: address already in use exit
status 1
```

Take another look at the signature of `ListenAndServe` and the way we are calling it. Remember what we were saying about why we were using `log.Fatal`?

If you do get this error message it means that you are already running an application on your computer that is using port `8080`, this could be another instance of your program or it could be another application. You can check that you do not have another instance running by checking the running processes:

```
$ ps -aux | grep 'go run'
```

If you do see another `go run ./basic_http_example.go` then you can simply kill it and retry. If you do not have another instance running, then you probably have some other software that is bound to this port. Try changing the port on line **10** and restart your program.

To test the server, open a new browser and type in the URI `http://127.0.0.1:8080/helloworld` and if things are working correctly you should see the following response from the server:

```
Hello World
```

Congratulations, that's the first step into microservice mastery. Now that we have our first program running, let's take a closer look at how we can return and accept JSON.

Reading and writing JSON

Thanks to the `encoding /json` package, which is built into the standard library encoding and decoding JSON to and from Go types is both fast and easy. It implements the simplistic `Marshal` and `Unmarshal` functions; however, if we need them, the package also provides `Encoder` and `Decoder` types that allow us greater control when reading and writing streams of JSON data. In this section, we are going to examine both of these approaches, but first let's take a look at how simple it is to convert a standard Go `struct` into its corresponding JSON string.

Marshalling Go structs to JSON

To encode JSON data, the `encoding/json` package provides the `Marshal` function, which has the following signature:

```
func Marshal(v interface{}) ([]byte, error)
```

This function takes one parameter, which is of type `interface`, so pretty much any object you can think of since `interface` represents any type in Go. It returns a tuple of `([]byte, error)`, you will see this return style quite frequently in Go, some languages implement a try catch approach that encourages an error to be thrown when an operation cannot be performed, Go suggests the pattern `(return type, error)`, where the error is `nil` when an operation succeeds.

In Go, unhandled errors are a bad thing, and whilst the language does implement `Panic` and `Recover`, which resemble exception handling in other languages, the situations where you should use these are quite different (see *The Go Programming Language*, Kernaghan). In Go, the `panic` function causes normal execution to stop and all deferred function calls in the Go routine are executed, the program will then crash with a log message. It is generally used for unexpected errors that indicate a bug in the code and good robust Go code will attempt to handle these runtime exceptions and return a detailed `error` object back to the calling function.

This pattern is exactly what is implemented with the `Marshal` function. In the instance that `Marshal` cannot create a JSON encoded byte array from the given object, which could be due to a runtime panic, then this is captured and an error object detailing the problem is returned to the caller.

Let's try this out, expanding on our existing example, instead of simply printing a string from our handler, let's create a simple `struct` for the response and return this instead.

Example 1.1 `reading_writing_json_1/reading_writing_json_1.go`

```
type helloWorldResponse struct {
    Message string
}
```

In our handler, we will create an instance of this object, set the message, then use the `Marshal` function to encode it to a string before returning.

Let's see what that will look like:

```
func helloWorldHandler(w http.ResponseWriter, r *http.Request) {
  response := helloWorldResponse{Message: "HelloWorld"}
  data, err := json.Marshal(response)
  if err != nil {
    panic("Ooops")
  }

  fmt.Fprint(w, string(data))
}
```

Now, when we run our program again and refresh our browser, we see the following output rendered in valid JSON:

```
{"Message":"Hello World"}
```

This is awesome; however, the default behavior of `Marshal` is to take the literal name of the field and use this as the field in the JSON output. What if I prefer to use camel case and would rather see "message", could we just rename the field in the `helloWorldResponse` struct?

Unfortunately we can't, as in Go, lowercase properties are not exported, `Marshal` will ignore these and will not include them in the output.

All is not lost as the `encoding/json` package implements `struct` field attributes that allow us to change the output for the property to anything we choose.

Example 1.2 `reading_writing_json_2/reading_writing_json_2.go`

```
type helloWorldResponse struct {
  Message string `json:"message"`
}
```

Using the `struct` field's tags, we can have greater control of how the output will look. In the preceding example, when we marshal this `struct` the output from our server would be:

```
{"message":"Hello World"}
```

This is exactly what we want, but we can use field tags to control the output even further. We can convert object types and even ignore a field altogether if we need to:

```
type helloWorldResponse struct {
// change the output field to be "message"
   Message   string `json:"message"`
   // do not output this field
   Author  string `json:"-"`
   // do not output the field if the value is empty
   Date    string `json:",omitempty"`
   // convert output to a string and rename "id"
   Id    int    `json:"id, string"`
}
```

Channel, complex types, and functions cannot be encoded in JSON; attempting to encode these types will result in an `UnsupportedTypeError` being returned by the `Marshal` function.

It also can't represent cyclic data structures; if your `stuct` contains a circular reference then `Marshal` will result in an infinite recursion, which is never a good thing for a web request.

If we want to export our JSON prettily formatted with indentation, we can use the `MarshallIndent` function, this allows you to pass an additional parameter of `string` to specify what you would like the indent to be. Two spaces right, not a tab?

```
func MarshalIndent(v interface{}, prefix, indent string) ([]byte, error)
```

The astute reader might have noticed that we are decoding our `struct` into a byte array and then writing that to the response stream, this does not seem to be particularly efficient and in fact it is not. Go provides `Encoders` and `Decoders`, which can write directly to a stream, since we already have a stream with the `ResponseWriter` then let's do just that.

Before we do, I think we need to look at the `ResponseWriter` a little to see what is going on there.

The `ResponseWriter` is an interface that defines three methods:

```
// Returns the map of headers which will be sent by the
// WriteHeader method.
Header()

// Writes the data to the connection. If WriteHeader has not
// already been called then Write will call
// WriteHeader(http.StatusOK).
Write([]byte) (int, error)

// Sends an HTTP response header with the status code.
WriteHeader(int)
```

If we have a `ResponseWriter` interface, how can we use this with `fmt.Fprint(w io.Writer, a ...interface{})`? This method requires a `Writer` interface as a parameter and we have a `ResponseWriter` interface. If we look at the signature for `Writer` we can see that it is:

```
Write(p []byte) (n int, err error)
```

Because the `ResponseWriter` interface implements this method, it also satisfies the interface `Writer` and therefore any object that implements `ResponseWriter` can be passed to any function that expects `Writer`.

Amazing, Go rocks, but we have not answered our question, *Is there any better way to send our data to the output stream without marshalling to a temporary object before we return it?*

The `encoding/json` package has a function called `NewEncoder` this returns us an `Encoder` object that can be used to write JSON straight to an open writer and guess what; we have one of those:

```
func NewEncoder(w io.Writer) *Encoder
```

So instead of storing the output of `Marshal` into a byte array, we can write it straight to the HTTP response.

Example 1.3 `reading_writing_json_3/reading_writing_json_3.go`:

```
func helloWorldHandler(w http.ResponseWriter, r *http.Request) {
    response := HelloWorldResponse{Message: "HelloWorld"}
    encoder := json.NewEncoder(w)
    encoder.Encode(&response)
}
```

We will look at benchmarking in a later chapter, but to see why this is important we have created a simple benchmark to check the two methods against each other, have a look at the output.

Example 1.4 `reading_writing_json_2/reading_writing_json_2.go`:

```
$go test -v -run="none" -bench=. -benchtime="5s" -benchmem

BenchmarkHelloHandlerVariable-8  20000000  511 ns/op  248 B/op  5 allocs/op
BenchmarkHelloHandlerEncoder-8  20000000  328 ns/op  24 B/op  2 allocs/op
BenchmarkHelloHandlerEncoderReference-8  20000000  304 ns/op  8 B/op  1
allocs/op
PASS
ok  github.com/building-microservices-with-
go/chapter1/reading_writing_json_2  24.109s
```

Using `Encoder` rather than marshalling to a byte array is nearly 50% faster. We are dealing with nanoseconds here so that time may seem irrelevant, but it isn't; this was two lines of code. If you have that level of inefficiency throughout the rest of your code then your application will run slower, you will need more hardware to satisfy the load and that will cost you money. There is nothing clever in the differences between the two methods all we have done is understood how the standard packages work and chosen the correct option for our requirements, that is not performance tuning, that is understanding the framework.

Unmarshalling JSON to Go structs

Now we have learned how we can send JSON back to the client, what if we need to read input before returning the output? We could use URL parameters and we will see what that is all about in the next chapter, but commonly you will need more complex data structures that involve the service to accept JSON as part of an HTTP `POST` request.

Applying similar techniques that we learned in the previous section to write JSON, reading JSON is just as easy. To decode JSON into a `stuct` field the `encoding/json` package provides us with the `Unmarshal` function:

```
func Unmarshal(data []byte, v interface{}) error
```

The `Unmarshal` function works in the opposite way to `Marshal`; it allocates maps, slices, and pointers as required. Incoming object keys are matched using either the `struct` field name or its tag and will work with a case-insensitive match; however, an exact match is preferred. Like `Marshal`, `Unmarshal` will only set exported `struct` fields, those that start with an upper-case letter.

We start by adding a new `struct` field to represent the request, whilst `Unmarshal` can decode the JSON into an `interface{}`, which would be of `map[string]interface{} // for JSON objects type` or: `[]interface{} // for JSON arrays`, depending if our JSON is an object or an array.

In my opinion it is much clearer to the readers of our code if we explicitly state what we are expecting as a request. We can also save ourselves work by not having to manually cast the data when we come to use it.

Remember two things:

- You do not write code for the compiler, you write code for humans to understand
- You will spend more time reading code than you do writing it

Taking these two points into account we create a simple `struct` to represent our request, which will look like this:

Example 1.5 `reading_writing_json_4/reading_writing_json_4.go`:

```
type helloWorldRequest struct {
  Name string `json:"name"`
}
```

Again, we are going to use `struct` field tags as whilst we could let `Unmarshal` do case-insensitive matching so `{"name": "World}` would correctly unmarshal into the `struct` the same as `{"Name": "World"}`, when we specify a tag we are being explicit about the request form and that is a good thing. In terms of speed and performance it is also about 10% faster, and remember, performance matters.

To access the JSON sent with the request we need to take a look at the `http.Request` object passed to our handler. The following listing does not show all the methods on the request, just the ones we are going to be immediately dealing with, for full documentation I recommend checking out the documentation at `https://godoc.org/net/http#Request`:

```
type Requests struct {
...
  // Method specifies the HTTP method (GET, POST, PUT, etc.).
  Method string

// Header contains the request header fields received by the server. The
type Header is a link to map[string] []string.
Header Header

// Body is the request's body.
Body io.ReadCloser
...
}
```

The JSON that has been sent with the request is accessible in the `Body` field. Body implements the interface `io.ReadCloser` as a stream and does not return a `[]byte` or a `string`. If we need the data contained in the body, we can simply read it into a byte array, as shown in the following example:

```
body, err := ioutil.ReadAll(r.Body)
if err != nil {
     http.Error(w, "Bad request", http.StatusBadRequest)
     return
}
```

Here is something we'll need to remember. We are not calling `Body.Close()`, if we were making a call with a client we would need to do this as it is not automatically closed, however, when used in a `ServeHTTP` handler, the server automatically closes the request stream.

To see how this all works inside our handler, we can look at the following handler:

```
func helloWorldHandler(w http.ResponseWriter, r *http.Request) {

  body, err := ioutil.ReadAll(r.Body)
```

```
    if err != nil {
      http.Error(w, "Bad request", http.StatusBadRequest)
              return
    }

    var request helloWorldRequest
    err = json.Unmarshal(body, &request)
    if err != nil {
      http.Error(w, "Bad request", http.StatusBadRequest)
              return
    }

  response := helloWorldResponse{Message: "Hello " + request.Name}

    encoder := json.NewEncoder(w)
    encoder.Encode(response)
}
```

Let's run this example and see how it works. To test, we can simply use the `curl` command to send a request to the running server. If you feel more comfortable using a GUI tool than Postman (which is available for the Google Chrome browser), they will work just fine or feel free to use your preferred tool:

```
$ curl localhost:8080/helloworld -d '{"name":"Nic"}'
```

You should see the following response:

```
{"message":"Hello Nic"}
```

What do you think will happen if you do not include a body with your request?

```
$ curl localhost:8080/helloworld
```

If you guessed correctly, that you would get a `HTTP status 400 Bad Request`, then you win a prize:

```
func Error(w ResponseWriter, error string, code int)
```

Errors reply to the request with the given message and status code. Once we have sent this, we need to return stopping further execution of the function as this does not close the `ResponseWriter` interface and return flow to the calling function automatically.

Just before you think you are done, have a go and see if you can improve the performance of the handler. Think about the things we were talking about when marshaling JSON.

Got it?

Well if not here is the answer, again all we are doing is using the `Decoder`, which is the opposite of the `Encoder` that we used in writing JSON. It has an instant 33% performance increase and less code too.

Example 1.6 `reading_writing_json_5/reading_writing_json_5.go`:

```
func helloWorldHandler(w http.ResponseWriter, r *http.Request) {

  var request HelloWorldRequest
  decoder := json.NewDecoder(r.Body)

  err := decoder.Decode(&request)
  if err != nil {
    http.Error(w, "Bad request", http.StatusBadRequest)
            return
  }

  response := HelloWorldResponse{Message: "Hello " + request.Name}

  encoder := json.NewEncoder(w)
  encoder.Encode(response)
}
```

Now we can see just how easy it is to encode and decode JSON with Go, I would recommend taking five minutes now to spend some time digging through the documentation for the `encoding/json` package (`https://golang.org/pkg/encoding/json/`) as there is a whole lot more that you can do with this.

Routing in net/http

Even a simple microservice will need the capability to route requests to different handlers dependent on the requested path or method. In Go this is handled by the `DefaultServeMux` method which is an instance of `ServerMux`. Earlier in this chapter, we briefly covered that when nil is passed to the handler parameter for the `ListenAndServe` function then the `DefaultServeMux` method is used. When we call the `http.HandleFunc("/helloworld", helloWorldHandler)` package function we are actually just indirectly calling `http.DefaultServerMux.HandleFunc(…)`.

The Go HTTP server does not have a specific router instead any object which implements the `http.Handler` interface is passed as a top level function to the `Listen()` function, when a request comes into the server the `ServeHTTP` method of this handler is called and it is responsible for performing or delegating any work. To facilitate the handling of multiple routes the HTTP package has a special object called `ServerMux`, which implements the `http.Handler` interface.

There are two functions to adding handlers to a `ServerMux` handler:

```
func HandlerFunc(pattern string, handler func(ResponseWriter, *Request))
func Handle(pattern string, handler Handler)
```

The `HandleFunc` function is a convenience function that creates a handler who's `ServeHTTP` method calls an ordinary function with the `func(ResponseWriter, *Request)` signature that you pass as a parameter.

The `Handle` function requires that you pass two parameters, the pattern that you would like to register the handler and an object that implements the `Handler` interface:

```
type Handler interface {
  ServeHTTP(ResponseWriter, *Request)
}
```

Paths

We already explained how `ServeMux` is responsible for routing inbound requests to the registered handlers, however the way that the routes are matched can be quite confusing. The `ServeMux` handler has a very simple routing model it does not support wildcards or regular expressions, with `ServeMux` you must be explicit about the registered paths.

You can register both fixed rooted paths, such as `/images/cat.jpg`, or rooted subtrees such as `/images/`. The trailing slash in the rooted subtree is important as any request that starts with `/images/`, for example `/images/happy_cat.jpg`, would be routed to the handler associated with `/images/`.

If we register a path `/images/` to the handler foo, and the user makes a request to our service at `/images` (note no trailing slash), then `ServerMux` will forward the request to the `/images/` handler, appending a trailing slash.

If we also register the path `/images` (note no trailing slash) to the handler bar and the user requests `/images` then this request will be directed to bar; however, `/images/` or `/images/cat.jpg` will be directed to foo:

```
http.Handle("/images/", newFooHandler())
http.Handle("/images/persian/", newBarHandler())
http.Handle("/images", newBuzzHandler())
/images                   => Buzz
/images/                  => Foo
/images/cat               => Foo
/images/cat.jpg           => Foo
/images/persian/cat.jpg   => Bar
```

Longer paths will always take precedence over shorter ones so it is possible to have an explicit route that points to a different handler to a catch all route.

We can also specify the hostname, we could register a path such as `search.google.com/` and `/ServerMux` would forward any requests to `http://search.google.com` and `http://www.google.com` to their respective handlers.

If you are used to a framework based application development approach such as using Ruby on Rails or ExpressJS you may find this router incredibly simple and it is, remember that we are not using a framework but the standard packages of Go, the intention is always to provide a basis that can be built upon. In very simple cases the `ServeMux` approach more than good enough and in fact I personally don't use anything else. Everyone's needs are different however and the beauty and simplicity of the standard packages makes it incredibly simple to build your own route as all is needed is an object which implements the `Handler` interface. A quick trawl through google will surface some very good third party routers but my recommendation for you is to learn the limitations of `ServeMux` first before deciding to choose a third-party package it will greatly help with your decision process as you will know the problem you are trying to solve.

Convenience handlers

The `net/http` package implements several methods that create different types of convenience handlers, let's examine these.

FileServer

A `FileServer` function returns a handler that serves HTTP requests with the contents of the filesystem. This can be used to serve static files such as images or other content that is stored on the file system:

```
func FileServer(root FileSystem) Handler
```

Take a look at the following code:

```
http.Handle("/images", http.FileServer(http.Dir("./images")))
```

This allows us to map the contents of the file system path `./images` to the server route `/images`, `Dir` implements a file system which is restricted to a specific directory tree, the `FileServer` method uses this to be able to serve the assets.

NotFoundHandler

The `NotFoundHandler` function returns a simple request handler that replies to each request with a `404 page not found reply`:

```
func NotFoundHandler() Handler
```

RedirectHandler

The `RedirectHandler` function returns a request handler that redirects each request it receives to the given URI using the given status code. The provided code should be in the 3xx range and is usually `StatusMovedPermanently`, `StatusFound`, or `StatusSeeOther`:

```
func RedirectHandler(url string, code int) Handler
```

StripPrefix

The `StripPrefix` function returns a handler that serves HTTP requests by removing the given prefix from the request URL's path and then invoking `h` handler. If a path does not exist, then `StripPrefix` will reply with an HTTP 404 not found error:

```
func StripPrefix(prefix string, h Handler) Handler
```

TimeoutHandler

The `TimeoutHandler` function returns a `Handler` interface that runs `h` with the given time limit. When we investigate common patterns in `Chapter 6`, *Microservice Frameworks*, we will see just how useful this can be for avoiding cascading failures in your service:

```
func TimeoutHandler(h Handler, dt time.Duration, msg string) Handler
```

The new handler calls `h.ServeHTTP` to handle each request, but if a call runs for longer than its time limit, the handler responds with a `503 Service Unavailable` response with the given message `(msg)` in its body.

The last two handlers are especially interesting as they are, in effect, chaining handlers. This is a technique that we will go into more in-depth in a later chapter as it allows you to both practice clean code and also allows you to keep your code DRY.

I may have lifted most of the descriptions for these handlers straight from the Go documentation and you probably have already read these because you have read the documentation right? With Go, the documentation is excellent and writing documentation for your own packages is heavily encouraged, even enforced, if you use the `golint` command that comes with the standard package then this will report areas of your code which do not conform to the standards. I really recommend spending a little time browsing the standard docs when you are using one of the packages, not only will you learn the correct usage, you may learn that there is a better approach. You will certainly be exposed to good practice and style and you may even be able to keep working on the sad day that Stack Overflow stops working and the entire industry grinds to a halt.

Static file handler

Whilst we are mostly going to be dealing with APIs in this book, it is a useful illustration to see how the default router and paths work by adding a secondary endpoint.

As a little exercise, try to modify the code in `reading_writing_json_5/reading_writing_json_5.go` to add an endpoint `/cat`, which returns the cat picture specified in the URI. To give you a little hint, you are going to need to use the `FileServer` function on the `net/http` package and your URI will look something like `http://localhost:8080/cat/cat.jpg`.

Did it work the first time or did you forget to add the `StripPrefix` handler?

Example 1.7 `reading_writing_json_6/reading_writing_json_6.go`:

```
cathandler := http.FileServer(http.Dir("./images"))
http.Handle("/cat/", http.StripPrefix("/cat/", cathandler))
```

In the preceding example, we are registering a `StripPrefix` handler with our path `/cat/`. If we did not do this, then the `FileServer` handler would be looking for our image in the `images/cat` directory. It is also worth reminding ourselves about the difference with `/cat` and `/cat/` as paths. If we registered our path as `/cat` then we would not match `/cat/cat.jpg`. If we register our path as `/cat/`, we will match both `/cat` and `/cat/whatever`.

Creating handlers

We will now finish off our examples here by showing how you can create a `Handler` rather than just using `HandleFunc`. We are going to split the code that performs the request validation for our `helloworld` endpoint and the code that returns the response out into separate handlers to illustrate how it is possible to chain handlers.

Example 1.8 `chapter1/reading_writing_json_7.go`:

```
type validationHandler struct {
  next http.Handler
}

func newValidationHandler(next http.Handler) http.Handler {
  return validationHandler{next: next}
}
```

The first thing we need to do when creating our own `Handler` is to define a `struct` field that will implement the methods in the `Handlers` interface. Since in this example, we are going to be chaining handlers together, the first handler, which is our validation handler, needs to have a reference to the next in the chain as it has the responsibility for calling `ServeHTTP` or returning a response.

For convenience, we have added a function that returns us a new handler; however, we could have just set the next field. This method, however, is better form as it makes our code a little easier to read and when we need to pass complex dependencies to the handler using a function to create, it keeps things a little neater:

```
func (h validationHandler) ServeHTTP(rw http.ResponseWriter, r *http.Request) {
  var request helloWorldRequest
```

```
39    decoder := json.NewDecoder(r.Body)
40
41    err := decoder.Decode(&request)
42    if err != nil {
43      http.Error(rw, "Bad request", http.StatusBadRequest)
44      return
45    }
46
47    h.next.ServeHTTP(rw, r)
48 }
```

The previous code block illustrates how we would implement the `ServeHTTP` method. The only interesting thing to note here is the statement that begins at line **44**. If an error is returned from decoding the request, we write a 500 error to the response, the handler chain would stop here. Only when no error is returned do we call the next handler in the chain and we do this simply by invoking its `ServeHTTP` method. To pass the name decoded from the request, we are simply setting a variable:

```
type helloWorldHandler struct{}

func newHelloWorldHandler() http.Handler {
  return helloWorldHandler{}
}

func (h helloWorldHandler) ServeHTTP(rw http.ResponseWriter, r
*http.Request) {
  response := helloWorldResponse{Message: "Hello " + name}

  encoder := json.NewEncoder(rw)
  encoder.Encode(response)
}
```

The `helloWorldHandler` type that writes the response does not look too different from when we were using a simple function. If you compare this to *example 1.6*, you will see that all we really have done is remove the request decoding.

Now the first thing I want to mention about this code is that it is purely to illustrate how you can do something, not that you should do something. In this simple case, splitting the request validation and response sending into two handlers adds a lot of needless complexity and it is not really making our code DRYer. The technique, however, is useful. When we examine authentication in a later chapter, you will see this pattern as it allows us to centralize our authentication logic and share it among handlers.

Context

The problem with the previous pattern is that there is no way that you can pass the validated request from one handler to the next without breaking the `http.Handler` interface, but guess what Go has us covered. The context package was listed as experimental for several years before finally making it in to the standard package with Go 1.7. The `Context` type implements a safe method for accessing request-scoped data that is safe to use simultaneously by multiple Go routines. Let's take a quick look at this package and then update our example to see it in use.

Background

The `Background` method returns an empty context that has no values; it is typically used by the main function and as the top-level `Context`:

```
func Background() Context
```

WithCancel

The `WithCancel` method returns a copy of the parent context with a cancel function, calling the cancel function releases resources associated with the context and should be called as soon as operations running in the `Context` type are complete:

```
func WithCancel(parent Context) (ctx Context, cancel CancelFunc)
```

WithDeadline

The `WithDeadline` method returns a copy of the parent context that expires after the current time is greater than deadline. At this point, the context's `Done` channel is closed and the resources associated are released. It also passes back a `CancelFunc` method that allows manual cancellation of the context:

```
func WithDeadline(parent Context, deadline time.Time) (Context, CancelFunc)
```

WithTimeout

The `WithTimeout` method is similar to `WithDeadline` except you pass it a duration for which the `Context` type should exist. Once this duration has elapsed, the `Done` channel is closed and the resources associated with the context are released:

```
func WithTimeout(parent Context, timeout time.Duration) (Context,
CancelFunc)
```

WithValue

The `WithValue` method returns a copy of the parent `Context` in which the `val` value is associated with the key. The `Context` values are perfect to be used for request-scoped data:

```
func WithValue(parent Context, key interface{}, val interface{}) Context
```

Why not attempt to modify *example 1.7* to implement a request scoped context. The key could be in the previous sentence; every request needs its own context.

Using contexts

You probably found that rather painful, especially if you come from a background in a framework such as Rails or Spring. Writing this kind of code is not really something you want to be spending your time on, building application features is far more important. One thing to note however is that neither Ruby or Java have anything more advanced in their base packages. Thankfully for us, over the seven years that Go has been in existence, many excellent people have done just that, and when looking at frameworks in `Chapter 3`, *Introducing Docker*, we will find that all of this complexity has been taken care of by some awesome open source authors.

In addition to the adoption of context into the main Go release version 1.7 implements an important update on the `http.Request` structure, we have the following additions:

```
func (r *Request) Context() context.Context
```

The `Context()` method gives us access to a `context.Context` structure which is always non nil as it is populated when the request is originally created. For inbound requests the `http.Server` manages the lifecycle of the context automatically cancelling it when the client connection closes. For outbound requests, `Context` controls cancellation, by this we mean that if we cancel the `Context()` method we can cancel the outgoing request. This concept is illustrated in the following example:

```
70 func fetchGoogle(t *testing.T) {
71   r, _ := http.NewRequest("GET", "https://google.com", nil)
72
73   timeoutRequest, cancelFunc := context.WithTimeout(r.Context(),
1*time.Millisecond)
74   defer cancelFunc()
75
76   r = r.WithContext(timeoutRequest)
77
78   _, err := http.DefaultClient.Do(r)
79   if err != nil {
80     fmt.Println("Error:", err)
81   }
82 }
```

In line **74**, we are creating a timeout context from the original in the request, and unlike an inbound request where the context is automatically cancelled for you we must manually perform this step in an outbound request.

Line **77** implements the second of the two new context methods which have been added to the `http.Request` object:

```
func (r *Request) WithContext(ctx context.Context) *Request
```

The `WithContext` object returns a shallow copy of the original request which has the context changed to the given `ctx` context.

When we execute this function we will find that after 1 millisecond the request will complete with an error:

```
Error: Get https://google.com: context deadline exceeded
```

The context is timing out before the request has a change to complete and the do method immediately returns. This is an excellent technique to use for outbound connections and thanks to the changes in Go 1.7 is now incredibly easy to implement.

What about our inbound connection Let's see how we can update our previous example. Example 1.9 updates our example to show how we can leverage the `context` package to implement Go routine safe access to objects. The full example can be found in `reading_writing_json_8/reading_writing_json_8.go` but all of the modification we need to make are in the two `ServeHTTP` methods for our handlers:

```
41 func (h validationHandler) ServeHTTP(rw http.ResponseWriter, r *http.Request) {
42   var request helloWorldRequest
43   decoder := json.NewDecoder(r.Body)
44
45   err := decoder.Decode(&request)
46   if err != nil {
47     http.Error(rw, "Bad request", http.StatusBadRequest)
48     return
49   }
50
51   c := context.WithValue(r.Context(), validationContextKey("name"), request.Name)
52   r = r.WithContext(c)
53
54   h.next.ServeHTTP(rw, r)
55 }
```

If we take a quick look at our `validationHandler` you will see that when we have a valid request, we are creating a new context for this request and then setting the value of the `Name` field in the request into the context. You might also wonder what is going on with line **51**. When you add an item to a context such as with the `WithValue` call, the method returns a copy of the previous context, to save a little time and add a little confusion, we are holding a pointer to the context, so in order to pass this as a copy to `WithValue`, we must dereference it. To update our pointer, we must also set the returned value to the value referenced by the pointer hence again we need to dereference it. The other think we need to look at with this method call is the key, we are using `validationContextKey` this is an explicitly declared type of string:

```
type validationContextKey string
```

The reason we are not just using a simple string is that context often flows across packages and if we just used string then we could end up with a key clash where one package within your control is writing a `name` key and another package which is outside of your control is also using the context and writing a key called `name`, in this instance the second package would inadvertently overwrite your context value. By declaring a package level type `validationContextKey` and using this we can ensure that we avoid these collisions:

```
func (h helloWorldHandler) ServeHTTP(rw http.ResponseWriter, r
*http.Request) {
  name := r.Context().Value(validationContextKey("name")).(string)
  response := helloWorldResponse{Message: "Hello " + name}

  encoder := json.NewEncoder(rw)
  encoder.Encode(response)
}
```

To retrieve the value, all we have to do is obtain the context and then call the `Value` method casting it into a string.

RPC in the Go standard library

As expected, the Go standard library has fantastic support for RPC right out-of-the-box. Let's look at a few examples of how we can use this.

Simple RPC example

In this simple example, we will see how we can use the standard RPC package to create a client and server that use a shared interface to communicate over RPC. We will follow the typical Hello World example that we ran through when learning the `net/http` package and see just how easy it is to build an RPC-based API in go:

`rpc/server/server.go`:

```
type HelloWorldHandler struct{}

func (h *HelloWorldHandler) HelloWorld(args *contract.HelloWorldRequest,
reply *contract.HelloWorldResponse) error {
  reply.Message = "Hello " + args.Name
  return nil
}
```

Like our example on creating REST APIs using the standard library for RPC, we will also define a handler. The difference between this handler and `http.Handler` is that it does not need to conform to an interface; as long as we have a `struct` field with methods on it we can register this with the RPC server:

```
func Register(rcvr interface{}) error
```

The `Register` function, which is in the `rpc` package, publishes the methods that are part of the given interface to the default server and allows them to be called by clients connecting to the service. The name of the method uses the name of the concrete type, so in our instance if my client wanted to call the `HelloWorld` method, we would access it using `HelloWorldHandler.HelloWorld`. If we do not wish to use the concrete types name, we can register it with a different name using the `RegisterName` function, which uses the provided name instead:

```
func RegisterName(name string, rcvr interface{}) error
```

This would enable me to keep the name of the `struct` field to whatever is meaningful to my code; however, for my client contract I might decide to use something different such as `Greet`:

```
func StartServer() {
  helloWorld := &HelloWorldHandler{}
  rpc.Register(helloWorld)

  l, err := net.Listen("("tcp", fmt.Sprintf(":%(":%v", port))
  if err != nil {
    log.Fatal(fmt.Sprintf("("Unable to listen on given port: %s", err))
  }

  for {
    conn, _ := l.Accept()
    go rpc.ServeConn(conn)
  }
}
```

In the `StartServer` function, we first create a new instance of our handler and then we register this with the default RPC server.

Unlike the convenience of `net/http` where we can just create a server with `ListenAndServe`, when we are using RPC we need to do a little more manual work. In line **23**, we are creating a socket using the given protocol and binding it to the IP address and port. This gives us the capability to specifically select the protocol we would like to use for the server, `tcp`, `tcp4`, `tcp6`, `unix`, or `unixpacket`:

```
func Listen(net, laddr string) (Listener, error)
```

The `Listen()` function returns an instance that implements the `Listener` interface:

```
type Listener interface {
  // Accept waits for and returns the next connection to the listener.
  Accept() (Conn, error)

  // Close closes the listener.
  // Any blocked Accept operations will be unblocked and return errors.
  Close() error

  // Addr returns the listener's network address.
  Addr() Addr
}
```

To receive connections, we must call the `Accept` method on the listener. If you look at line **29**, you will see that we have an endless for loop, this is because unlike `ListenAndServe` which blocks for all connections, with an RPC server we handle each connection individually and as soon as we deal with the first connection we need to continue to again call `Accept` to handle subsequent connections or the application would exit. Accept is a blocking method so if there are no clients currently attempting to connect to the service then `Accept` will block until one does. Once we receive a connection then we need to call the `Accept` method again to process the next connection. If you look at line **30** in our example code, you will see we are calling the `ServeConn` method:

```
func ServeConn(conn io.ReadWriteCloser)
```

The `ServeConn` method runs the `DefaultServer` method on the given connection, and will block until the client completes. In our example, we are using the go statement before running the server so that we can immediately process the next waiting connection without blocking for the first client to close its connection.

In terms of communication protocol, `ServeConn` uses the `gob` wire format `https://golang.org/pkg/encoding/gob/`, we will see when we look at JSON-RPC how we can use a different encoding.

The `gob` format was specifically designed to facilitate Go to Go-based communication and was designed around the idea of something easier to use and possibly more efficient than the likes of protocol buffers, this comes at a cost of cross language communication.

With gobs, the source and destination values and types do not need to correspond exactly, when you send `struct`, if a field is in the source but not in the receiving `struct`, then the decoder will ignore this field and the processing will continue without error. If a field is present in the destination that is not in the source, then again the decoder will ignore this field and will successfully process the rest of the message. Whilst this seems like a minor benefit, it is a huge advancement over the RPC messages of old such as JMI where the exact same interface must be present on both the client and server. This level of inflexibility with JMI introduced tight coupling between the two code bases and caused no end of complexity when it was required to deploy an update to our application.

To make a request to our client we can no longer simply use curl as we are no longer are using the HTTP protocol and the message format is no longer JSON. If we look at the example in `rpc/client/client.go` we can see how to implement a connecting client:

```
13 func CreateClient() *rpc.Client {
14   client, err := rpc.Dial("tcp", fmt.Sprintf("localhost:%v", port))
15   if err != nil {
16     log.Fatal("dialing:", err)
17   }
18
19   return client
20 }
```

The previous block shows how we need to setup `rpc.Client`, the first thing we need to do on line **14** is to create the client itself using the `Dial()` function in the `rpc` package:

```
func Dial(network, address string) (*Client, error)
```

We then use this returned connection to make a request to the server:

```
func PerformRequest(client *rpc.Client)
contract.HelloWorldResponse {
  args := &contract.HelloWorldRequest{Name: "World"}
  var reply contract.HelloWorldResponse

  err := client.Call("HelloWorldHandler.HelloWorld", args, &reply)
  if err != nil {
```

```
28      log.Fatal("error:", err)
29    }
30
31    return reply
32 }
```

In line **26**, we are using the `Call()` method on the client to invoke the named function on the server:

```
func (client *Client) Call(serviceMethod string, args interface{}, reply
interface{}) error
```

`Call` is a blocking function which waits until the server sends a reply writing the response assuming there is no error to the reference of our `HelloWorldResponse` passed to the method and if an error occurs when processing the request this is returned and can be handled accordingly.

RPC over HTTP

In the instance that you need to use HTTP as your transport protocol then the `rpc` package can facilitate this by calling the `HandleHTTP` method.

The `HandleHTTP` method sets up two endpoints in your application:

```
const (
  // Defaults used by HandleHTTP
  DefaultRPCPath   = "/_goRPC_"
  DefaultDebugPath = "/debug/rpc"
)
```

If you point your browser at the `DefaultDebugPath` you can see details for the registered endpoints, there are two things to note:

- This does not mean you can communicate easily with your API from a web browser. The messages are still `gob` encoded so you would need to write a gob encoder and decoder in JavaScript, which I am not actually sure is possible. It was certainly never the intent of the package to support this capability and therefore I would not advise this action, a JSON or JSON-RPC based message is much better suited to this use case.
- The debug endpoint is not going to provide you with auto-generated documentation for your API. The output is fairly basic and the intention seems to be so you can track the number of calls made to an endpoint.

All that said there may be a reason why you need to use HTTP, possibly your network does not allow any other protocol or potentially you have a load balancer that is not capable of dealing with pure TCP connections. We can also take advantage of HTTP headers and other metadata which is not available using a pure TCP request.

`rpc_http/server/server.go`

```
22 func StartServer() {
23   helloWorld := &HelloWorldHandler{}
24   rpc.Register(helloWorld)
25   rpc.HandleHTTP()
26
27   l, err := net.Listen("tcp", fmt.Sprintf(":%v", port))
28   if err != nil {
29       log.Fatal(fmt.Sprintf("Unable to listen on given port: %s", err))
30   }
31
32   log.Printf("Server starting on port %v\n", port)
33
34   http.Serve(l, nil)
35 }
```

If we look at line **25**, in the preceding example, we can see we are calling the `rpc.HandleHTTP` method, this is a requirement using HTTP with RPC as it will register the HTTP handlers we mentioned earlier with the `DefaultServer` method. We then call the `http.Serve` method and pass it the listener we are creating in line **27**, we are setting the second parameter to be `nil` as we wish to use the `DefaultServer` method. This is exactly the same method that we looked at in the previous examples when we were looking at RESTful endpoints.

JSON-RPC over HTTP

In this last example, we will look at the `net/rpc/jsonrpc` package that provides a built-in codec for serializing and deserializing to the JSON-RPC standard. We will also look at how we can send these responses over HTTP, whilst you may ask why not just use REST, and to some extent I will agree with you, it is an interesting example to be able to see how we can extend the standard framework.

The `StartServer` method contains nothing we have not seen before it is the standard `rpc` server setup, the main difference is line **42** where instead of starting the RPC server we are starting an `http` server and passing the listener to it along with a handler:

`rpc_http_json/server/server.go`

```
33 func StartServer() {
34  helloWorld := new(HelloWorldHandler)
35  rpc.Register(helloWorld)
36
37  l, err := net.Listen("tcp", fmt.Sprintf(":%v", port))
38  if err != nil {
39    log.Fatal(fmt.Sprintf("Unable to listen on given port: %s", err))
40  }
41
42 http.Serve(l, http.HandlerFunc(httpHandler))
43 }
```

The handler we are passing to the server is where the magic happens:

```
45 func httpHandler(w http.ResponseWriter, r *http.Request) {
46   serverCodec := jsonrpc.NewServerCodec(&HttpConn{in: r.Body, out: w})
47   err := rpc.ServeRequest(serverCodec)
48   if err != nil {
49     log.Printf("Error while serving JSON request: %v", err)
50   http.Error(w, "Error while serving JSON request, details have been
logged.", 500)
51   return
52   }
53 }
```

In line **46**, we are calling the `jsonrpc.NewServerCodec` function and passing to it a type that implements `io.ReadWriteCloser`. The `NewServerCodec` method returns a type that implements `rpc.ClientCodec`, which has the following methods:

```
type ClientCodec interface {
  // WriteRequest must be safe for concurrent use by multiple goroutines.
  WriteRequest(*Request, interface{}) error
  ReadResponseHeader(*Response) error
  ReadResponseBody(interface{}) error

  Close() error
}
```

A `ClientCodec` type implements the writing of RPC request and reading RPC responses. To write a request to the connection a client calls the `WriteRequest` method. To read the response, the client must call `ReadResponseHeader` and `ReadResponseBody` as a pair. Once the body has been read, it is the client's responsibility to call the `Close` method to close the connection. If a nil interface is passed to `ReadResponseBody` then the body of the response should be read and then discarded:

```
type HttpConn struct {
  in  io.Reader
  out io.Writer
}

func (c *HttpConn) Read(p []byte) (n int, err error)  { return c.in.Read(p) }
func (c *HttpConn) Write(d []byte) (n int, err error) { return c.out.Write(d) }
func (c *HttpConn) Close() error                      { return nil }
```

The `NewServerCodec` method requires that we pass it a type that implements the `ReadWriteCloser` interface. As we do not have such a type passed to us as parameters in the `httpHandler` method we have defined our own type, `HttpConn`, which encapsulates the `http.Request` body, which implements `io.Reader`, and the `ResponseWriter` method, that implements `io.Writer`. We can then write our own methods that proxy the calls to the reader and writer creating a type that has the correct interface.

And that is it for our short intro to RPC with the standard libraries; we will see when we look at some frameworks more in depth in `Chapter 3`, *Introducing Docker*, how these can be used to build a production microservice.

Summary

That's it for this chapter, we have just written our first microservice in Go and only using the standard library, you should now have an appreciation of just how powerful the standard library is providing us with many of the features we need to write RESTful and RPC-based microservices. We have also looked at encoding and decoding data using the `encoding/json` package and how we can create light weight messaging by using `gobs`.

As you progress through this book, you will see how the many, wonderful open source packages build on these foundations to make Go such a fantastic language for microservice development, and by the end of the book you will have all the knowledge required for successfully building microservices in Go.

2
Designing a Great API

Regardless of whether you are experienced in building APIs and microservices and looking for the techniques on how you can apply them with Go or you are completely new to the world of microservices, it is worth spending the time to read this chapter.

Writing an API contract feels part art, part science and, when you discuss your design with other engineers, you will most certainly agree to disagree, not to the level of tabs versus spaces, but there is certainly something personal about API contracts.

In this chapter, we will look at the two most popular options, which are RESTful and RPC. We will examine the semantics of each approach, which will equip you with the knowledge to argue your case when the inevitable discussion (read argument) occurs. Choosing between REST or RPC may be entirely down to your current environment. If you currently have services running that implement a RESTful approach, then I suggest you stick with it, likewise if you now use RPC. One thing I would suggest is that you read the entire chapter to understand the semantics, pros, and cons of each approach.

RESTful APIs

The term **REST** was suggested by Roy Fielding in his Ph.D. dissertation in the year 2000. It stands for **Representational State Transfer** and is described as:

> *"REST emphasizes scalability of component interactions, generality of interfaces, independent deployment of components, and intermediary components to reduce interaction latency, enforce security and encapsulate legacy systems."*

Having an API that conforms to the REST principles is what makes it RESTful.

URIs

One of the main components in the HTTP protocol is a URI. **URI** stands for **Uniform Resource Identifiers** and is the method by which you will access the API. You may be asking what the difference between a URI and a URL (Uniform Resource Locator) is? When I started to write this chapter, I wondered about this myself and did what any self-respecting developer would do, which is to head over to Stack Overflow. Unfortunately, my confusion only grew as there were lots of detailed answers, none of which I found particularly enlightening. Time to head over to the inner circle of hell also known as W3C standards to look up the RFC for the official answer.

In short, there is no difference, a URL is a URI that identifies a resource by its network location, and it is acceptable to interchange the terms when describing a resource entirely.

The clarification document published back in 2001 (`http://www.w3.org/TR/uri-clarification`) goes on to explain that in the early to mid-90s there was an assumption that an identifier is cast into one or two classes. An identifier might specify the location of a resource (URL) or its name (Uniform Resource Name URN) independent of location. A URI could either be a URL or a URN. Using this example, `http://` would be a URL scheme and `isbn:` a URN scheme. However, this changed over time and the importance of the additional level of hierarchy lessened. The view changed that an individual scheme does not need to be cast into one of a discrete set of types.

The conventional approach is that `http:` is a URI scheme and `urn:` is also a URI scheme. URNs take the form `urn:isbn:n-nn-nnnnnn-n`, `isbn:` is a URN namespace identifier, not a URN scheme or a URI scheme.

Following this view, the term URL does not refer to a formal partition of URI space rather, URL is an informal concept; a URL is a type of URI that identifies a resource via its network location.

For the rest of this book, we will use the term URI and when we do we will be talking about a method to access a resource that is running on a remote server.

URI format

RFC 3986, which was published in 2005 `https://www.ietf.org/rfc/rfc3986.txt`, defines the format that makes valid URIs:

```
URI = scheme "://" authority "/" path [ "?" query] ["#" fragment"]
URI = http://myserver.com/mypath?query=1#document
```

We are will use the path element in order to locate an endpoint that is running on our server. In a REST endpoint, this can contain parameters as well as a document location. The query string is equally important, as you will use this to pass parameters such as page number or ordering to control the data that is returned.

Some general rules for URI formatting:

- A forward slash / is used to indicate a hierarchical relationship between resources
- A trailing forward slash / should not be included in URIs
- Hyphens - should be used to improve readability
- Underscores _ should not be used in URIs
- Lowercase letters are preferred as case sensitivity is a differentiator in the `path` part of a URI

The concept behind many of the rules is that a URI should be easy to read and to construct. It should also be consistent in the way that it is built so you should follow the same taxonomy for all the endpoints in your API.

URI path design for REST services

Paths are broken into documents, collections, stores, and controllers.

Collections

A collection is a directory of resources typically broken by parameters to access an individual document. For example:

```
GET /cats   -> All cats in the collection
GET /cats/1 -> Single document for a cat 1
```

When defining a collection, we should always use a plural noun such as `cats` or `people` for the collection name.

Documents

A document is a resource pointing to a single object, similar to a row in a database. It has the ability to have child resources that may be both sub-documents or collections. For example:

```
GET /cats/1           -> Single document for cat 1
GET /cats/1/kittens   -> All kittens belonging to cat 1
GET /cats/1/kittens/1 -> Kitten 1 for cat 1
```

Controller

A controller resource is like a procedure, this is typically used when a resource cannot be mapped to standard **CRUD** (**create**, **retrieve**, **update**, and **delete**) functions.

The names for controllers appear as the last segment in a URI path with no child resources. If the controller requires parameters, these would typically be included in the query string:

```
POST /cats/1/feed            -> Feed cat 1
POST /cats/1/feed?food=fish ->Feed cat 1 a fish
```

When defining a controller name we should always use a verb. A verb is a word that indicates an action or a state of being, such as `feed` or `send`.

Store

A store is a client-managed resource repository, it allows the client to add, retrieve, and delete resources. Unlike a collection, a store will never generate a new URI it will use the one specified by the client. Take a look at the following example that would add a new cat to our store:

```
PUT /cats/2
```

This would add a new cat to the store with an ID of `2`, if we had posted the new cat omitting the ID to a collection the response would need to include a reference to the newly defined document so we could later interact with it. Like controllers we should use a plural noun for store names.

CRUD function names

When designing great REST URIs we never use a CRUD function name as part of the URI, instead we use a HTTP verb. For example:

```
DELETE /cats/1234
```

We do not include the verb in the name of the method as this is specified by the HTTP verb, the following URIs would be considered an anti-pattern:

```
GET /deleteCat/1234
DELETE /deleteCat/1234
POST /cats/1234/delete
```

When we look at HTTP verbs in the next section this will make more sense.

HTTP verbs

The commonly used HTTP verbs are:

- `GET`
- `POST`
- `PUT`
- `PATCH`
- `DELETE`
- `HEAD`
- `OPTIONS`

Each of these methods has a well-defined semantic within the context of our REST API and the correct implementation will help your user understand your intention.

GET

The `GET` method is used to retrieve a resource and should never be used to mutate an operation, such as updating a record. Typically, a body is not passed with a `GET` request; however, it is not an invalid `HTTP` request to do so.

Request:

```
GET /v1/cats HTTP/1.1
```

Response:

```
HTTP/1.1 200 OK
Content-Type: application/json
Content-Length: xxxx

{"name": "Fat Freddie's Cat", "weight": 15}
```

POST

The `POST` method is used to create a new resource in a collection or to execute a controller. It is typically a non-idempotent action, in that multiple posts to create an element in a collection that will create multiple elements not updated after the first call.

The `POST` method is always used when calling controllers as the actions of this is considered non-idempotent.

Request:

```
POST /v1/cats HTTP/1.1
Content-Type: application/json
Content-Length: xxxx

{"name": "Felix", "weight": 5}
```

Response:

```
HTTP/1.1 201 Created
Content-Type: application/json
Content-Length: 0
Location: /v1/cats/12343
```

PUT

The `PUT` method is used to update a mutable resource and must always include the resource locator. The `PUT` method calls are also idempotent in that multiple requests will not mutate the resource to a different state than the first call.

Request:

```
PUT /v1/cats HTTP/1.1
Content-Type: application/json
Content-Length: xxxx

{"name": "Thomas", "weight": 7 }
```

Response:

```
HTTP/1.1 201 Created
Content-Type: application/json
Content-Length: 0
```

PATCH

The `PATCH` verb is used to perform a partial update, for example, if we only wanted to update the name of our cat we could make a `PATCH` request only containing the details that we would like to change.

Request:

```
PATCH /v1/cats/12343 HTTP/1.1
Content-Type: application/json
Content-Length: xxxx

{"weight": 9}
```

Response:

```
HTTP/1.1 204 No Body
Content-Type: application/json
Content-Length: 0
```

In my experience PATCH updates are rarely used, the general convention is to use a PUT and to update the whole object, this not only makes the code easier to write but also makes an API which is simpler to understand.

DELETE

The `DELETE` verb is used when we want to remove a resource, generally we would pass the ID of the resource as part of the path rather than in the body of the request. This way, we have a consistent method for updating, deleting, and retrieving a document.

Request:

```
DELETE /v1/cats/12343 HTTP/1.1
Content-Type: application/json
Content-Length: 0
```

Response:

```
HTTP/1.1 204 No Body
Content-Type: application/json
Content-Length: 0
```

HEAD

A client would use the `HEAD` verb when they would like to retrieve the headers for a resource without the body. The `HEAD` verb is typically used in place of a `GET` verb when a client only wants to check if a resource exists or to read the metadata.

Request:

```
HEAD /v1/cats/12343 HTTP/1.1
Content-Type: application/json
Content-Length: 0
```

Response:

```
HTTP/1.1 200 OK
Content-Type: application/json
Last-Modified: Wed, 25 Feb 2004 22:37:23 GMT
Content-Length: 45
```

OPTIONS

The `OPTIONS` verb is used when a client would like to retrieve the possible interactions for a resource. Typically, the server will return an `Allow` header, which will include the `HTTP` verbs that can be used with this resource.

Request:

```
OPTIONS /v1/cats/12343 HTTP/1.1
Content-Length: 0
```

Response:

```
HTTP/1.1 200 OK
Content-Length: 0
Allow: GET, PUT, DELETE
```

URI query design

It is perfectly acceptable to use a query string as part of an API call; however, I would refrain from using this to pass data to the service. Instead the query should be used to perform actions such as:

- Paging
- Filtering
- Sorting

If we need to make a call to a controller, we discussed earlier that we should use a `POST` request as this is most likely a non-idempotent request. To pass data to the service, we should include the data inside of the body. However, we could use a query string to filter the action of the controller:

```
POST /sendStatusUpdateEmail?$group=admin
{
  "message": "All services are now operational\nPlease accept our
             apologies for any inconvenience caused.\n
             The Kitten API team"
}
```

In the preceding example, we would send a status update email with the message included in the body of the request, because we are using the group filter passed in the query string we could restrict the action of this controller to only send to the admin group.

If we had added the message to the query string and not passed a message body, then we would potentially be causing two problems for ourselves. The first is that the max length for a URI is 2083 characters. The second is that generally a `POST` request would always include a request body. Whilst this is not required by the `HTTP` specification, it would be expected behavior by the majority of your users.

Response codes

When writing a great API, we should use `HTTP` status codes to indicate to the client the success or failure of the request. In this chapter, we will not be taking a comprehensive look at all the status codes available; there are many resources on the Internet that have this information. We will provide some sources for further reading, what we will do is look at the status codes that you as a software engineer will want your microservice to return.

Currently, it is a generally held consensus that this is good practice as it allows the client to immediately determine the status of a request without having to dive into the request body to gain further insight. In the instance of a failure and APIs that always return a `200 OK` response to the user with a message body containing further information is not good practice as it requires the client to have to inspect the body to determine outcome. It also means that the message body will contain additional information other than the object that it should represent. Consider the following bad practice:

Bad request body:

```
POST /kittens
RESPONSE HTTP 200 OK
{
  "status": 401,
  "statusMessage": "Bad Request"
}
```

Successful request:

```
POST /kittens
RESPONSE HTTP 201 CREATED
{
  "status": 201,
  "statusMessage": "Created",
  "kitten": {
    "id": "1234334dffdf23",
    "name": "Fat Freddy'sFreddy's Cat"
  }
}
```

Imagine if you were writing a client for the preceding request, you need to add logic to your application to check the status node in the response before you could read and process the returned kitten.

Now consider something even worse:

And even worse failure:

```
POST /kittens
RESPONSE HTTP 200 OK
{
  "status": 400,
  "statusMessage": "Bad Request"
}
```

And even worse success:

```
POST /kittens
RESPONSE HTTP 200 OK
{
  "id": "123434jhjh3433",
  "name": "Fat Freddy'sFreddy's Cat"
}
```

If your API author had done something like the preceding example, you need to check to see if the response that has been returned is an error or the kitten that you were expecting. The number of WTFs per minute you would utter whilst coding a client for this API would not endear you to its author. These might seem like extreme examples, but there are instances like this out in the wild, at some point in my career I'm fairly sure I have been guilty of such a crime, but then I had not read this book.

What the author in their best intention has done is try to take the HTTP status codes too literally. W3C RFC2616 states that the HTTP status code relates to the attempt to understand and satisfy the request (`https://www.w3.org/Protocols/rfc2616/rfc2616-sec6.html#sec6.1.1`); however, this is a little ambiguous when you look at some of the individual status codes. Modern consensus is that it is OK to use HTTP status codes to indicate the processing state of an API request not just the server's ability to process the request. Consider how we could make these requests better by implementing this approach.

A good example of a failure:

```
POST /kittens
RESPONSE HTTP 400 BAD REQUEST
{
  "errorMessage": "Name should be between 1 and 256 characters in
  length and only contain [A-Z] - ['-.]"
}
```

A good example of a success:

```
POST /kittens
RESPONSE HTTP 201 CREATED
{
  "id": "123hjhjh2322",
  "name": "Fat Freddy'sFreddy's cat"
}
```

This is far more semantic; the user only ever needs to read the response in the instance of a failure if they require further information. In addition to this we can provide a standard error object that is used across all the endpoints of our API, which provides further but non-required information to determine why a request failed. We will look at error objects in a little while, but for now let's look at HTTP status codes more in depth.

2xx Success

2xx status codes indicate that the clients request has been successfully received and understood.

200 OK

This is a generic response code indicating that the request has succeeded. The response accompanying this code is generally:

- `GET`: An, an entity corresponding to the requested resource
- `HEAD`: The, the header fields corresponding to the requested resource without the message body
- `POST`: An, an entity describing or containing the result of the action

201 Created

The created response is sent when a request succeeds and the result is that a new entity has been created. Along with the response it is common that the API will return a `Location` header with the location of the newly created entity:

```
201 Created
Location: https://api.kittens.com/v1/kittens/123dfdf111
```

It is optional to return an object body with this response type.

204 No Content

This status informs the client that the request has been successfully processed; however, there will be no message body with the response. For example, if the user makes a `DELETE` request to the collection then the response may return a 204 status.

3xx Redirection

The 3xx indicate class of status codes indicates that the client must take additional action to complete the request. Many of these status codes are used by CDNs and other content redirection techniques, however, code 304 can exceptionally useful when designing our APIs to provide semantic feedback to the client.

301 Moved Permanently

This tells the client that the resource they have requested has been permanently moved to a different location. Whilst this is traditionally used to redirect a page or resource from a web server it can also be useful to us when we are building our APIs. In the instance that we rename a collection we could use a 301 redirect to send the client to the correct location. This however should be used as an exception rather than the norm. Some clients do not implicitly follow 301 redirect and implementing this capability adds additional complexity for your consumers.

304 Not Modified

This response is generally used by a CDN or caching server and is set to indicate that the response has not been modified since the last call to the API. This is designed to save bandwidth and the request will not return a body, but will return a `Content-Location` and `Expires` header.

4xx Client Error

In the instance of an error caused by a client, not the server, the server will return a 4xx response and will always return an entity that gives further details on the error.

400 Bad Request

This response indicates that the request could not be understood by the client due to a malformed request or due to a failure of domain validation (missing data, or an operation that would cause invalid state).

401 Unauthorized

This indicates that the request requires user authentication and will include a `WWW-Authenticate` header containing a challenge applicable to the requested resource. If the user has included the required credentials in the `WWW-Authenticate` header, then the response should include an error object that may contain relevant diagnostic information.

403 Forbidden

The server has understood the request, but is refusing to fulfill it. This could be due to incorrect access level to a resource not that the user is not authenticated.

If the server does not wish to make the fact that a request is not able to access a resource due to access level public, then it is permissible to return a `404 Not found` status instead of this response.

404 Not Found

This response indicates that the server has not found anything matching the requested URI. No indication is given of whether the condition is temporary or permanent.

It is permissible for the client to make multiple requests to this endpoint as the state may not be permanent.

405 Method Not Allowed

The method specified in the request is not allowed for the resource indicated by the URI. This may be when the client attempts to mutate a collection by sending a `POST`, `PUT`, or `PATCH` to a collection that only serves retrieval of documents.

408 Request Timeout

The client did not produce a request within the time that the server is prepared to wait. The client may repeat the request without modification at a later time.

5xx Server Error

Response status codes within the 500 range indicate that something has gone "Bang", the server knows this and is sorry for the situation.

The RFC advises that an error entity should be returned in the response explaining whether this is permanent or temporary and containing an explanation of the error. When we look at our chapter on security we will look at the recommendation about not giving too much information away in error messages as this state may have been engineered by a user in the attempt to compromise your system and by returning things such as a stack trace or other internal information with a 5xx error can actually help to compromise your system. With this in mind it is currently common that a 500 error will just return something very generic.

500 Internal Server Error

A generic error message indicating that something did not go quite as planned.

503 Service Unavailable

The server is currently unavailable due to temporary overloading or maintenance. There is a rather useful pattern that you can implement to avoid cascading failure in the instance of a malfunction in which the microservice will monitor its internal state and in the case of failure or overloading will refuse to accept the request and immediately signal this to the client. We will look at this pattern more in chapter xx; however, this instance is probably where you will be wanting to return a 503 status code. This could also be used as part of your health checks.

HTTP headers

Request headers are a really important part of the HTTP request and response process and implementing a standard approach helps your users to transition from one API to another. In this sub section, we will not cover all the possible headers that you can use in your API, but we will look at the most common headers for full information on the HTTP protocol please take a look at RFC 7231 `https://tools.ietf.org/html/rfc7231`. This document contains a comprehensive overview of the current standard.

Standard request headers

Request headers provide additional information for the request and the response of your API. Think of them like metadata for the operation. They can be used to augment other data for the response that does not belong in the body itself such as the content encoding. They can also be utilized by the client to provide information that can help the server process the response. Where possible we should always use the standard headers as this gives consistency to your user and provides them with a common standard across multiple endpoints from many different vendors.

Authorization - string

Authorization is one of the most commonly used request headers, even if you have a public read only API I advise you to ask the user to authorize their requests. By requesting that the user authorizes a request, you have the capability to perform operations such as user level logging and rate limiting. Quite often you may see authorization conducted with a custom request header such as "X-API-Authorization". I would recommend you do not use this approach as the standard Authorization header as specified by the W3C RFC 2616 (`https://www.w3.org/Protocols/rfc2616/rfc2616-sec14.html`) has all the capability we need. Many companies such as Twitter and PayPal use this header to authenticate requests let's. Let's look at a simple example from Twitter's developer documentation to see how this can be implemented:

```
Authorization:
        OAuth oauth_consumer_key="xvz1evFS4wEEPTGEFPHBog",
              oauth_nonce="kYjzVBB8Y0ZFabxSWbWovY3uYSQ2pTgmZeNu2VS4cg",
              oauth_signature="tnnArxj06cWHq44gCs1OSKk%2FjLY%3D",
              oauth_signature_method="HMAC-SHA1",
              oauth_timestamp="1318622958",
              oauth_token="370773112-
GmHxMAgYyLbNEtIKZeRNFsMKPR9EyMZeS9weJAEb",
              oauth_version="1.0"
```

The header is in the form of `[Authorization method] [Comma separated URL encoded values]`. This clearly informs the server that the authorization type is OAuth and the various components of this authorization follow this in a comma delaminated format. By following this standard approach you can enable your consumers to use a third-party library that implements this standard and thus save them the work of having to build a bespoke implementation.

Date

Timestamp of the request in RFC 3339 format.

Accept - content type

The requested content type for the response, such as:

- `application/xml`
- `text/xml`
- `application/json`
- `text/javascript` (for JSONP)

Accept-Encoding - gzip, deflate

REST endpoints should always support gzip and deflate encoding, when applicable.

Implementing gzip support in Go is relatively straightforward; we showed how it is possible to implement middleware into your microservices in `Chapter 1`, *Introduction to Microservices*. In the following example, we will use this technique to create a gzip response writer.

The core of writing a response in a gzipped format is the `compress/gzip` package, which is part of the standard library. It allows you to create a `Writer` interface that implements `ioWriteCloser` wrapping an existing `io.Writer`, which writes to the given writer using the gzip compression:

```
func NewWriter(w io.Writer) *Writer
```

To create our handler we are going to write the `NewGzipHandler` function, this returns a new `http.Handler` that will wrap our standard output handler.

The first thing we need to do is create our own `ResponseWriter` that embeds `http.ResponseWriter`.

Example 2.1 `chapter2/gzip/gzip_deflate.go`:

```
type GzipResponseWriter struct {
  gw *gzip.Writer
  http.ResponseWriter
}
```

The core method for this is the implementation of the `Write` method:

```
func (w GzipResponseWriter) Write(b []byte) (int, error) {
  if _, ok := w.Header()["Content-Type"] !ok {
    // If content type is not set, infer it from the uncompressed body.
  w.Header().Set("Content-Type", http.DetectContentType(b))
  }
  return w.gw.Write(b)
}
```

If you look at the implementation for `Write` in the standard `http.Response` struct there is a whole load of stuff going on in there that we neither want to lose or re-implement because the `gzip.Writer` object is created with a writer when we call `Write` on it, it then in turn calls write on `http.Response` and we lose none of the complexity.

Internally in our `NewGzipHandler` our handler checks to see if the client has sent the `Accept-Encoding` header and if so we will write the response using the `GzipResponseWriter` method if the client has requested uncompressed content then we only call `ServeHttp` with the standard `ResponseWriter`:

```
type GZipHandler struct {
 next http.Handler
}

func (h *GZipHandler) ServeHTTP(w http.ResponseWriter, r *http.Request) {
 encodings := r.Header.Get("Accept-Encoding")

 if strings.Contains(encodings, "gzip") {
     h.serveGzipped(w, r)
 } else if strings.Contains(encodings, "deflate") {
     panic("Deflate not implemented")
 } else {
     h.servePlain(w, r)
 }
}

func (h *GZipHandler) serveGzipped(w http.ResponseWriter, r *http.Request) {
 gzw := gzip.NewWriter(w)
 defer gzw.Close()

 w.Header().Set("Content-Encoding", "gzip")
 h.next.ServeHTTP(GzipResponseWriter{gzw, w}, r)
}

func (h *GZipHandler) servePlain(w http.ResponseWriter, r *http.Request)
{
 h.next.ServeHTTP(w, r)
}
```

This is by no means a comprehensive example and there are many open source packages like the one from the team at the NY Times (`https://github.com/NYTimes/gziphandler`), which manages this for you.

As a little programming test, why not try and modify this example to implement `DEFLATE`.

Standard response headers

All services should return the following headers.

- `Date`: The date that the request was processed in RFC 3339 format.
- `Content-Type`: The content type of the response.
- `Content-Encoding`: gzip or deflate.
- `X-Request-ID/X-Correlation-ID`: Whilst you may not directly request your clients to implement this header it may be something that you add to requests when you call downstream services. When you are trying to debug a service that is running in production it can be incredibly useful to be able to group all the requests by a single transaction ID. A common practice that we will see when we look at logging and monitoring is to store all logs in a common database such as Elastic Search. By setting the standard way of working when building many connected microservices that they pass the correlation ID with each downstream call you will be able to query your logs in Kibana or another log query tool and group them into a single transaction:

  ```
  X-Request-ID: f058ebd6-02f7-4d3f-942e-904344e8cde
  ```

Returning errors

In the instance of failure, users of your API should be able to write one piece of code that handles errors across different endpoints. A standard error entity will help your consumers by enabling them to write DRY code whenever an error caused by client or server occurs.

The Microsoft API guidelines recommend the following format for these entities:

```
{
  "error": {
    "code": "BadArgument",
    "message": "Previous passwords may not be reused",
    "target": "password",
    "innererror": a {
      "code": "PasswordError",
  "innererror": {
    "code": "PasswordDoesNotMeetPolicy",
    "minLength": "6",
    "maxLength": "64",
    "characterTypes": ["lowerCase","upperCase","number","symbol"],
    "minDistinctCharacterTypes": "2",
    "innererror": {
      "code": "PasswordReuseNotAllowed"
    }
```

```
            }
        }
    }
}
```

ErrorResponse: Object

The `ErrorResponse` is the top level object which will be returned by our response and contains the following fields:

Property	**Type**	**Required**	**Description**
error	Error	✓	The error object.

Error: Object

The `Error` object is the detail for our error response; it provides full detail for the reason that the error occurred:

Property	**Type**	**Required**	**Description**
Code	`String` (enumerated)	✓	One of a server-defined set of error codes.
Message	`String`	✓	A human-readable representation of the error.
Target	`String`	-	The target of the error.
Details	`Error[]`	-	An array of details about specific errors that led to this reported error.
`innererror`	InnerError	-	An object containing more specific information than the current object about the error.

InnerError: Object

Property	Type	Required	Description
Code	`String`	-	A more specific error code than was provided by the containing error.
`innererror`	InnerError	-	An object containing more specific information than the current object about the error.

Microsoft has provided an excellent API guidelines resource, you can read more about returning errors by looking at the following link:

`https://github.com/Microsoft/api-guidelines/blob/master/Guidelines.md#51-errors`

Accessing APIs from JavaScript

Web browsers implement a sandbox mechanism that restricts resources in one domain from accessing resources in another. For example, you may have an API that allows the modification and retrieval of user data and a website that provides an interface for this API. If the browser did not implement the "same-origin policy" and assuming the user did not log out of their session then it would be possible for a malicious page to send a request to the API and modify it without you knowing.

To get around this, there are two methods that can be implemented by your microservice to allow this access, **JSONP** which stands for (**JSON with Padding**) and **CORS** (**Cross-Origin Resource Sharing**).

JSONP

JSONP is pretty much a hack, and it is implemented by most browsers that do not implement the later CORS standard. It is restricted to `GET` requests only and works by getting round the issue that while `XMLHTTPRequest` is blocked from making requests to third-party servers, there are no restrictions on HTML script elements.

A JSONP request inserts a `<script src="...">` element into the browsers DOM with the API's URI as the `src` target. This component returns a function call with the JSON data as a parameter, and when this loads, the function executes passing the data to the callback.

JavaScript callback is defined in the code:

```
function success(data) {
  alert(data.message);
}
```

This is the response from the API call:

```
success({"message":"Hello World"})
```

To denote a request for data to be returned as JSONP, generally the `callback=functionName` parameter is added to the URI, in our example this would be `/helloworld?callback=success`. Implementing this is particularly straightforward let's take a look at our simple Go `helloworld` example and see how we can modify this to implement JSONP.

One thing to note is the `Content-Type` header that we are returning. We are no longer returning `application/json` as we are not returning JSON we are actually returning JavaScript so we must set the `Content-Type` header accordingly:

```
Content-Type: application/javascript
```

Example `chapter2/jsonp/jsonp.go`:

Let's take a quick look at an example of how we can send JSONP with Go, our response object is going to be exactly the same as the ones in `Chapter 1`, *Introduction to Microservices*:

```
type helloWorldResponse struct {
 Message string `json:"message"`
}
```

The difference is all in the handler, if we look at line **30** we are checking to see if there is a callback parameter in the query string. This would be provided by the client and indicates the function they expect to be called when the response is returned:

```
23 func helloWorldHandler(w http.ResponseWriter, r *http.Request) {
24  response := helloWorldResponse{Message: "HelloWorld"}
25  data, err := json.Marshal(response)
26  if err != nil {
27    panic("Ooops")
28 }
29
30  callback := r.URL.Query().Get("callback")
31  if callback != "" {
32    r.Headers().Add("Content-Type", "application/javascript")
33    fmt.Fprintf(w, "%s(%s)", callback, string(data))
34  } else {
```

```
35     fmt.Fprint(w, string(data))
36   }
37 }
```

To return our response in JSONP format all we need to do is wrap the standard response to a JavaScript function call. In line **33**, we are taking the callback function name that was passed by the client and encapsulating the response we would normally send. The resultant output would look something like this:

Request:

```
GET /helloworld?callback=hello
```

Response:

```
hello({"message":"Hello World"})
```

CORS

Assuming your users are using a desktop browser that has been released in the last five years, or a mobile browser such as iOS 9 or Android 4.2+, then implementing CORS will be more than enough. `http://caniuse.com/#feat=cors` says that it is over 92% of all Internet users. I was looking forward to bashing IE for the lack of full adoption; however, since this has been supported since IE8 I will have to complain about mobile users.

CORS is a W3C proposal to standardize cross-origin requests from the browser. It works by the browsers built in `HTTP` client making an `OPTIONS` request to a URI before the real request.

If the server at the other end returns a header that contains the origin of the domain from which the script is being loaded, then the browser will trust the server and will allow a cross-site request to be made:

```
Access-Control-Allow-Origin: origin.com
```

Implementing this in Go is quite straightforward and we could create a middleware to globally manage this for us. For simplicity, in our example we have hard coded this into the handler:

Example 2.2 chapter2/cors/cors.go

```
25 if r.Method == "OPTIONS" {
26  w.Header().Add("Access-Control-Allow-Origin", "*")
27  w.Header().Add("Access-Control-Allow-Methods", "GET")
28  w.WriteHeader(http.StatusNoContent)
29  return
30 }
```

In line **25**, we detect if the request method is `OPTIONS` and instead of returning the response we return the `Access-Control-Allow-Origin` header that the client is expecting. In our example, we are simply returning `\*`, which means all domains are allowed to interact with this API. This is not the safest implementation and quite often you will request your API users to register the domains that will be interacting with the API and restrict the `Allow-Origin` to only include those domains. In addition to the `Allow-Origin` header we are also returning the following:

```
Access-Control-Allow-Methods: GET
```

This tells the browser that it can only make `GET` requests to this URI and that it is forbidden to make `POST`, `PUT`, and so on. This is an optional header, but it can be used to enhance your user's security when interacting with the API. One thing to note is that we are not sending back a `200 OK` response we are using `204 No Content` since it is invalid to return a body with an `OPTIONS` request.

RPC APIs

RPC stands for remote procedure call; it is a method of executing a function or method on a remote machine. RPC has been around since the dawn of time and there are many different types of RPC technology some of which relies on there being an interface definition (SOAP, Thrift Protocol Buffers). This interface definition can make it easier to generate client and server stubs for different technology stacks. Generally, the interface is defined using a **DSL** (**domain specific language**) and a generator program will use this to create application clients and servers.

Where REST needs to use HTTP as a transport layer, RPC is not bound by this constraint, and while it is possible to send RPC calls over HTTP, you can use the lightness of TCP or even UDP sockets if you choose to.

RPC has seen a resurgence in use lately with many large-scale systems built by the likes of Uber, Google, Netflix, and so on are using RPC. Due to the speed and performance that you can get from the lower latency from not using HTTP and the smaller message size attained by implementing a binary message format rather than JSON or XML.

The detractors of RPC mention the tight coupling that can occur between the client and the server in that if you update the contract on the server then all the clients need to be updated too. With many modern RPC implementations this is less of a problem and in fact is no less a problem than you can have with RESTful APIs. Whilst old technology such as JMI was tightly bound, requiring the client and the server to share the same interface, modern implementations such as Protocol Buffers marshal the object sensibly and will not throw an error should there be minor differences. Thus by following the standard guidelines in the *Versioning APIs* section you have no less a problem than if you were implementing a RESTful API.

One of the benefits of RPC is that you can quickly generate a client for your users, this allows an abstraction from both the transport and the message type and allows them to depend upon an interface. As the creator you can change the underlying implementation of your application such as a move from Thrift to Proto buffers, without requiring the client to do anything other than use the latest version of your provided client. Versioning also allows you to retain the same backward compatibility that you can achieve with REST.

RPC API design

Some of the principles we have just discussed for creating a good RESTful API can also apply to RPC. However; one of the main differences is that you may not be using HTTP as your transport; therefore you are not always going to be able to use HTTP status codes as an indicator of success or failure. **RPC** stands for **Remote Procedure Call** and dates way back before the Internet. It was originally conceived as a way to execute a procedure that could be running in a separate application on the same machine or even potentially on the network. While we take this for granted now, back in the 90s this was cutting edge. Unfortunately, frameworks such as CORBA and Java RMI gave RPC a bad name and even now if you speak to an opponent of RPC they will most likely bring these two frameworks up. The benefits, however, were performance, using binary serialization is incredibly efficient on the network and we no longer have the tight coupling that RMI and CORBA enforced. We are also not trying to do anything too clever; we are no longer attempting to share an object across two processes we are taking a more functional approach, that is, methods that return immutable objects. This gives us the best of both worlds; the simplicity of interoperation and the speed and small payload of binary messages.

RPC message frameworks

These days we are no longer coupled to having the same interface implementation on both the client and the server, this would not adhere to our mantra of independently versionable and deployable. Thankfully frameworks are more flexible we can take the same approach as we do with REST, it is OK to add, however, removing elements or changing the signatures of a method must trigger a version update.

Gob

We have already looked at gob in the previous chapter but as a quick re-cap, the gob format was specifically designed to facilitate Go to Go-based communication and was structured around the idea of something easier to use and possibly more efficient than the likes of protocol buffers, this comes at a cost of cross-language communication.

gob object definition:

```
type HelloWorldRequest struct {
  Name string
}
```

More information about gob can be found in the Go documentation at `https://golang.org/pkg/encoding/gob/`

Thrift

The Thrift framework was created by Facebook and was open sourced in 2007. It is currently maintained by the Apache Software Foundation. The main aims of Thrift are:

- **Simplicity**: Thrift code is straightforward and approachable, free of unnecessary dependencies
- **Transparency**: Thrift conforms to the most common idioms in all languages
- **Consistency**: Niche, language-specific features belong in extensions, not in the core library
- **Performance**: Strive for performance first, elegance second

This is a thrift service definition:

```
struct User {
  1: string name,
  2: i32 id,
  3: string email
}
```

```
struct Error {
  1: i32 code,
  2: string detail
}

service Users {
  Error createUser(1: User user)
}
```

Find more information on Apache Thrift at `https://thrift.apache.org`.

Protocol Buffers

Protocol Buffers are a Google product, and they have just entered their third revision. Protocol Buffers take the approach of providing a DSL that the generator (written in C) reads and can generate client and server stubs for over ten languages, the primary ten are maintained by Google and encompass: Go, Java, C, JavaScript for NodeJS.

Protocol Buffers is a pluggable architecture, so it is possible to write your own plugins to generate all kinds of endpoints not just RPC; however, RPC is the main use case as they are coupled to the gRPC framework.

gRPC was designed by Google to be a fast and language agnostic RPC framework, which originated from an internal project where latency and speed were of the utmost importance in Google's architecture. By default, gRPC uses protocol buffers as the method for serializing and de-serializing structured data. An example of this DSL is shown in the following example.

Protocol buffer service definition:

```
service Users {
  rpc CreateUser (User) returns (Error) {}
}

message User {
  required string name = 1;
  required int32 id = 2;
  optional string email = 3;
}

message Error {
  optional code int32 = 1
  optional detail string = 2
}
```

Find more information on Protocol Buffers at
`https://developers.google.com/protocol-buffers/`.

JSON-RPC

JSON-RPC is an attempt at a standard way of representing objects for RPC using JSON. This removes the need to decode any proprietary binary protocol at the expense of transfer speed. There is no requirement for any particular client or server to serve this data format, TCP sockets, and the ability to write strings that pretty much most all programming languages can manage are all you require.

Unlike Thrift and Protocol Buffers, JSON-RPC sets the standard for the message serialization.

JSON-RPC implements some nice features that allow the batching of requests; every request contains an `id` parameter, which is established by the client. When the server responds it will return the same identifier allowing the client to understand to which request a response relates.

This is a JSON-RPC serialized request:

```
{
  "jsonrpc": "2.0",
  "method": "Users.v1.CreateUser",
  "params": {
    "name": "Nic Jackson",
    "id": 12335432434
  },
  "id": 1
}
```

This is a JSON-RPC serialized response:

```
{
  "jsonrpc": "2.0",
  "result": {...},
  "id": 1
}
```

Find more information on JSON-RPC 2.0 at `http://www.jsonrpc.org/specification`.

Filtering

When we looked at RESTful APIs we discussed the concept of using the query string to perform filtering actions such as:

- Paging
- Filtering
- Sorting

Obviously, if we are writing an RPC API, we do not have the luxury of a query string; however, implementing these concepts is incredibly useful. As long as we are consistent there is no reason at all that we cannot define a parameter on our request object for the filter condition:

```
{
 "jsonrpc": "2.0",
 "method": "Users.v1.GetUserLog",
 "params": {
   "name": "Nic Jackson",
   "id": 12335432434,
   "filter": {
     "page_start": 1,  //optional
     "page_size" : 10,  //optional
     "sort": "name DESC" //optional
   },
 "id": 1
}
```

This is just an example and you will probably choose to implement something specific to your own needs, however, the key is consistency. If we use this same object for every method, we can be reasonably sure that our users will be cool with this.

Versioning APIs

API versioning is something you should think about from the very beginning and avoid as long as you can. In general, you will need to make changes to your API, however, having to maintain *n* different versions can be a royal pain in the backside, so doing the upfront design thinking at the beginning can save you a whole load of trouble.

Before we look at how you can version your API, which is quite straightforward let's look at when you should version.

You would increment your API version number when you introduce a breaking change.

Breaking changes include:

- Removing or renaming APIs or API parameters
- Changing the type of an API parameter, for example, from integer to string
- Changes to response codes, error codes, or fault contracts
- Changes to the behavior of an existing API

Things that do not involve a breaking change include:

- Adding parameters to a returned entity
- Adding additional endpoints or functionality
- Bug fixes or other maintenance that does not include items in the breaking changes list

Semantic versioning

Microservices should implement the Major versioning scheme. Quite often, designers will elect to only implement a Major version number and imply `.0` for the minor version as according to the semantic versioning principles `http://semver.org` a Minor version would generally indicate the addition of functionality that has been implemented in a backwards compatible way. This could be adding additional endpoints to your API. It can be argued that since this would not affect the client's ability to interact with your API you should not worry about Minor versions and only concentrate on major as the client will not need to request a particular version without these additions in order to function.

When versioning APIs I think it is cleaner to drop the minor version and only concentrate on major version. We would take this approach for two reasons:

- The URI becomes more readable, and dots are only used as network location separators. When using an RPC API dots are only used to separate `API.VERSION.METHOD` and make everything easier to read.
- We should be inferring through our API versioning that change is a big thing and has an impact on the function of the client. Internally we can still use `Major.Minor`; however, this does not need to be something to the client as they will not have the capability to elect to use minor versions of the API.

Versioning formats for REST APIs

To allow the client to request a particular API version, there are three common ways you can do this.

It can be done as part of the URI:

```
https://myserver.com/v1/helloworld
```

It can also be done as a query string parameter:

```
https://myserver.com/helloworld?api-version=1
```

Finally, It can be done by using a custom HTTP header:

```
GET https://myserver.com/helloworld
api-version: 2
```

Whichever way you implement versioning is up to you and your team, but it should play a big part in your upfront design thinking. Once you have decided on an option stick, to it as providing a consistent and great experience for your consumers should be one of your primary goals.

Versioning formats for RPC APIs

Versioning RPC can be a little more difficult as most likely you are not using HTTP as your transport. However, this is still possible. The best way to deal with this is the namespace of your handlers.

In the go base packages, you have the capability to give your handler a name, `Greet.v1.HelloWorld`.

Naming for RPC

With RPC you do not have the luxury of using HTTP verbs to confer the intent of the API, for example, you have the collection users. With an HTTP API you would be able to split up the various actions using `GET`, `POST`, `DELETE`, and so on. This is not possible with an RPC API and you need to think in the same way as if you were writing methods inside your Go code, so for example:

```
GET /v1/users
```

The preceding code might be written as an RPC method as follows:

```
Users.v1.Users
GET /v1/users/123434
```

Alternatively, it might be written as an RPC method as follows:

```
Users.v1.User
```

Sub collections become a little less semantic, whereas in a RESTful API you would be able to do the following:

```
GET /v1/users/12343/permissions/1232
```

You cannot do this with an RPC API and you must explicitly specify the method as a separate entity:

```
Permissions.v1.Permission
```

The method name also needs to infer the action that the API is going to perform; you cannot rely on the use of HTTP verbs, so in the instance that you have a method that can delete a user you would have to add the delete verb into the method call, for example:

```
DELETE /v1/users/123123
```

The preceding code would become:

```
Users.v1.DeleteUser
```

Object type standardization

Whether you are using custom binary serialization, JSON, or JSON-RPC you need to think about how your user is going to handle the object at the other side of the transaction. Many of the serialization packages Protocol Buffers such as protocol buffers and Thrift that use stubs to generate client code will happily deal with serialization of simple types such as Dates into native types that enable your consumer to easily use and manipulate these objects. However, if you are using JSON or JSON-RPC there is no concept of a Date as a native type therefore it can be useful to fall back to ISO standards which the user of the client can easily deserialize. The Microsoft API design guidelines provide some good advice on how to handle Dates and Durations.

Dates

When returning a date, you should always use the `DateLiteral` format and preferably the `Iso8601Literal`. If you do need to send back a date in a format other than `Iso8601Literal`, then you can use a `StructuredDateLiteral` format, which allows you to specify the kind as part of the returned entity.

The informal `Iso8601Literal` format is the simplest method to use and should be understandable by almost any client consuming your API:

```
{"date": "2016-07-14T16:00Z"}
```

The more formal `StucturedDateLiteral` does not return a string, but an entity that contains two properties, `kind` and `value`:

```
{"date": {"kind": "U", "value": 1471186826}}
```

The permissible kinds are:

- `C`: **CLR**; number of milliseconds since midnight January 1 00
- `E`: **ECMAScript**; number of milliseconds since midnight, January 1, 1970
- `I`: **ISO 8601**; a string limited to the ECMAScript subset
- `O`: **OLE Date**; integral part is the number of days since midnight, December 31, 1899, and fractional part is the time within the day (0.5 = midday)
- `T`: **Ticks**; number of ticks (100-nanosecond intervals) since midnight January 1, 1601
- `U`: **UNIX**; number of seconds since midnight, January 1, 1970
- `W`: **Windows**; number of milliseconds since midnight January 1, 1601
- `X`: **Excel**; as for O, but the year 1900 is incorrectly treated as a leap year, and day 0 is "January 0 (zero)"

Durations

Durations are serialized to conform with ISO 8601 and are represented by the following format:

```
P[n]Y[n]M[n]DT[n]H[n]M[n]S
```

- `P`: This is the duration designator (historically called "period") placed at the start of the duration representation
- `Y`: This is the year designator that follows the value for the number of years
- `M`: This is the month designator that follows the value for the number of months
- `W`: This is the week designator that follows the value for the number of weeks
- `D`: This is the day designator that follows the value for the number of days
- `T`: This is the time designator that precedes the time components of the representation
- `H`: This is the hour designator that follows the value for the number of hours
- `M`: This is the minute designator that follows the value for the number of minutes
- `S`: This is the second designator that follows the value for the number of seconds

For example, `P3Y6M4DT12H30M5S` represents a duration of "three years, six months, four days, twelve hours, thirty minutes, and five seconds".

Intervals

Again part of the ISO 8601 specification is if you need to receive or send an interval you can use the following format:

- Start and end, such as `2007-03-01T13:00:00Z/2008-05-11T15:30:00Z`
- Start and duration, such as `2007-03-01T13:00:00Z/P1Y2M10DT2H30M`
- Duration and end, such as `P1Y2M10DT2H30M/2008-05-11T15:30:00Z`
- Duration only, such as `P1Y2M10DT2H30M`, with additional context information

Find more information on JSON serialization of dates and times at `https://github.com/Microsoft/api-guidelines/blob/master/Guidelines.md#113-json-serialization-of-dates-and-times`.

Documenting APIs

Documenting APIs is incredibly useful whether you intend the API to be consumed internally by other teams in your company, external users, or even only yourself. You will thank yourself for spending the time to document the operations of the API and keep this up to date. Keeping documentation up to date should not be an arduous task. There are many applications that can generate documentation automatically from your source code, so all you need to do is run this application as part of your build workflow.

REST based-based APIs

Currently three primary standards are fighting it out to become the queen of REST API documentation:

- Swagger
- API Blueprint
- RAML

Swagger

Swagger was designed by SmartBear and has been chosen to be part of the Open API Initiative; this potentially gives it the greatest chance of adoption as a standard for documenting RESTful APIs. The Open API Initiative (`https://openapis.org`) however is an industry body and whether it gains the recognition that the W3C has around web standards is probably dependent on more big names joining.

Documentation is written in YAML, and various code generation tools can both write Swagger documentation from source code as well as being able to generate client SDKs. The standard is comprehensive in its feature list and is also relatively simple to write as well as being well understood by the developer community.

The code example of Swagger is shown as follows:

```
/pets:
  get:
    description: Returns all pets from the system that the user has access
to
    produces:
      - application/json
    responses:
      '200':
        description: A list of pets.
```

```
    schema:
      type: array
      items:
        $ref: '#/definitions/Pet'

definitions:
  Pet:
    type: object
    properties:
      name:
  type: string
    description: name of the pet
```

Find more information on Swagger at `http://swagger.io`.

API Blueprint

API Blueprint is an open standard designed by Apiary and released under the MIT license. It ties closely into Apiary's products. However, it can be used on its own, and there are a variety of open source tools that read and write the format.

Documentation is written in Markdown, which can make authoring the documentation feel a little more natural rather than dealing with nested layers of objects.

The code example for API Blueprint is shown as follows:

```
FORMAT: 1A

# Data Structures

## Pet (object)
+ name: Jason (string) - Name of the pet.

# Pets [/pets]

Returns all pets from the system that the user has access to'to'

## Retrieve all pets [GET]
+ Response 200 (application/json)
+ Attributes (array[Pet])
```

Find more information on API Blueprint at `https://apiblueprint.org`.

RAML

RAML stands for **RESTful API Modelling Language** and is written in `YAML` format. It aims to allow the definition of a human-readable format that describes resources, methods, parameters, responses, media types, and other HTTP constructs that form the basis of your API.

The code example for RAML is shown as follows:

```
#%RAML 1.0
title: Pets API
mediaType: [ application/json]
types:
  Pet:
    type: object
    properties:
      name:
        type: string
        description: name of the pet
/pets:
  description: Returns all pets from the system that the user has access to
  get:
    responses:
      200:
        body: Pet[]
```

Find more information on RAML at `http://raml.org`.

RPC based-based APIs

With RPC APIs there is an argument that your contract is your documentation, in the following example we define the interface using the protocol buffers DSL and would make any necessary comments to assist the consumer as required. The predominant theory to follow is one of self-documenting code that your methods and parameter names should infer intent and enough description to negate the use of comments.

Protocol buffer example:

```
// The greeting service definition.
service Users {
  // Create user creates a user in the system with the given User details,
  // it returns an Error message which will be nil on a successful
operation
  rpc CreateUser (User) returns (Error) {}
}
```

```
// Person describes a user entity
message User {
  // name is a required field and represents the name of
  required string name = 1;
  // id is the unique identifier for the user in the sytem
  required int32 id = 2;
  // email is the users email address and is an optional field
  optional string email = 3;
}

message Error {
  optional code int32 = 1
  optional detail string = 2
}
```

Which standard you choose is entirely dependent on you, your workflow, your team standards, and your users. It will vary from case to case, however, once you choose an approach in the same way as you do with naming conventions you should stick to a consistent style across all of your APIs.

Summary

In this chapter, we did not spend much time looking at code; however, we have looked at some essential concepts around writing a great API, which is as important as being able to write the code.

The bulk of this chapter has been concerned with RESTful APIs as unlike RPC we need to be a little more descriptive in their use. We also have the capability to leverage the principles of HATEOAS, which we do not have when using RPC.

In the next chapter, we will start to look at some of the fantastic frameworks that exist in the Go community, so we can start applying these principles and furthering our advancement to microservice mastery.

3
Introducing Docker

Before we go any further with this book, we need to look at a little thing called Docker, before we begin don't forget to clone the example code repository `https://github.com/building-microservices-with-go/chapter3.git`.

Introducing Containers with Docker

Docker is a platform that has risen to prominence in the last three years; it was born out of the desire to simplify the process of building, shipping, and running applications. Docker is not the inventor of the container, Jacques Gélinas created the VServer project back in 2001, and since then the other main projects have been LXC from IBM and rkt from CoreOS.

If you would like to read more about the history, then I recommend this excellent blog post by Redhat: `http://rhelblog.redhat.com/2015/08/28/the-history-of-containers`, this section is going to concentrate on Docker which is by far the most popular current technology.

The concept of a container is process isolation and application packaging. To quote Docker:

> *A container image is a lightweight, stand-alone, executable package of a piece of software that includes everything needed to run it: code, runtime, system tools, system libraries, settings.*
>
> ...
>
> *Containers isolate software from its surroundings, for example, differences between development and staging environments and help reduce conflicts between teams running different software on the same infrastructure.*

Where they benefit application development is that we can take advantage of this when deploying these applications as it allows us to pack them closer together, saving on hardware resources.

From a development and test lifecycle, containers give us the capability to run production code on our development machines with no complicated setup; it also allows us to create that `Clean Room` environment without having different instances of the same database installed to trial new software.

Containers have become the primary choice for packaging microservices, and as we progress through the examples in this book, you will learn how invaluable it is to your workflow.

Containers work by isolating processes and filesystems from each other. Unless explicitly specified, containers cannot access each other's file systems. They also cannot interact with one another via TCP or UDP sockets unless again specified.

Docker is made up of many parts; however, at its core is the Docker Engine, a lightweight application runtime with features for orchestration, scheduling networking, and security. Docker Engine can be installed anywhere on a physical or virtual host, and it supports both Windows and Linux. Containers allow developers to package large or small amounts of code and their dependencies together into an isolated package.

We can also draw from a huge array of pre-created images, just about all software vendors from MySQL to IBM's WebSphere have an official image that is available for us to use.

Docker also uses Go, in fact nearly all of the code that goes into the Docker Engine and other applications are written in Go.

Rather than write an essay on how Docker works, let's examine each of the features by example. By the end of this chapter, we will take one of the simple examples that we created in `Chapter 1`, *Introduction to Microservices*, and create a Docker image for it.

Installing Docker

Head over to `https://docs.docker.com/engine/installation/` and install the correct version of Docker on your machine. You will find versions for Mac, Windows, and Linux.

Running our first container

To validate Docker has been installed correctly, let's run our first container, **hello-world** is actually an image, an image is an immutable snapshot of a container. Once we start these with the following command they become containers, think of it like types and instances, a type defines fields and methods making up behavior. An instance is a living instantiation of this type, you can assign other types to the fields and call the methods to perform actions.

```
$ docker run --rm hello-world
```

The first thing you should see is:

```
Unable to find image 'hello-world:latest' locally
latest: Pulling from library/hello-world
c04b14da8d14: Pull complete
Digest:
sha256:0256e8a36e2070f7bf2d0b0763dbabdd67798512411de4cdcf9431a1feb60fd9
Status: Downloaded newer image for hello-world:latest
```

When you execute a `docker run` the first thing the engine does is check to see if you have the image installed locally. If it doesn't then it connects to the default registry, in this case, `https://hub.docker.com/` to retrieve it.

Once the image has been downloaded, the daemon can create a container from the downloaded image, all the output is streamed to the output on your terminal:

```
Hello from Docker!
This message shows that your installation appears to be working correctly.
```

The `--rm` flag tells the Docker engine to remove the container and delete any resources such as volumes it was using on exit. Unless we would like to re-start a container at some point it is good practice to use the `--rm` flag to keep our filesystem clean, otherwise, all of the temporary volumes which are created will sit around and consume space.Let's try something a little more complicated, this time, we will start a container and create a shell inside of it to show how you can navigate to the internal file system. Execute the following command in your terminal:

```
$ docker run -it --rm alpine:latest sh
```

Alpine is a lightweight version of Linux and is perfect for running Go applications. The `-it` flags stand for **interactive terminal** it maps the standard in from your terminal to the input of the running container. The `sh` statement after the name of the image we want to run is the name of the command we would like to execute in the container when it starts.

If all went well, you should now be inside a shell of the container. If you check the current directory by executing the `ls` command, you will see the following, which hopefully is not the directory you were in before running the command:

```
bin     etc     lib      media   proc    run     srv     tmp     var
dev     home    linuxrc  mnt     root    sbin    sys     usr
```

This is the root folder of the newly started container, containers are immutable, so any changes you make to the file system in a running container is disposed of when the container is stopped. While this may seem to be a problem, there are solutions for persisting data, which we will look at in a little bit, however, for now, the important concept to remember is that:

> *"Containers are immutable instances of images, and the data volumes are by default non-persistent"*

You need to remember this when designing your services, to illustrate how this works take a look at this simple example.

Open another terminal and execute the following command:

```
$ docker ps
```

You should see the following output:

```
CONTAINER ID        IMAGE               COMMAND             CREATED
STATUS              PORTS               NAMES
43a1bea0009e        alpine:latest       "sh"                6 minutes ago
Up 6 minutes                            tiny_galileo
```

The `docker ps` command queries the engine and returns a list of the containers, by default this only shows the running containers, however, if we add the `-a` flag we can also see stopped containers.

The Alpine Linux container that we started earlier is currently running, so jump back to your previous terminal window and create a file in the root file system:

```
$ touch mytestfile.txt
```

If we list the directory structure again, we can see that a file has been created in the root of the file system:

```
bin          lib          mytestfile.txt  sbin         usr
dev          linuxrc      proc            srv          var
etc          media        root            sys
home         mnt          run             tmp
```

Now exit the container using the `exit` command and run `docker ps` again, you should see the following output:

```
CONTAINER ID        IMAGE               COMMAND             CREATED
STATUS              PORTS               NAMES
```

If we add the `-a` flag command to see stopped containers too, we should see the container we started earlier:

```
CONTAINER ID        IMAGE               COMMAND             CREATED
STATUS                     PORTS               NAMES
518c8ae7fc94        alpine:latest       "sh"                5 seconds ago
Exited (0) 2 seconds ago                       pensive_perlman
```

Now, start another container again using the `docker run` command and list the directory contents in the root folder.

No `mytestfile.txt` right? The reason this does not exist is because of the principle we were discussing earlier, which I think is important to mention again as if this is the first time you have used Docker it will catch you out:

> *"Containers are immutable instances of images, and the data volumes are by default non-persistent."*

There is something worth noting, however, unless you explicitly remove a container it will persist in a stopped state on the Docker host.

Removing containers is important to remember for two reasons; the first is that if you do not remember this, you will fill up the disk on your host quickly as every time you create a container Docker will allocate space on the host for the container volumes. The second is that the container can be restarted.

Restarted that sounds cool, in fact, it is a handy feature, not something you should use in your production environment, for that you need to remember the golden rule and design your application accordingly:

> *"Containers are immutable instances of images, and the data volumes are by default non-persistent."*

However, the use of Docker extends far beyond simply running applications for your microservices. It is an awesome way to manage your development dependencies without cluttering up your development machine. We will look at that a little later on, but for now, we are interested in how we can restart a stopped container.

If we execute the `docker ps -a` command, we will see that we now have two stopped containers. The oldest one is the first container we started to which we added our `mytestfile.txt`. This is the one we want to restart, so grab the ID of the container and execute the following command:

```
$ docker start -it [container_id] sh
```

Again, you should be in a shell at the root of the container if you check the directory contents what do you think you will find?

That's right, `mytestfile.txt`; this is because when you restarted the container, the engine remounted the volumes that were attached the first time you ran the command. These are the same volumes you mutated to add the file as mentioned earlier.

So we can restart our container; however, I just want to repeat the golden rule one last time:

> *"Containers are immutable instances of images, and the data volumes are by default non-persistent."*

When running in a production environment, you cannot ensure that you can restart a container. There are a million reasons for this, one of the main ones that we will look at more in depth when we look at orchestration is that containers are generally run on a cluster of hosts. Since there is no guarantee which host the container will be restarted on or even that the host the container was previously running on actually exists. There are many projects that attempt to solve this, but the best approach is to avoid the complexity altogether. If you need to persist files, then store them in something that is designed for the job such as Amazon S3 or Google Cloud Storage. Design your applications around this principle and you will spend far less time panicking when the inevitable happens, and your super sensitive data container disappears.

OK, before we look at Docker volumes in more depth let's clean up after ourselves.

Exit your container and get back to the shell on the Docker host. If we run `docker ps -a` ,we will see that there are two stopped containers. To remove these, we can use the `docker rm containerid` command.

Run this now using the first `containerid` in your list, if this is successful, the container ID you asked to be removed would be echoed back to you, and the container will is deleted.

If you want to remove all the stopped containers you can use the following command:

```
$ docker rm -v $(docker ps -a -q)
```

The `docker ps -a -q` the `-a` flag will list all the containers including the stopped ones, -`q` will return a list of the container IDs rather than the full details. We are passing this as a parameter list to `docker rm`, which will remove all the containers in the list.

To avoid having to remove a container we can use the `--rm` flag when starting a new container. This flag tells Docker to remove the container when it stops.

Docker volumes

We have seen how Docker containers are immutable; however, there are some instances when you may wish to write some files to a disk or when you want to read data from a disk such as in a development setup. Docker has the concept of volumes, which can be mounted either from the host running the Docker machine or from another Docker container.

Union filesystem

To keep our images efficient and compact Docker uses the concept of a Union File System. The Union filesystem allows us to represent a logical file system by grouping different directories and or files together. It uses a **Copy on Write** technique, which copies the layer when we modify the file system, this way we only use about 1MB of space when creating a new image. When data is written to the file system Docker copies the layer and puts it on the top of the stack. When building images and extending existing images we are leveraging this technique, also when starting an image and creating a container the only difference is this writable layer, which means we do not need to copy all the layers every time and fill up our disk.

Mounting volumes

The `-v`, or `--volume` parameter allows you to specify a pair of values corresponding to the file system you wish to mount on the host and the path where you would like to mount the volume inside the container.

Let's try our example from earlier, but this time mounting a volume on the local file system:

```
$ docker run -it -v $(pwd):/host alpine:latest /bin/sh
```

If you change into the host folder, you will see that there is access to the same folder from where you ran the `docker run` command. The syntax for the values for `-v` is `hostfolder:destinationfolder`, one thing I think is important to point out is that these paths need to be absolute, and you cannot use a relative path like `./` or `../foldername`. The volume you have just mounted has read/write access, any changes you make will be synchronized to the folder on the host so be careful to not go running `rm -rf *`. Creating Volumes on a production environment should be used very sparingly, I would advise that where possible you avoid doing it all together as in a production environment there is no guarantee if a container dies and is re-created that it will be replaced on the same host where it was previously. This means that any changes you have made to the volume will be lost.

Docker ports

When running web applications inside a container, it is quite common that we will need to expose some ports to the outside world. By default, a Docker container is completely isolated, and if you start a server running on port `8080` inside your container unless you explicitly specify that port is accessible from the outside, it will not be accessible.

Mapping ports is a good thing from a security perspective as we are operating on a principle of no trust. It is also effortless to expose these ports. Using one of the examples we created in `Chapter 1`, *Introduction to Microservices*, let's see just how easy this is.

Move to the folder where you checked out the sample code, and run the following Docker command:

```
$ docker run -it --rm -v $(pwd):/src -p 8080:8080 -w /src golang:alpine
/bin/sh
```

The `-w` flag we are passing is to set the working directory that means that any command we run in the container will be run inside this folder. When we start the shell, you will see that rather than having to change into the folder we specify in the second part of the volume mounting we are already in that folder and can run our application. We are also using a slightly different image this time. We are not using `alpine:latest`, which is a lightweight version of Linux, we are using `golang:alpine`, which is a version of Alpine with the most recent Go tools installed.

If we start our application using the `go run main.go` command; we should see the following output:

```
2016/09/02 05:53:13 Server starting on port 8080
```

Now change to another shell and try to curl the API endpoint:

```
$ curl -XPOST localhost:8080/helloworld -d '{"name":"Nic"}'
```

You should see something like the following message returned:

```
{"message":"Hello Nic"}
```

If we run the `docker ps` command to inspect the running containers, we will see that there are no ports exposed. Go back to your previous terminal window and kill the command and then exit the container.

This time, when we start it, we will add the `-p` argument to specify the port. Like volumes, this takes a pair of values separated by a colon `(:)`. The first is the destination port on the host that we would like to bind to the second is the source port on the Docker container to which our application is bound.

Because this binds to the port on the host machine, in the same way that you would not be able to start the program locally twice because of the port binding, you cannot do this with the host port mappings in Docker either. Of course, you can start multiple instances of your code in separate containers and bind to different ports, and we will see how you can do that in just a bit.

But first let's take a look at that port command, rather than starting a container and creating a shell to run our application we can do this in one command by replacing the `/bin/sh` command with our `go run` command. Give that a try and see if you can get your application running.

Got it?

You should have typed something like the following:

```
$ docker run -it --rm -v $(pwd):/src -w /src -p 8080:8080 golang:alpine go
run reading_writing_json_8.go
```

Now try your `curl` to send some data to the API again, you should see the following output:

```
{"message":"Hello Nic"}
```

Like volumes, you can specify multiple instances of the `-p` argument, which enables you to set up the binding for multiple ports.

Removing a container starting with an explicit name

Containers that start with a name parameter are not automatically removed even if you specify the `--rm` argument. To remove a container started in this way, we must manually use the `docker rm` command. If we append the `-v` option to the command, we can also remove the volumes that are associated with it. We should really do this now, or when we try to recreate the container later in the chapter, you might be left a little puzzled:

```
$ docker rm -v server
```

Docker networking

I never intended this chapter to be a full reproduction of the official Docker documentation; I am just trying to explain some of the key concepts that will help you as you progress through the rest of this book.

Docker networking is an interesting topic, and by default, Docker supports the following network modes:

- bridge
- host
- none
- overlay

Bridge networking

The bridge network is the default network that your containers will connect to when you launch them; this is how we were able to join our containers together in the last example. To facilitate this, Docker uses some of the core Linux capabilities such as networking namespaces and virtual Ethernet interfaces (or `veth` interfaces).

When the Docker engine starts, it creates the `docker0` virtual interface on the host machine. The `docker0` interface is a virtual Ethernet bridge that automatically forwards packets between any other network interfaces that are attached to it. When a container starts it creates a `veth` pair, it gives one to the container, which becomes its `eth0`, and the other connects to the `docker0` bridge.

Host networking

The host network is essentially the same network that the Docker engine is running on. When you connect a container to the host network all of the ports that are exposed by the container are automatically mapped to the hosts, it also shares the IP address of the host. While this may seem like a nice convenience, Docker was always designed to be capable of running multiple instances of the same container on the engine, and since you can only bind a socket to one port in Linux using the `host network` limits this feature.

The host network can also pose a security risk to your container as it is no longer protected by the principle of no trust and you no longer have the ability to explicitly control if a port is exposed or not. That being said, due to the efficiencies of host networking it may in some instances be appropriate to connect a container to the host network if you anticipate that it is going to heavily use the network. An API gateway might be one such example, this container would still be possible to route requests to other API containers that are sitting on the bridge network.

No network

Removing your container from any network might in some instances be something you wish to do. Consider the situation where you have an application that only processes data stored in a file. Utilizing the principle of no trust, we may determine that the securest thing to do is to not connect it to any container and to only allow it to write to a volume that is mounted on the host. Attaching your container to the `none` network provides exactly this capability, and while the use case might be somewhat limited it is there, and it's nice to know about it.

Overlay network

The Docker overlay network is a unique Docker network that is used to connect containers running on separate hosts to one another. With the bridge network as we have already learned, network communication is localized to the Docker host and this is generally fine when you are developing software. When you run your code in production however, all this changes, as you will typically be running multiple hosts, each running multiple containers as part of your high availability setup. The containers still need to talk to one another, and while we could route all traffic through an **ESB** (**enterprise service bus**), this is a little bit of an anti-pattern in the microservice world. The recommended approach as we will see in a later chapter, is for the service to be responsible for its own discovery and load balancing client calls. The Docker overlay network solves this problem, it is in effect a network tunnel between machines which passes the traffic unmodified over the physical network. The problem with the overlay is that you can no longer rely on Docker to update the `etc/hosts` file for you, and you must depend on a dynamic service registry.

Custom network drivers

Docker also supports plugins for networking, based around its open source `libnetwork` project, you can write custom networking plugins that can replace the networking subsystem of the Docker engine. They also give the capability for you to connect non-Docker applications to your container network such as a physical database server.

Weaveworks

Weaveworks is one of the most popular plugins, it gives you the capability to securely link your Docker hosts and also provides a whole host of additional tools such as service discovery with weavedns and visualization with weavescope, so you can see how your network is connected together.

`https://www.weave.works`

Project Calico

Project Calico attempts to solve the speed and efficiency problems that using virtual LANs, bridging, and tunneling can cause. It achieves this by connecting your containers to a vRouter, which then routes traffic directly over the L3 network. This can give huge advantages when you are sending data between multiple data centers as there is no reliance on NAT and the smaller packet sizes reduce CPU utilization.

https://www.projectcalico.org

Creating custom bridge networks

Implementing a custom overlay network is beyond the scope of this book, however, understanding how you can create custom bridge networks is something that we should look at as Docker-Compose, which we are going to introduce later in this chapter, utilizes these concepts.

Like many of the Docker tools, creating a bridge network is quite straightforward. To see the currently running networks on your Docker engine, we can execute the following command:

```
$ docker network ls
```

The output should be something like the following:

```
NETWORK ID          NAME                DRIVER              SCOPE
8e8c0cc84f66        bridge              bridge              local
0c2ecf158a3e        host                host                local
951b3fde8001        none                null                local
```

You will find that there are three networks created by default, which is three of the ones we discussed earlier. Because these are default networks, we are unable to remove these, Docker requires these networks to function correctly and allowing you to remove them would be a bad thing indeed.

Creating a bridge network

To create a bridge network, we can use the following command:

```
$ docker network create testnetwork
```

Run this now in your terminal and list the networks again to see the results.

You will see that there is now a fourth network in your list that uses the bridge driver and that has the name you specified as one of the arguments. By default, when you create a network, it uses the `bridge` as a default driver, of course, it is possible to create a network to a custom driver, and this can be easily facilitated by specifying the additional argument, `-d drivername`.

Connecting containers to a custom network

To connect a container to a custom network, let's again use the example application that we created in `Chapter 1`, *Introduction to Microservices*:

```
$ docker run -it --rm -v $(pwd):/src -w /src --name server --
network=testnetwork golang:alpine go run main.go
```

Did you get the error message that the name is already in use because you forgot to remove the container in the earlier section? If so, it might be time to head back a few pages.

Assuming all went well, you should see the server starting message, now let's try to curl the container using the same command we executed earlier:

```
$ docker run --rm appropriate/curl:latest curl -i -XPOST
server:8080/helloworld -d '{"name":"Nic"}'
```

You should have received the following error message:

```
curl: (6) Couldn't resolve host 'server'
```

This was expected, have a go to see if you can update the `docker run` command to make it work with our API container.

Got it?

If not, here is the modified command with the added network argument:

```
$ docker run --rm --network=testnetwork appropriate/curl:latest curl -i -
XPOST server:8080/helloworld -d '{"name":"Nic"}'
```

This command should have worked just fine the second time, and you should see the expected output. Now remove the server container, and we will take a look at how you can write your own Docker files.

Writing Dockerfiles

Dockerfiles are the recipes for our images; the define the base image, software to be installed and give us the capability to set the various structure that our application needs.

In this section, we are going to look at how we can create a Docker file for our example API. Again, this is not going to be a comprehensive overview of how Dockerfiles work as there are many books and online resources that exist for that explicit purpose. What we will do is to look at the salient points that will give us the basics.

The first thing we are going to do is build our application code as when we package this into a Docker file we will be executing a binary, not using the `go run` command. The image we are going to create will have only the software installed that we need to run our application. Limiting the software installed is a Docker best practice when creating images as it reduces the attack surface by only including what is necessary.

Building application code for Docker

We are going to execute a slightly different command for creating our files from the usual `go build`:

```
$ CGO_ENABLED=0 GOOS=linux GOARCH=386 go build -a -installsuffix cgo -
ldflags '-s' -o server
```

In the preceding command, we are passing the argument `-ldflags '-s'`, this argument passes the `-s` argument to the linker when we build the application and tells it to statically link all dependencies. This is very useful when we use the popular Scratch container as a base; Scratch is the lightest base you can get it has no application frameworks or applications this is opposed to Ubuntu, which takes about 150MB. The difference between Scratch and Ubuntu is that Scratch does not have access to the standard C library `GLibC`.

If we do not build a static binary, then it will not execute if we try to run it in a Scratch container. The reason for this is that while you may think that your Go application is a static binary it still has a dependency on `GLibC`, both the `net` and the `os/user` packages link to `GLibC` so if we are to run our application with a Scratch base image we need to statically link this. The benefit, however, is an incredibly small image, we end up with an image which is roughly 4MB in size, exactly the size of our compile Go application.

Because the Docker engine is running on Linux, we also need to build our Go binary for the Linux architecture. Even if you are using Docker for Mac or Docker for Windows, what is happening under the hood is that the Docker engine is running a lightweight virtual machine on either `HyperV` or the Mac's `xhyve` virtual machine.

If you are not using Linux to run your go build command and since Go has excellent capability for cross-platform compilation, you don't need to do much. All you do need to do is prefix the architecture variables `GOOS=linux GOARCH=386` to your go build command as we did in the earlier example.

Now that we have created a binary for our application, let's take a look at the Docker file:

```
1 FROM scratch
2 MAINTAINER jackson.nic@gmail.com
3
4 EXPOSE 8080
5
6 COPY ./server ./
7
8 ENTRYPOINT ./server
```

FROM

The `FROM` instruction set the base image for subsequent instructions. You can use any image that is either stored in a remote registry or locally on your Docker Engine. When you execute `docker build`, if you do not already have this image, then Docker will pull it from the registry as the first step of the build process. The format for the `FROM` command is the same as you would use when issuing a `docker run` command it is either:

- `FROM image` // assuming latest
- `FROM image:tag` // where you can specify a tag to use

In **line 1**, we are using the image name scratch, this is a particular kind of image, which is basically a blank canvas. We could use Ubuntu or Debian or Alpine or pretty much anything really, but since all we need to run our Go application is the application itself then we can use scratch to produce the smallest possible image.

MAINTAINER

The `MAINTAINER` instruction allows you to set the author of the generated image. This is an optional instruction; however, it can be good practice to include this even if you are not planning on publishing your image to the public registry.

EXPOSE

The EXPOSE instruction informs Docker that the container listens on the specified networks ports at runtime. Expose does not make the ports accessible to the host; this function still needs to be performed with the -p mapping.

COPY

The COPY instruction copies files from the source in the first part of this instruction to the destination specified in the second part:

- COPY <src> <dest>
- COPY ["<src>", "<dest>"] // useful when paths contain whitespace

The <src> in the COPY instruction may contain wildcards with the matching done using Go's filepath.Match rules.

Note:

- <src> must be part of the context for the build, you cannot specify relative folders such as ../;
- A root / specified in the <src> will be the root of the context
- A root / specified in the <dest> will map to the containers root file system
- Specifying a COPY instruction without a destination will copy the file or folder into the WORKDIR with the same name as the original

ENTRYPOINT

An ENTRYPOINT allows you to configure the executable that you would like to run when your container starts. Using ENTRYPOINT makes it possible to specify arguments as part of the docker run command which is appended to the ENTRYPOINT.

ENTRYPOINT has two forms:

- ENTRYPOINT ["executable", "param1", "param2"] // preferred form
- ENTRYPOINT command param1 param2 //shell form

For example, in our Docker file, we are specifying the `ENTRYPOINT ./server`. This is our Go binary that we would like to run. When we start our container with the following `docker run helloworld` command, we do not need to explicitly tell the container to execute the binary and launch the server. We can, however, pass additional arguments to the application via the `docker run` command arguments; these would then be appended to the `ENTRYPOINT` before the application is run. For example:

```
$ docker run --rm helloworld --config=/configfile.json
```

The preceding command would append the arguments to the executed statement defined in the entry point, which would be the equivalent of executing the following shell command:

```
$ ./server --config=configfile.json
```

CMD

The CMD instruction has three forms:

- `CMD ["executable", "param1", "param2"]` // exec form
- `CMD ["param1", "param2"]` // append default parameters to `ENTRYPOINT`
- `CMD command param1 param2` // shell form

When `CMD` is used to provide default arguments for the `ENTRYPOINT` instruction then both the `CMD` and `ENTRYPOINT` instructions should be specified using the `JSON` array format.

If we specify a default value for `CMD`, we can still override it by passing the command arguments to the `docker run` command.

Only one `CMD` instruction is permitted in a Docker file.

Good practice for creating Dockerfiles

Taking all of this into account, we need to remember how the union file system works in Docker and how we can leverage it to create small and compact images. Every time we issue a command in the Dockerfile, Docker will create a new layer. When we mutate this command, the layer must be completely recreated and potentially all the following layers too, which can dramatically slow down your build. It is therefore recommended a good practice that you should attempt to group your commands as tightly as possible to reduce the possibility of this occurring.

Quite often, you will see Dockerfiles which instead of having a separate `RUN` command for every command we would like to execute, we chain these using standard bash formatting.

For example, consider the following, which would install software from a package manager.

Bad Practice:

```
RUN apt-get update
RUN apt-get install -y wget
RUN apt-get install -y curl
RUN apt-get install -y nginx
```

Good Practice:

```
RUN apt-get update && \
    apt-get install -y wget curl nginx
```

The second example would only create one layer, which in turn would create a much smaller and more compact image, it is also good practice to organize your COPY statements placing the statement which changes the least further up in the Dockerfile, this way you avoid invalidation of subsequent layers even if there are no changes to these layers.

Building images from Dockerfiles

To build an image from our Dockerfile, we can execute a straightforward command:

```
$ docker build -t testserver .
```

Breaking this down the `-t` argument is the tag we wish to give the container, this takes the form name:tag, If we omit the `tag` portion of the argument as we have in our example command, then the tag `latest` will be automatically assigned.

If you run `docker images`, you will see that our `testserver` image has been given this tag.

The final argument is the context we would like to send to the Docker Engine. When you run a Docker build, the context is automatically forwarded to the server. This may seem strange, but you have to remember that it is not uncommon that the Docker Engine will not be running on your local machine, and therefore it will not have access to your local filesystem. For this reason, we should be careful about where we are setting our context as it can mean that potentially a large amount of data is being sent to the engine, which will slow things down. Context then becomes the root for your `COPY` commands.

Now that we have our running container, let's test it out. Why not start a container from our newly built image and check the API by curling the endpoint:

```
$ docker run --rm -p 8080:8080 testserver
$ curl -XPOST localhost:8080/helloworld -d '{"name":"Nic"}'
```

Docker build context

When we run our Docker build command, we set the context path as the final argument. What actually happens when the command executes is that the context is transferred to the server. This can cause problems if you have a large source folder, so it is good practice to only send the files you need to be packaged inside the container or the files you need when building the container. There are two ways we can mitigate this problem. The first is to ensure that our context only has the files on it we require. Since this is not always possible we have a secondary option of using a `.dockerignore` file.

Docker Ignore files

The `.dockerignore` file is similar to a git ignore file before the CLI sends the context to the Engine, it excludes files and directories that match patterns in the `.dockerignore` file. It uses the patterns which are defined in Go's `filepath.Match` rules you can find more information about them in the following Go documentation: `https://godoc.org/path/filepath#Match`

Rule	Behavior
`# comment`	Ignored.
`*/temp*`	Exclude files and directories whose names start with temp in any immediate subdirectory of the root. For example, the plain file `/somedir/temporary.txt` is excluded, as is the directory `/somedir/temp`.
`*/*/temp*`	Exclude files and directories starting with temp from any subdirectory that is two levels below the root. For example, `/somedir/subdir/temporary.txt` is excluded.
`temp?`	Exclude files and directories in the root directory whose names are a one-character extension of temp. For example, `/tempa` and `/tempb` are excluded.

`https://docs.docker.com/engine/reference/builder/#/dockerignore-file`

Running Daemons in containers

One of the things you might be used to when deploying an application to a VM or physical server is to use a Daemon runner such as `initd` or `systemd` to ensure that the application is started in the background and continues to run even if it crashes. This is an anti-pattern when you are using Docker containers, for Docker to successfully stop the application it will attempt to kill the process running with PID 1. Daemons will generally start with PID 1 and start your application with another process ID, which will mean they are not killed when you stop the Docker container. This can cause containers to hang when the `docker stop` command is executed.

In the instance that you need to ensure that your application keeps running even after a crash then you delegate this responsibility to the orchestrator who is starting your Docker container. We will learn more about this when we look at orchestration in a later chapter.

Docker Compose

That was all super easy-ish, let's now take a look at a compelling feature of Docker that allows you to start multiple containers at once with your stack definition stored in a handy YAML file.

Installing Docker Compose on Linux

If you have either Docker for Mac or Docker for Windows installed then it already comes bundled with `docker-compose`, if however, you are using Linux, then you may need to install this yourself as it does not come as part of the default Docker package.

To install Docker Compose on Linux, execute the following command in your terminal:

```
$ curl -L
https://github.com/docker/compose/releases/download/1.8.0/docker-compose-`u
name -s`-`uname -m` > /usr/local/bin/docker-compose  && chmod +x
/usr/local/bin/docker-compose
```

Before we look at how we can run our application with `docker-compose`, let's take a look at the file we are going to run and some of the important facets of it:

```
1 version: '2'
2 services:
3   testserver:
4     image: testserver
5   curl:
6     image: appropriate/curl
7     entrypoint: sh -c  "sleep 3 && curl -XPOST testserver:8080/helloworld
-d '{\"name\":\"Nic\"}'"
```

Docker Compose files are written in YAML, inside this file you can define services that will make up your application. In our simple example, we are only describing two services. The first is our example code that we have just built and the second is a simple service that curls this API. As a production example, this is not particularly useful I admit, but it is only intended to show how to set up these files. As we progress through later chapters, we will heavily rely on compose files to create our databases and other data stores that make up our application.

Line 1 defines the version of the Docker compose file we are using, version 2 is the latest version and is a breaking change from version 1 which along with the `--link` directive is now deprecated and will be removed in a future release.

In **line 2** we define the services. Services are the containers that you would like to start with your stack. Each service has to have a unique name to the compose file, but not necessarily to all the containers running on your Docker Engine. To avoid conflicts when starting a stack, we can pass `-p projectname` to the `docker-compose up` command; this will prefix the name of any of our containers with the specified project name.

The minimum information you need to specify for a service is the image, which is the image you wish to start a container from. In the same way that `docker run` works, this can either be a local image on the Docker Engine or it can be a reference to an image in a remote registry. When you start a stack, compose will check to see if the image is available locally and if not it will automatically pull it from the registry.

Line 6 defines our second service; this is simply going to execute a command to curl a request to the API exposed by the first service.

In this service definition block, we are both specifying the image and an entry point.

Service startup

The previous command looks a little weird, but there is a gotcha with Docker compose, which quite a few people fall foul too, there is no real way for compose to know when an application is running. Even if we use the `depends-on` configuration, we are only informing compose that there are dependencies and that it should control the start order of the services.

```
sh -c  "sleep 3 && curl -XPOST testserver:8080/helloworld -d
'{\"name\":\"Nic\"}'"
```

All compose will do is check that the container has been started. The general problem occurs with a misunderstanding that a container being started equals it is ready to receive requests. More often than not this is not the case, it can take time for your application to start and be ready to accept requests. If you have a dependency like we have specified in our entry point to curl the endpoint in another service, then we cannot assume that the dependent service is ready for requests before we execute our command. We will cover a pattern for dealing with this in `Chapter 6`, *Microservice Frameworks*, but for now we can be aware that:

> *"Container started, and service ready is not the same thing."*

In our simple example, we know that it roughly takes a second or so for the service to start, so we will just sleep for three seconds to give it plenty of time to get ready before executing our command. This method is not good practice, and it is only to illustrate how we can use compose to link services. In reality, you would probably never start a single command like we are here in your compose file.

When you use a Docker network, Docker automatically adds a mapping to the containers `resolve.conf` pointing to the built in Docker DNS server, we can then contact other containers connected to the same network by referencing them by name. Looking at our curl command, this DNS capability is exactly what allows us to use the hostname testserver.

OK, time to test it out, run the following command from your terminal:

```
$ docker-compose up
```

All being well you should see the following message returned in the output:

```
{"message":"Hello Nic"}
```

Ctrl + *C* will exit compose, however, since we did run this with the `docker run` command and passed the arguments `--rm` to remove the container, we need to ensure that we clean up after ourselves. To remove any stopped container that you have started with `docker-compose`, we can use the particular compose command `rm` and pass the `-v` argument to remove any associated volumes:

```
$ docker-compose rm -v
```

Specifying the location of a compose file

Whenever you run `docker-compose`, it looks for a file named `docker-compose.yml` in the current folder as a default file. To specify an alternate file, we can pass the `-f` argument to compose with a path to the compose file we would like to load:

```
$ docker-compose -f ./docker-compose.yml up
```

Specifying a project name

As we discussed earlier when we start `docker-compose`, it will create services with the given names in your Compose file appending the project name `default` to them. If we need to run multiple instances of this compose file, then `docker-compose` will not start another instance as it will check to see if any services are running with the given names first. To override this, we can specify the project name replacing the default name of `default`. To do this we just need to specify the `-p projectname` argument to our command as follows:

```
$ docker-compose -p testproject up
```

This will then create two containers:

- `testproject_testserver`
- `testproject_curl`

Summary

In summary, we have learned how to work with Docker in this chapter, and while this is only a brief overview, I suggest you head over to the documentation and read more in depth on the concepts of Dockerfiles, Composefiles, the Docker Engine, and Docker Compose. Docker is an invaluable tool for development, testing, and production and as we progress through the following chapters, we will use these concepts extensively. In the next chapter, we are going to look at testing, which builds on all of the things you have learned so far.

4
Testing

When you try to define what testing is, you will come up with a multitude of answers, and many of us will not understand the full benefits of testing until we've been burnt by buggy software or we have tried to change a complex code base which has no tests.

When I tried to define testing, I came up with the following:

> *"The art of a good night's sleep is knowing you will not get woken by a support call and the piece of mind from being able to confidently change your software in an always moving market."*

OK, so I am trying to be funny, but the concept is correct. Nobody enjoys debugging poorly written code, and indeed, nobody enjoys the stress caused when a system fails. Starting out with a mantra of quality first can alleviate many of these problems.

Over the last 20 years, techniques like TDD have become commonplace. In some instances, it is not as common as I would like, but at least people are talking about testing now. In some ways, we have the Agile Alliance to thank for this:

> *the principle of releasing little and often provides significant business benefits; the downside (or the benefit, depending on your viewpoint) to releasing little and often is that you can no longer spend three months running through a regression test suite before you release to market.*

In my office, context switching is one of the biggest complaints. Nobody enjoys having to drop what they are doing to investigate a problem on work that they or even a colleague may have carried out months or years ago. We want to be moving forward; and to ensure we can do that, we have to make sure that what we have previously delivered meets the specification and is of high enough quality to meet the client's requirement.

I also mentioned a change in my definition, and one of the biggest problems with change is the concern that the change you are making may have an undesirable effect on another part of the system. This effect applies to microservices as well as large monolithic systems.

What if I also told you that the side effect of code that is easy to test is probably well-written code that is loosely coupled and has the right abstractions?

Testing, however, is not just about the developer: there is a definite need for manual testing by people detached from the code base. This exploratory testing can bring out missing requirements or incorrect assumptions. In itself, this is a specialized field and way beyond the scope of this book, so we are going to concentrate on the kind of testing that you should be doing.

The testing pyramid

Mike Cohn is credited with having created the concept of a testing pyramid in his book *Succeeding with Agile*. The concept is that your cheapest (fastest) tests to run, which will be your unit tests, go at the bottom of the pyramid; service level integration tests are on top of this, and at the very top, you place full end-to-end tests, which are the costliest element. Because this is a pyramid, the number of tests gets smaller as you move up the pyramid.

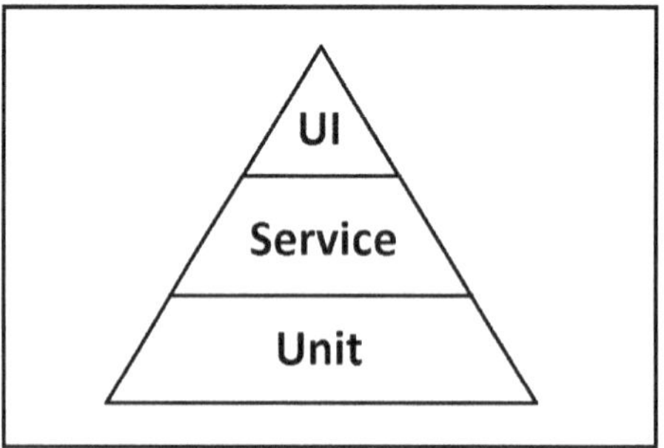

In the early days of automated testing, all the testing was completed at the top of the pyramid. While this did work from a quality perspective, it meant the process of debugging the area at fault would be incredibly complicated and time-consuming. If you were lucky, there might be a complete failure which could be tracked down to a stack trace. If you were unlucky, then the problem would be behavioral; and even if you knew the system inside out, it would involve plowing through thousands of lines of code and manually repeating the action to reproduce the failure.

Outside-in development

When writing tests, I like to follow a process called outside-in development. With outside-in development, you start by writing your tests almost at the top of the pyramid, determine what the functionality is going to be for the story you are working on, and then write some failing test for this story. Then you work on implementing the unit tests and code which starts to get the various steps in the behavioral tests to pass.

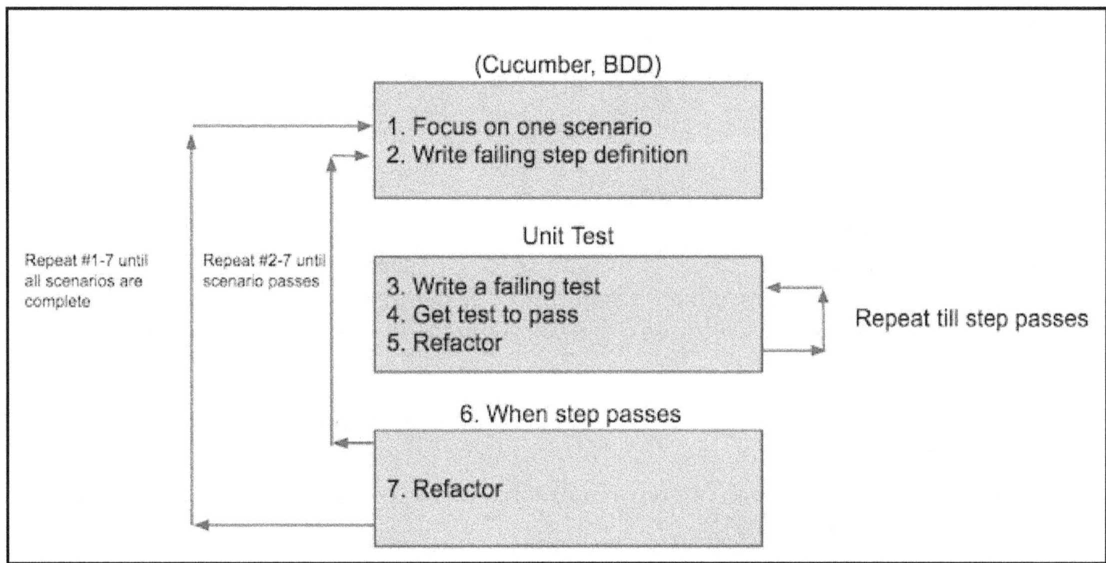

This initial specification also becomes the living documentation for your system. We will go into more detail as to how you can create this later in this chapter, but more often than not it is written in a language like **Gherkin** and is defined by working in a group with a domain specialist like a product owner, a developer, and a testing expert. The intention behind Gherkin is to create a universal language that everyone understands. This ubiquitous language uses verbs and nouns that have special meaning to the team, and which is almost always domain-specific, but should also be understandable to outsiders.

```
Feature: As a user when I call the search endpoint, I would like to receive
a list of kittens
```

The feature is the story which, in an agile environment is owned by the product owner. The feature is then broken down into scenarios which explain in greater detail the qualities that the code must have to be acceptable.

```
Scenario: Invalid query
 Given I have no search criteria
```

```
When I call the search endpoint
Then I should receive a bad request message
```

When we get to the section on BDD in a little while we will examine this in greater depth; we will also look at a framework for Go for writing and executing Cucumber specifications. Now, however, I am going to break the rules of outside in development by showing you how to write great unit tests in Go. The concepts we are about to learn will be greatly beneficial when we do start to look at BDD, so I think it is best we cover them first. Like the previous chapters, it will be useful to you when reading through this chapter to have the source code handy; you can clone the code from the following location: `https://github.com/building-microservices-with-go/chapter4.git`

Unit tests

Our unit tests go right down to the bottom of the pyramid. This book was never intended to be a lesson in TDD, there are plenty of better places to learn that. We will, however, take a look at the testing framework which is built into Go. Before we do that, let's just remind ourselves of the three laws of testing as defined by the awesome Uncle Bob Martin in his book *Clean Code*:

- **First law**: You may not write production code until you have written a failing unit test
- **Second law**: You may not write more of a unit test than is sufficient to fail, and not compiling is failing
- **Third law**: You may not write more production code than is sufficient to pass the currently failing test

One of the most effective ways to test a microservice in Go is not to fall into the trap of trying to execute all the tests through the HTTP interface. We need to develop a pattern that avoids creating a physical web server for testing our handlers, the code to create this kind of test is slow to run and incredibly tedious to write. What need to be doing is to test our handlers and the code within them as unit tests. These tests will run far quicker than testing through the web server, and if we think about the coverage, we will be able to test the wiring of the handlers in the Cucumber tests that execute a request to the running server which overall gives us 100% coverage of our code.

`main.go`

```
func main() {
  err := http.ListenAndServe(":2323", &handlers.SearchHandler{})
  if err != nil {
    log.Fatal(err)
```

```
    }
}
```

You will see in the main function that we have split the handlers out into a separate package. Breaking up the code in this way allows us to test these in isolation, so let's go ahead and write some unit tests for our `SearchHandler`.

The convention is that we define our test files in the same folder as the package to which they belong, and we name them the same as the file they are testing followed by `_test`. For our example, we are going to write some tests for our `SearchHandler` which lives in the `handlers/search.go` file; therefore our test file will be named `handlers/search_test.go`.

The signature for a test method looks like this:

```
func TestXxx(*testing.T)
```

The name of the test must have a particular name beginning with `Test` and then immediately following this an uppercase character or number. So we could not call our test `TestmyHandler`, but we could name it `Test1Handler` or `TestMyHandler`.

Again, drawing on Uncle Bob's wisdom, we need to think about the names of our tests as carefully as we would the names for our methods in our production code.

The first test we are going to write is the one who will validate that search criteria have been sent with the request and the implementation is going to look like this:

```
func TestSearchHandlerReturnsBadRequestWhenNoSearchCriteriaIsSent(t
*testing.T) {
  handler := SearchHandler{}
  request := httptest.NewRequest("GET", "/search", nil)
  response := httptest.NewRecorder()

  handler.ServeHTTP(response, request)

  if response.Code != http.StatusBadRequest {
    t.Errorf("Expected BadRequest got %v", response.Code)
  }
}
```

The net/http/httptest package has two fantastic convenience methods for us NewRequest and NewResponse, if you are familiar with unit testing concepts, then one of the fundamentals isolate dependency. Often we replace the dependencies with Mocks or Spies which allow us to test the behavior of our code without having to execute code in the dependencies. These two functions enable us to do exactly this; they generate Mock versions of the dependent objects http.Request and http.ResponseWriter.

httptest.NewRequest

The first line we need to pay attention to is line **11**: the net/http/httptest package has some nice convenience methods for us. The NewRequest method returns an incoming server request which we can then pass to our http.Handler:

```
func NewRequest(method, target string, body io.Reader) *http.Request
```

We can pass parameters to the method and the target, which is either the path or an absolute URL. If we only pass a path, then example.com will be used as our host setting. Finally, we can give it an io.Reader file which will correspond to the body of the request; if we do not pass a nil value then Request.ContentLength is set.

httptest.NewRecorder

In line **12** we are creating a ResponseRecorder type: this is going to be our instance of ResponseWriter that we pass to the handler. Because a handler has no return function to validate correct operation, we need to check what has been written to the output. The ResponseRecorder type is an implementation of http.ResponseWriter which does just that: it records all the mutations we make so that it is later possible to make our assertions against it.

```
type ResponseRecorder struct {
        Code      int           // the HTTP response code from WriteHeader
        HeaderMap http.Header   // the HTTP response headers
        Body      *bytes.Buffer // if non-nil, the bytes.Buffer to append
written data to
        Flushed   bool
        // contains filtered or unexported fields
 }
```

All we then need to do is to call the ServeHTTP method with our dummy request and response and then assert that we have the correct outcome.

Go does not have an assertion library as you would find with RSpec or JUnit. We will look at a third-party framework later in this chapter, but for now, let's concentrate on the standard packages.

In line **16**, we are checking to see if the response code returned from the handler is equal to the expected code `http.BadRequest`. If it is not, then we call the Errorf method on the testing framework.

ErrorF

```
func (c *T) Errorf(format string, args ...interface{})
```

The `Errorf` function takes the parameters of a format string and a variadic list of parameters; internally this calls the `Logf` method before calling `Fail`.

If we run our tests by running the command `go test -v -race ./...`, we should see the following output:

```
=== RUN   TestSearchHandlerReturnsBadRequestWhenNoSearchCriteriaIsSent
--- FAIL: TestSearchHandlerReturnsBadRequestWhenNoSearchCriteriaIsSent
(0.00s)
     search_test.go:17: Expected BadRequest got 200
 FAIL
 exit status 1
 FAIL    github.com/nicholasjackson/building-microservices-in-
 go/chapter5/handlers    0.016s
```

The `-v` flag will print the output in a verbose style, and it will also print all the text written to the output by the application, even if the test succeeds.

The `-race` flag enables Go's race detector which holds discover bugs with concurrency problems. A data race occurs when two Go routines access the same variable concurrently, and at least one of the accesses is a write. The race flag adds a small overhead to your test run, so I recommend you add it to all executions.

Using `-./...` as our final parameter allows us to run all our tests in the current folder as well as the child folders, it saves us from manually having to construct a list of packages or files to test.

Now we have a failing test we can go ahead and write the implementation to make the test pass:

```
decoder := json.NewDecoder(r.Body)
defer r.Body.Close()

request := new(searchRequest)
err := decoder.Decode(request)
if err != nil {
  http.Error(rw, "Bad Request", http.StatusBadRequest)
  return
}
```

When we rerun the tests, we can see that they have succeeded:

```
=== RUN   TestSearchHandlerReturnsBadRequestWhenNoSearchCriteriaIsSent
--- PASS: TestSearchHandlerReturnsBadRequestWhenNoSearchCriteriaIsSent
(0.00s)
PASS
ok      github.com/nicholasjackson/building-microservices-in-
go/chapter5/handlers    1.022s
```

This output is awesome; but what if passing a query to the request with a blank string constitutes a failure? Time to write another test:

```
func TestSearchHandlerReturnsBadRequestWhenBlankSearchCriteriaIsSent(t
*testing.T) {
  handler := SearchHandler{}
  data, _ := json.Marshal(searchRequest{})
  request := httptest.NewRequest("POST", "/search",
bytes.NewReader(data))
  response := httptest.NewRecorder()

  handler.ServeHTTP(response, request)

  if response.Code != http.StatusBadRequest {
    t.Errorf("Expected BadRequest got %v", response.Code)
  }
}
```

This test is very similar to the last one; the only difference is that we are passing some JSON in the request body. While this test will fail correctly, we should take the lead from Uncle Bob and refactor this to make it more readable:

```
func TestSearchHandlerReturnsBadRequestWhenBlankSearchCriteriaIsSent(t
*testing.T) {
  r, rw, handler := setupTest(&searchRequest{})

```

```
    handler.ServeHTTP(rw, r)

    if rw.Code != http.StatusBadRequest {
      t.Errorf("Expected BadRequest got %v", rw.Code)
    }
}
```

We have refactored our test to add a setup method which is shared across the two tests, the intention behind this is to keep our tests focused on three core areas:

- Setup
- Execute
- Assert

Bad tests with duplicated code can be worse than bad code: your tests should be clear, easy to understand and contain the same care that you would add to your production code.

Now, if the test fails, we can go ahead and update our code to implement the feature:

```
if err != nil || len(request.Query) < 1 {
       http.Error(rw, "Bad Request", http.StatusBadRequest)
       return
   }
```

All we needed to do was make a simple modification to our `if` statement. As our system grows in complexity and we find more cases for what constitutes an invalid search query, we will refactor this into a separate method; but, for now, this is the minimum we need to do to make the test pass.

Dependency injection and mocking

To get the tests that return items from the `Search` handler to pass, we are going to need a data store. Whether we implement our data store in a database or a simple in-memory store we do not want to run our tests against the actual data store as we will be checking both data store and our handler. For this reason, we are going to need to manage the dependencies on our handler so that we can replace them in our tests. To do this, we are going to use a technique called dependency injection where we will pass our dependencies into our handler rather than creating them internally.

This method allows us to replace these dependencies with stubs or mocks when we are testing the handler, making it possible to control the behavior of the dependency and check how the calling code responds to this.

Before we do anything, we need to create our dependency. In our simple example, we are going to create an in-memory data store which has a single method:

```
Search(string) []Kitten
```

To replace the type with a mock, we need to change our handler to depend on an interface which represents our data store. We can then interchange this with either an actual data store or a mock instance of the store without needing to change the underlying code:

```
type Store interface {
    Search(name string) []Kitten
}
```

We can now go ahead and create the implementation for this. Since this is a simple example, we are going to hardcode our list of kittens as a slice and the search method will just select from this slice when the criteria given as a parameter matches the name of the kitten.

OK, great; we now have our data store created, so let's see how we are going to modify our handler to accept this dependency. It is quite simple: because we created a struct which implements the `ServeHTTP` method, we can just add our dependencies onto this struct:

```
Search {
    Store data.Store
}
```

Note how we are using a reference to the interface rather than the concrete type, which allows us to interchange this object with anything that implements the store interface.

Now, back to our unit tests: we would like to ensure that, when we call the `ServeHTTP` method with a search string, we are querying the data store and returning the kittens from it.

To do this, we are going to create a mock instance of our data store. We could create the mock ourselves; however, there is an excellent package by Matt Ryer who incidentally is also a Packt author. Testify (`https://github.com/stretchr/testify.git`) has a fully featured mocking framework with assertions. It also has an excellent package for testing the equality of objects in our tests and removes quite a lot of the boilerplate code we have to write.

In the data package, we are going to create a new file called `mockstore.go`. This structure will be our mock implementation of the data store:

```
// MockStore is a mock implementation of a datastore for testing purposes
type MockStore struct {
```

```
7   mock.Mock
8 }
9
10 //Search returns the object which was passed to the mock on setup
11 func (m *MockStore) Search(name string) []Kitten {
12   args := m.Mock.Called(name)
13
14   return args.Get(0).([]Kitten)
15 }
```

In line **6**, we are defining our `MockStore` object. There is nothing unusual about this, except you will note that it is embedding the `mock.Mock` type. Embedding Mock will give us all of the methods on the `mock.Mock` struct.

When we write the implementation for our search method, we are first calling the `Called` method and passing it the arguments that are sent to `Search`. Internally, the mock package is recording that this method was called and with what parameters so that we can later write an assertion against it:

```
args := m.Mock.Called(name)
```

Finally, we are returning `args.Get(0).(Kitten)`. When we call the `Called` method, the mock returns us a list of arguments that we provided in the setup. We are casting this to our output type and returning to the caller. Let's take a quick look at the test method and see how this works.

Line **57** is the start of our test setup. The first thing we are going to do is to create an instance of our `MockStore`. We then set this as a dependency for our `Search` handler. If we skip back up the file to line **38**, you will see that we are calling the `On` method on our `mockStore`. The `On` method is a setup method for the mock and has the signature:

```
func (c *Call) On(methodName string, arguments ...interface{}) *Call
```

If we do not call the `On` method with the parameter `Search` then when we call the `Search` method in our code we will get an exception from the test saying that `Search` has been called yet has not been setup. One of the reasons why I like to use mocking rather than a simple Stub is this ability to assert that a method has been called and we can explicitly dictate the behavior that the code under test is allowed to exhibit. This way we can ensure that we are not doing work the output of which has not been tested.

In our instance, we are setting up the condition that, when the `Search` method is called with the parameter `Fat Freddy's Cat`, we would like to return an array of kittens.

The assertion is that we are calling the `Search` method on the data store and passing it the query that was sent in the HTTP response. Using assertions in this way is a handy technique as it allows us to test the unhappy path such as when a data store may not be able to return data due to an internal error or another reason. If we were trying to test this with an integration test, it could be tough to persuade the database to fail on demand.

Why don't you spend five minutes as a little exercise and go ahead and write this code to finish off?

Did it all work? Don't worry if not, you can just check out the example code to see where you have gone wrong, but I hope that the process is useful. You can see how you can take a measured approach through two layers of testing to produce a working application. These tests are now your safety net: whenever you change the code to add a new feature, you can be sure that you are not breaking something unintentionally.

Code coverage

Code coverage is an excellent metric to ensure that the code you are writing has adequate coverage.

The most simplistic way of getting a readout of test coverage is to execute our tests with the `-cover` option:

```
go test -cover ./...
```

If we run this against our example code in the root folder of our example code we will see the following output:

```
$go test -cover ./...
? github.com/building-microservices-with-go/chapter4 [no test files]
ok github.com/building-microservices-with-go/chapter4/data 0.017s coverage:
20.0% of statements
ok github.com/building-microservices-with-go/chapter4/features 0.018s
coverage: 0.0% of statements [no tests to run]
ok github.com/building-microservices-with-go/chapter4/handlers 0.018s
coverage: 100.0% of statements
```

Now our handlers look beautiful: we have 100% coverage of this package. However, our data package is only reporting 20% coverage. Before we get too alarmed at this, let's take a look at what we are trying to test.

If we first examine the `datastore.go` file, this is only an interface and therefore does not have any test files; however, the `memorystore.go` does. This file is well covered with 100% test coverage for this file. The files that are letting us down are our mock class and our MongoDB implementation.

Now the mock type I am not too bothered about, but the Mongo store is an interesting problem.

This type would be incredibly difficult to test due to the dependency on the MongoDB. We could create a mock implementation of the Mongo package to test our code, but this could be more complicated than the implementation. There are however some critical areas where we could make mistakes in this class. Consider line **26**:

```
c := s.DB("kittenserver").C("kittens")
```

This line retrieves the collection `kittens` from the database `kittenserver`. If we make a simple spelling mistake here, then our application will not work. We do not want to wait until this code gets out into production to see that this is happening. We also do not want to have to manually test this as, in a larger application, this could be considerably time-consuming. Integration tests are really where our Cucumber tests shine. If you remember, we are writing some very high-level end-to-end tests to make sure that the input into our API results in the correct output. Because this is running against an actual database, if we had made such an error, then it would be picked up. So, while the Go coverage report states that we are not covered, it's because we have higher level tests that the Go test is not looking at, so we are covered. The central area where we could run into problems would be by omitting line **23**.

If we do not close the connection to the database after we have opened it, we are going to be leaking connections; after a while, we may find that we can no longer open another as the pool is exhausted. There is no simple way to test this, but there is, however, a way to catch the problem post-deploy. When we look at logging and monitoring in `Chapter 7`, *Logging and Monitoring*, we will see how we can expose such information to help us ensure our production system is functioning correctly.

Behavioral Driven Development

Behavioral Driven Development (**BDD**) and is a technique often executed by an application framework called **Cucumber**. It was developed by Dan North and was designed to create a common ground between developers and product owners. In theory, it should be possible to test complete coverage of the system with BDD; however, since this would create a significant number of slow running tests it is not the best approach. What we should be doing is defining the boundaries of our system, and we can save the granularity for our unit tests.

In our Three Amigos group, we discuss the facets of the feature and what the essential qualities of it are and start to write scenarios.

Sad path

```
Scenario: User passes no search criteria
  Given I have no search criteria
  When I call the search endpoint
  Then I should receive a bad request message
```

Happy path

```
Scenario: User passes valid search criteria
  Given I have valid search criteria
  When I call the search endpoint
  Then I should receive a list of kittens
```

These scenarios are quite a simple example, but I think you can understand how, when using this language with non-technical people, it would be quite straightforward to come up with these descriptions. From an automation perspective what we then do is to write the steps which correspond to each of these `Given`, `When`, and `Then` statements.

For this book, we are going to take a look at the GoDog framework which allows us to implement the step definitions in Go. We will first need to install the application you can do this by running the command: `fgo get github.com/DATA-DOG/godog/cmd/godog`

If we look at `features/search.feature` we can see that we have implemented this feature and the scenarios.

If we run the `godog ./` command to run these tests without first creating the features, we should see the following error message:

```
Feature: As a user when I call the search endpoint, I would like to receive
a list of kittens

Scenario: Invalid query
# features/search.feature:4
    Given I have no search criteria
    When I call the search endpoint
    Then I should receive a bad request message

Scenario: Valid query
# features/search.feature:9
    Given I have valid search criteria
    When I call the search endpoint
    Then I should receive a list of kittens

2 scenarios (2 undefined)
6 steps (6 undefined)
321.121µs
```

You can implement step definitions for undefined steps with these snippets:

```
func iHaveNoSearchCriteria() error {
    return godog.ErrPending
}

func iCallTheSearchEndpoint() error {
    return godog.ErrPending
}

func iShouldReceiveABadRequestMessage() error {
    return godog.ErrPending
}

func iHaveAValidSearchCriteria() error {
    return godog.ErrPending
}

func iShouldReceiveAListOfKittens() error {
    return godog.ErrPending
}

func FeatureContext(s *godog.Suite) {
    s.Step(`^I have no search criteria$`, iHaveNoSearchCriteria)
    s.Step(`^I call the search endpoint$`, iCallTheSearchEndpoint)
    s.Step(`^I should receive a bad request message$`,
```

```
iShouldReceiveABadRequestMessage)
    s.Step(`^I have a valid search criteria$`, iHaveAValidSearchCriteria)
    s.Step(`^I should receive a list of kittens$`,
iShouldReceiveAListOfKittens)
}
```

Usefully, this gives us the boilerplate to perform our steps; once we implement this and rerun the command we get a different message:

```
Feature: As a user when I call the search endpoint, I would like to receive
a list of kittens

   Scenario: Invalid query                        # search.feature:4
     Given I have no search criteria              # search_test.go:6 ->
github.com/nicholasjackson/building-microservices-in-
go/chapter5/features.iHaveNoSearchCriteria
     TODO: write pending definition
     When I call the search endpoint
     Then I should receive a bad request message

   Scenario: Valid query                          # search.feature:9
     Given I have a valid search criteria         # search_test.go:18 ->
github.com/nicholasjackson/building-microservices-in-
go/chapter5/features.iHaveAValidSearchCriteria
       TODO: write pending definition
     When I call the search endpoint
     Then I should receive a list of kittens

 2 scenarios (2 pending)
 6 steps (2 pending, 4 skipped)
 548.978µs
```

We can now start filling in the details for the steps which should fail as we have not yet written our code.

We can implement our code using plain Go which gives us the capability to use any of the interfaces and packages. Take a look at the example which corresponds to the method `iCallTheSearchEndpoint`:

```
func iCallTheSearchEndpoint() error {
  var request []byte

  response, err = http.Post("http://localhost:2323", "application/json",
bytes.NewReader(request))
  return err
}

func iShouldReceiveABadRequestMessage() error {
```

```
  if response.StatusCode != http.StatusBadRequest {
    return fmt.Errorf("Should have recieved a bad response")
  }

  return nil
}
```

Now we have some tests implemented we should run Cucumber tests as some of the steps should be passing. To test the system, we need to start our main application; we could split our main function out into a `StartServer` function, which could be called directly from Cucumber. However, that is omitting the fact that we forgot to call `StartServer` in the main function. For this reason, the best approach is to test the complete application in our Cucumber test from the outside in.

To do this, we are going to add a couple of new functions to the `features/search_test.go` file:

```
func FeatureContext(s *godog.Suite) {
  s.Step(`^I have no search criteria$`, iHaveNoSearchCriteria)
  s.Step(`^I call the search endpoint$`, iCallTheSearchEndpoint)
  s.Step(`^I should receive a bad request message$`, iShouldReceiveABadRequestMessage)
  s.Step(`^I have a valid search criteria$`, iHaveAValidSearchCriteria)
  s.Step(`^I should receive a list of kittens$`, iShouldReceiveAListOfKittens)

  s.BeforeScenario(func(interface{}) {
    startServer()
    fmt.Printf("Server running with pid: %v", server.Process.Pid)
  })

  s.AfterScenario(func(interface{}, error) {
    server.Process.Kill()
  })
}

var server *exec.Cmd

func startServer() {
  server = exec.Command("go", "run", "../main.go")
  go server.Run()
  time.Sleep(3 * time.Second)
}
```

In line **66**, we are using the `BeforeScenario` method on `godog`: this allows us to run a function before our scenario starts. We would use this for clearing up any data in the data store, but in our simple example, we are just going to start our application server. Later on in this chapter, we will look at a more complex example, which uses Docker Compose to start a stack of containers containing our server and a database.

The `startServer` function spawns a new process to run `go run ../main.go`. We have to run this in `gofunc` as we do not want the test to block. Line **81** contains a small pause to see if our server has started. In reality, we should be checking the health endpoint of the API, but for now, this will suffice.

Line **71** will execute after the scenario has finished and tears down our server. If we don't do this then the next time we try to start our server it will fail as the process will already be running and bound to the port.

Let's go ahead and run our Cucumber tests, and the output should look something like this:

```
Feature: As a user when I call the search endpoint, I would like to receive
a list of kittens
 Server running with pid: 91535
   Scenario: Invalid query                          # search.feature:4
     Given I have no search criteria                # search_test.go:17 ->
github.com/building-microservices-with-
go/chapter4/features.iHaveNoSearchCriteria
     When I call the search endpoint                # search_test.go:25 ->
github.com/building-microservices-with-
go/chapter4/features.iCallTheSearchEndpoint
     Then I should receive a bad request message # search_test.go:32 ->
github.com/building-microservices-with-
go/chapter4/features.iShouldReceiveABadRequestMessage
 Server running with pid: 91615
   Scenario: Valid query                        # search.feature:9
     Given I have a valid search criteria       # search_test.go:40 ->
github.com/building-microservices-with-
go/chapter4/features.iHaveAValidSearchCriteria
     Do not have a valid criteria
     When I call the search endpoint
     Then I should receive a list of kittens

 --- Failed scenarios:

     search.feature:10

 2 scenarios (1 passed, 1 failed)
 6 steps (3 passed, 1 failed, 2 skipped)
 6.010954682s
```

```
make: *** [cucumber] Error 1
```

Perfect! We are getting there, some of the steps are passing now, and one of the features is passing. We can now go ahead finish these tests off, but first, we need to look at how we can use Docker Compose to test against a real database.

Testing with Docker Compose

So far this has been relatively simple implementation, but it is not particularly useful as a real-world example. It is going to be pretty rare that you find yourself implementing an in-memory data store with only three items in it. More often than not you are going to be using a functioning database. Of course, the integration between a real database and our code needs testing; we need to ensure that the connection to the data store is correct and that the query we are sending to it is valid.

To do this, we need to spin up a real database and to do that we can use Docker-Compose as it is a fantastic way of starting our dependencies.

In our sample file `docker-compose.yml`, we have the following:

```
version: '2'
services:
  mongodb:
    image: mongo
    ports:
      - 27017:27017
```

When we run `docker-compose up` command, we will download the image of MongoDB and start an instance exposing these ports on our local host.

We now need to create a new struct in our project which is going to implement the store interface. We can then execute commands against the real database as opposed to using a mock or a simple in-memory store.

The implementation for `MongoStore` is quite straight forward. Looking at the file in `data/monogstore.go`, you will see that we have two additional methods not defined in our interface, namely:

```
DelleteAllKittens
InsertKittens
```

These are here because we need them for the setup of our functional tests.

If we look at our file `features/search_test.go` you will see that we have added a couple of extra calls to the `FeatureContext` method in our setup.

The first thing we are doing is to call the `waitForDB` method: because we cannot control when our Mongo instance is going to be ready to accept connections, we need to wait for it before kicking off the tests. The process is that we will try to create an instance to our `MongoStore` using the convenience method `NewMongoStore`, internally this is doing the following work:

```
// NewMongoStore creates an instance of MongoStore with the given connection string
func NewMongoStore(connection string) (*MongoStore, error) {
  session, err := mgo.Dial(connection)
  if err != nil {
    return nil, err
  }

  return &MongoStore{session: session}, nil
}
```

The `Dial` method attempts to connect to the instance of MongoDB specified in the connection string. If this connection fails, then an error is returned. In our code, if we receive an error, we return this to the caller of `NewMongoStore` with a nil instance of our struct. The `waitForDB` method works by repeatedly attempting to create this connection until it no longer receives an error. To avoid spamming the database while it is trying to start, we sleep for one second after every failed attempt, to a maximum time of 10 seconds. This method will block the main Go routine, but this is by design as we do not want the tests to execute until we are sure we have this connection:

```
func waitForDB() {
  var err error

  for i := 0; i < 10; i++ {
    store, err = data.NewMongoStore("localhost")
    if err == nil {
      break
    }
    time.Sleep(1 * time.Second)
  }
}
```

We have also added some code to the `BeforeScenario` setup: the first thing we are going to do is wipe our database clearing down any previous test data. Clearing data is an incredibly important step as, should we have had any methods which mutate the data; we would not get predictable test results after each run.

Finally, we insert the `setupData` method into our test data, and then we will proceed to execute the tests.

We now have quite a few things to do before we can test our code, we need to run docker-compose, perform our tests and then stop docker-compose. An efficient way of scripting this process is to use Makefiles, Makefiles have been around forever and are still the primary software build mechanisms for many applications. They allow us to define commands in a simple text file which we can then run by executing **make [command]**.

If we look at the Cucumber command in the Makefile in the example repository, we can see how we script the steps that need to be carried out to run our tests. We are starting our Mongo instance with `docker-compose`, running our Cucumber tests and then tearing the database down again:

```
cucumber:
    docker-compose up -d
    cd features && godog ./
    docker-compose stop
```

If you are wondering why we still need the `waitForDB` method when we are starting our database before running the tests, remember that Docker only knows when the primary process is executed. There can be a considerable lag between the commencement of the process and it being ready to accept connections. To run this we run `make cucumber` from the command line the result should be passing cucumber tests:

```
$make cucumber
docker-compose up -d
chapter4_mongodb_1 is up-to-date
cd features && godog ./
Feature: As a user when I call the search endpoint, I would like to receive
a list of kittens
Server running with pid: 88200
  Scenario: Invalid query # search.feature:4
    Given I have no search criteria # search_test.go:21 ->
github.com/building-microservices-with-
go/chapter4/features.iHaveNoSearchCriteria
    When I call the search endpoint # search_test.go:29 ->
github.com/building-microservices-with-
go/chapter4/features.iCallTheSearchEndpoint
    Then I should receive a bad request message # search_test.go:40 ->
github.com/building-microservices-with-
go/chapter4/features.iShouldReceiveABadRequestMessage
Server running with pid: 88468
  Scenario: Valid query # search.feature:9
    Given I have a valid search criteria # search_test.go:48 ->
github.com/building-microservices-with-
```

```
go/chapter4/features.iHaveAValidSearchCriteria
    When I call the search endpoint # search_test.go:29 ->
github.com/building-microservices-with-
go/chapter4/features.iCallTheSearchEndpoint
    Then I should receive a list of kittens # search_test.go:54 ->
github.com/building-microservices-with-
go/chapter4/features.iShouldReceiveAListOfKittens

2 scenarios (2 passed)
6 steps (6 passed)
7.028664s
docker-compose stop
Stopping chapter4_mongodb_1 ... done
```

That is all for this section, we have learned that, with a few well-placed patterns, it is easy to write a robust test suite that will keep us safe and sound asleep instead of getting up in the middle of the night to diagnose a broken system. In the next section, we are going to look at some of the fantastic features of Go to ensure that our code is fast and optimized.

Benchmarking and profiling

Go has two excellent ways to analyze the performance of your code. We have benchmark tests and the fantastic pprof.

Benchmarks

Benchmarking is a way of measuring the performance of your code by executing it multiple times with a fixed workload. We took a look at this briefly in `Chapter 1`, *Introduction to Microservices*, where we ascertained that the `json.Marshal` method was slower than the `json.Encode` method. While this is a useful feature, I find it tough to work out what I should benchmark. If I am writing an algorithm, then this is relatively straightforward. However, when writing a microservice that is predominately interacting with a database, it is far more challenging.

To demonstrate how easy it is to execute benchmarks in Go, take a look at `chandlers/search_bench_test.go`:

```
func BenchmarkSearchHandler(b *testing.B) {
  mockStore = &data.MockStore{}
  mockStore.On("Search", "Fat Freddy's Cat").Return([]data.Kitten{
    data.Kitten{
      Name: "Fat Freddy's Cat",
```

```
16      },
17    })
18
19    search := Search{DataStore: mockStore}
20
21    for i := 0; i < b.N; i++ {
22      r := httptest.NewRequest("POST", "/search",
      bytes.NewReader([]byte(`{"query":"Fat Freddy's Cat"}`)))
23      rr := httptest.NewRecorder()
24      search.ServeHTTP(rr, r)
25    }
26  }
```

The most important part of this code is hidden away at line **21**:

```
for n := 0; n < b.N; n++
```

When running a benchmark, Go needs to run it multiple times to get an accurate reason. The number of times that the benchmark will run is the field `N` on the benchmark's struct. Before setting this number, Go will execute a few iterations of your code to get an approximate measurement of the execution time.

We would execute our benchmark using the `go test-bench -benchmem` command:

```
go test -bench=. -benchmem
BenchmarkSearchHandler-8            50000          43183 ns/op        49142
B/op           68 allocs/op
PASS
ok      github.com/building-microservices-with-go/chapter4/handlers
2.495s
```

Here we are passing an additional flag to see the memory allocations for each execution. We know that our handler when running with the mock takes 43,183 nanoseconds or 0.043183 milliseconds to execute and performs 68 memory allocations. It'd be good if the code would run this fast when running in real life, but we might have to wait a few years before we see this level of speed from an API connected to a database.

One of the other nice features of benchmark tests is that we can run them and it outputs profiles which can be used with pprof:

```
go test -bench=. -cpuprofile=cpu.prof -blockprofile=block.prof -
memprofile=mem.prof
```

The output of this command will give us more information about where this time and memory is being consumed and can help us to optimize our code correctly.

Profiling

When we wish to take a look at the speed of our program, the best technique we can employ is profiling. Profiling automatically samples your running application while it is executing; and then we can compute that data, such as the running time of a particular function, into a statistical summary called a profile.

Go supports three different types of profiling:

- **CPU**: Identifies the tasks which require the most CPU time
- **Heap**: Identifies the statements responsible for allocating the most memory
- **Blocking**: Identifies the operations responsible for blocking Go routines for the longest time

If we would like to enable profiling on our application, we can do one of two things:

- Add `import "net/http/pprof"` to your startup file
- Manually start profiling

The first option is the most straightforward. You only add it to the beginning of your main Go file and, if you are not already running an HTTP web server, start one:

```
import _ "net/http/pprof"

go func() {
    log.Println(http.ListenAndServe("localhost:6060", nil))
}()
```

This method then exposes various paths on your HTTP server at `/debug/pprof/` which can then be accessed via a URL. The side effect of this, however, is that when this import statement is in your go file, then you will be profiling, which not only could slow down your application, but you also don't want to expose this information for public consumption.

Another method of profiling is to start the profiler when you start your application by passing some additional command line flags:

```
var cpuprofile = flag.String("cpuprofile", "", "write cpu profile to
file")
var memprofile = flag.String("memprofile", "", "write memory profile
to file")
var store *data.MongoStore

func main() {
  flag.Parse()
```

```
25
26    if *cpuprofile != "" {
27      fmt.Println("Running with CPU profile")
28      f, err := os.Create(*cpuprofile)
29      if err != nil {
30        log.Fatal(err)
31      }
32      pprof.StartCPUProfile(f)
33    }
34
35    sigs := make(chan os.Signal, 1)
36    signal.Notify(sigs, syscall.SIGINT, syscall.SIGTERM)
37
38    go func() {
39      <-sigs
40      fmt.Println("Finished")
41      if *memprofile != "" {
42        f, err := os.Create(*memprofile)
43        if err != nil {
44          log.Fatal(err)
45        }
46        runtime.GC()
47        pprof.Lookup("heap").WriteTo(f, 0)
48        defer f.Close()
49      }
50      if *cpuprofile != "" {
51        pprof.StopCPUProfile()
52      }
53
54      os.Exit(0)
55    }()
```

On line **26**, we are checking whether we have specified an output file for CPU profiling, and if so, we are creating the file and then starting the profiler with `pprof.StartCPUProfile(f)`, and passing it a reference to the file:

```
func StartCPUProfile(w io.Writer) error
```

The `StartCPUProfile` function enables the CPU profiling for the current process and buffers the output to `w`. While running, the CPU profiler will stop your application roughly 100 times per second and record the data.

To profile heap allocations, we use a slightly different command:

```
pprof.Lookup("heap").WriteTo(f, 0)
func Lookup(name string) *Profile
```

The `Lookup()` function returns the profile with the given name, or if no such profile exists, the predefined profiles available are:

```
goroutine    - stack traces of all current goroutines
heap         - a sampling of all heap allocations
threadcreate - stack traces that led to the creation of new OS threads
block        - stack traces that led to blocking on synchronization
primitives

fuc (p *Profile) WriteTo(w io.Writer, debug int) error
```

`WriteTo` outputs the profile to the given write in the pprof format. If we set the debug flag to `1`, then `WriteTo` will add comments to function names and line numbers instead of just hexadecimal addresses that pprof uses. These comments are so you can read the file without needing any special tooling.

If you look at the example code in the folder `benchmark`, you will find an example profile and the binary from which it was generated.

We can now run the pprof tool to examine what is going on. To do this, we need to run the tool on the command line and provide a reference to the binary that the profile was executed against, and also the profile:

```
go tool pprof ./kittenserver ./cpu.prof
```

The simplest command we can run is `top`. Top will show us the functions which consumed the most CPU during the execution of our application:

```
Entering interactive mode (type "help" for commands)
 (pprof) top
 24460ms of 42630ms total (57.38%)
 Dropped 456 nodes (cum <= 213.15ms)
 Showing top 10 nodes out of 163 (cum >= 790ms)
       flat  flat%   sum%        cum   cum%
    16110ms 37.79% 37.79%    16790ms 39.39%  syscall.Syscall
     2670ms  6.26% 44.05%     2670ms  6.26%  runtime._ExternalCode
     1440ms  3.38% 47.43%     1560ms  3.66%  syscall.Syscall6
      900ms  2.11% 49.54%      900ms  2.11%  runtime.epollctl
      830ms  1.95% 51.49%     2370ms  5.56%  runtime.mallocgc
      610ms  1.43% 52.92%     1470ms  3.45%  runtime.pcvalue
      510ms  1.20% 54.12%      510ms  1.20%  runtime.heapBitsSetType
      470ms  1.10% 55.22%     2810ms  6.59%  runtime.gentraceback
      470ms  1.10% 56.32%      470ms  1.10%  runtime.memmove
      450ms  1.06% 57.38%      790ms  1.85%  runtime.deferreturn
 (pprof)
```

The main offender in this instance is `syscall.Syscall`. If we look this up in the documentation, we find that package syscall contains an interface to the low-level operating system primitives.

On its own this output is not particularly useful, so let's generate a call graph which will show us more detail. We can do this again from the pprof tool. However, we do need to install Graphviz first. If you are using macOS then you can install this with brew:

```
brew install graphviz
```

If you are using a Linux based system and have the apt package manager, you can use that:

```
apt-get install graphviz
```

The output for this looks like this `benchmark/cpu.png`:

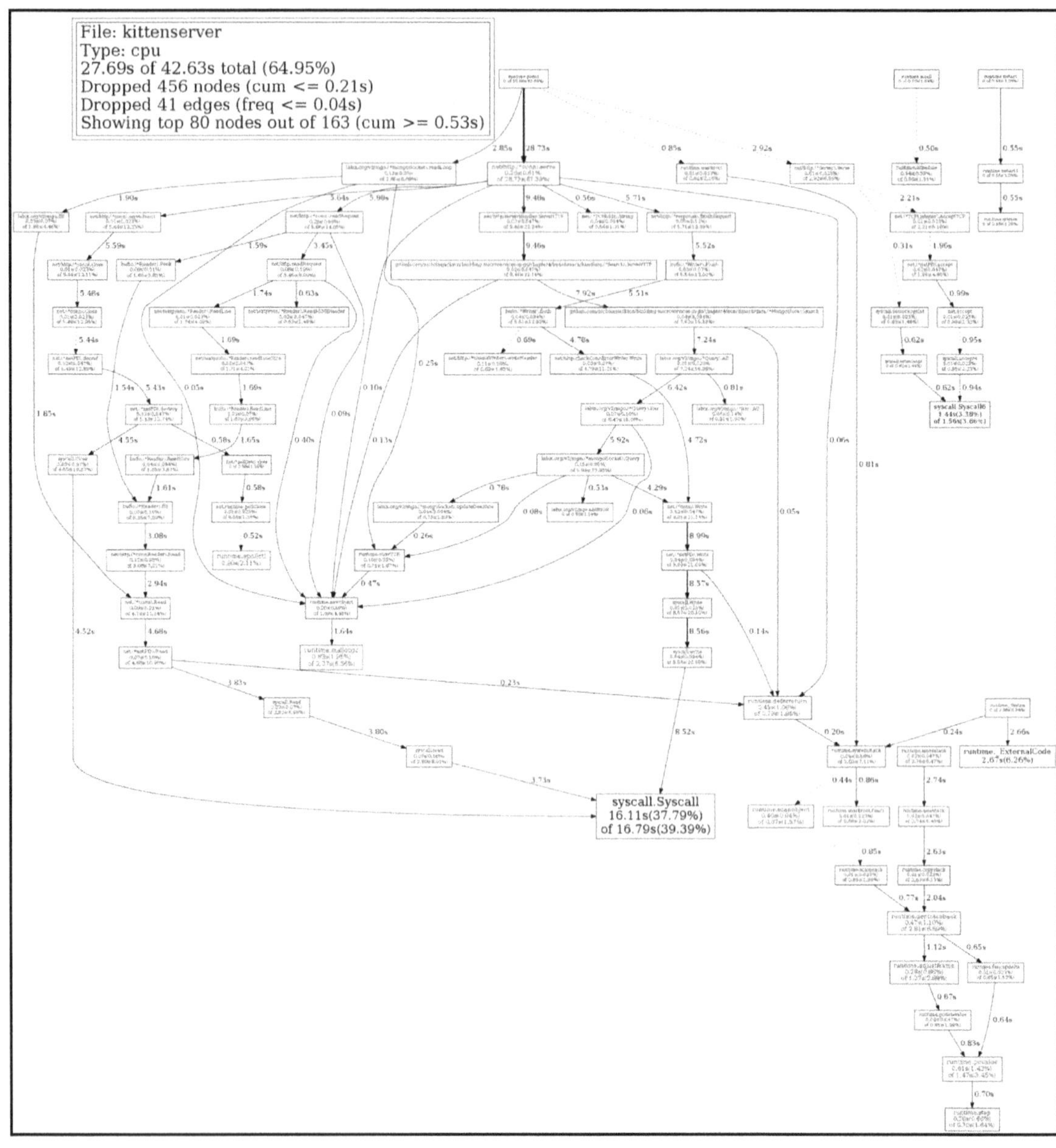

That is quite something! However, we can see that `syscall.Syscall` is in the largest font as it is responsible for consuming the most CPU. If we start here at the bottom and start tracing backward, we can see that the root of this seems to be our data store's search function.

To get a closer look at exactly where this is happening, we can use the list command and then pass the name of an object or method we would like to investigate further:

```
Entering interactive mode (type "help" for commands)
(pprof) list Search
Total: 42.63s
ROUTINE ======================== github.com//building-microservices-with-
go/chapter4/data.(*MongoStore).Search in github.com/building-microservices-
with-go/chapter4/data/mongostore.go
    40ms      7.92s (flat, cum) 18.58% of Total
       .          .     16:
       .          .     17:    return &MongoStore{session: session}, nil
       .          .     18:}
       .          .     19:
       .          .     20:// Search returns Kittens from the MongoDB
                        instance which have the name name
    40ms       40ms       21:func (m *MongoStore) Search(name string)
                          []Kitten {
       .      270ms     22:    s := m.session.Clone()
      .       10ms     23:    defer s.Close()
      .          .     24:
      .       20ms     25:    var results []Kitten
      .       70ms     26:    c := s.DB("kittenserver").C("kittens")
      .      7.30s     27:    err := c.Find(Kitten{Name:
                                 name}).All(&results)
       .          .     28:    if err != nil {
       .          .     29:        return nil
       .          .     30:    }
       .          .     31:
       .      210ms     32:    return results
       .          .     33:}
       .          .     34:
       .          .     35:// DeleteAllKittens deletes all the kittens
                        from the datastore
      .          .     36:func (m *MongoStore) DeleteAllKittens() {
      .          .     37:    s := m.session.Clone()
```

When we do this with the search method, we can see that a huge percentage of our CPU cycles were spent executing queries to MongoDB. If we look at the other route from `syscall.Syscall`, it shows that another large consumer is the `http.ResponseWriter` interface.

This output all makes sense as we are not doing anything too clever in our API; it just retrieves some data from a database. The nice thing about pprof is that we can use the same commands to query the heap usage.

Summary

In this chapter, you have learned some best practice approaches to testing microservices in Go. We have looked at the testing package, including some special features for dealing with requests and responses. We have also looked at writing integration tests with Cucumber.

Ensuring that your code works without fault, however, is only part of the job, we also need to make sure that our code is performant, and Go has some excellent tools for managing this too.

I would always recommend that you test your code and that you do this religiously. As for performance optimization, this is open for debate, no doubt you have heard comments that premature optimization is the root of all evil. However, this quote from Donald Knuth is much-misunderstood: he did not mean that you should never optimize until you have a problem; he said that you should only optimize what matters. With pprof, we have an easy way to figure out what, if anything, actually matters. Include the practice of profiling into your development routine, and you will have faster and more efficient applications, profiling is also an excellent technique to understand your application better when you are trying to track down that tricky bug.

> *"Programmers waste enormous amounts of time thinking about, or worrying about, the speed of noncritical parts of their programs, and these attempts at efficiency have a strong negative impact when debugging and maintenance are considered. We should forget about small efficiencies, say about 97% of the time: premature optimization is the root of all evil. Yet we should not pass up our opportunities in that critical 3%."*
> *- Donald Knuth*

5
Common Patterns

Before we take a look at some frameworks which can help you build microservices in Go, we should first look at some of the design patterns that will help you avoid failure.

I am not talking about software design patterns like factories or facades, but architectural designs like load balancing and service discovery. If you have never worked with microservice architecture before, then you may not understand why these are needed, but I hope that by the end of the chapter you will have a solid understanding why these patterns are important and how you can apply them correctly. If you have already successfully deployed a microservice architecture, then this chapter will give you greater knowledge of the underlying patterns which make your system function. If you have not had much success with microservices, then possibly you did not understand that you need the patterns I am going to describe.

In general, there is something for everyone, and we are going to look at not just the core patterns but some of the fantastic open source software which can do most of the heavy lifting for us.

The examples referenced in this chapter can be found at: `https://github.com/building-microservices-with-go/chapter5.git`

Design for failure

Anything that can go wrong will go wrong.

When we are building microservices, we should always be prepared for failure. There are many reasons for this, but the main one is that cloud computing networks can be flakey and you lose the ability to tune switching and routing, which would have given you an optimized system if you were running them in your data center. In addition to this, we tend to build microservice architectures to scale automatically, and this scaling causes services to start and stop in unpredictable ways.

What this means for our software is that we need to think about this failure up front while discussing upcoming features. We then need to design this into the software from the beginning, and as engineers, we need to understand these problems.

In his book *Designing Data-Intensive Applications*, Martin Kleppman makes the following comment:

> *The bigger a system gets, the more likely it is that one of its components is broken. Over time, broken things get fixed, and new things break, but in a system with thousands of nodes, it is reasonable to assume that something is always broken. If the error handling strategy consists of only giving up such a large system would never work.*

While this applies to more major systems, I would argue that the situation where you need to start considering failure due to connectivity and dependency begins once your estate reaches the size of *n+1*. This might seem a frighteningly small number, but it is incredibly relevant. Consider the following simplistic system:

You have a simple website which allows your users (who are all cat lovers) to register for updates from other cat lovers. The update is in the form of a simple daily e-mail, and you would like to send out a welcome e-mail once the form has been submitted by the user and the data saved into the database. Because you are a good microservice practitioner you have recognized that sending e-mails should not be the responsibility of the registration system, and instead you would like to devolve this to an external system. In the meantime, the service is growing in popularity; you have determined that you can save time and effort by leveraging the e-mail as an API service from MailCo. This has a simple RESTful contract and can support all your current needs, which allows you to get to market that little bit sooner.

The following diagram represents that simple microservice:

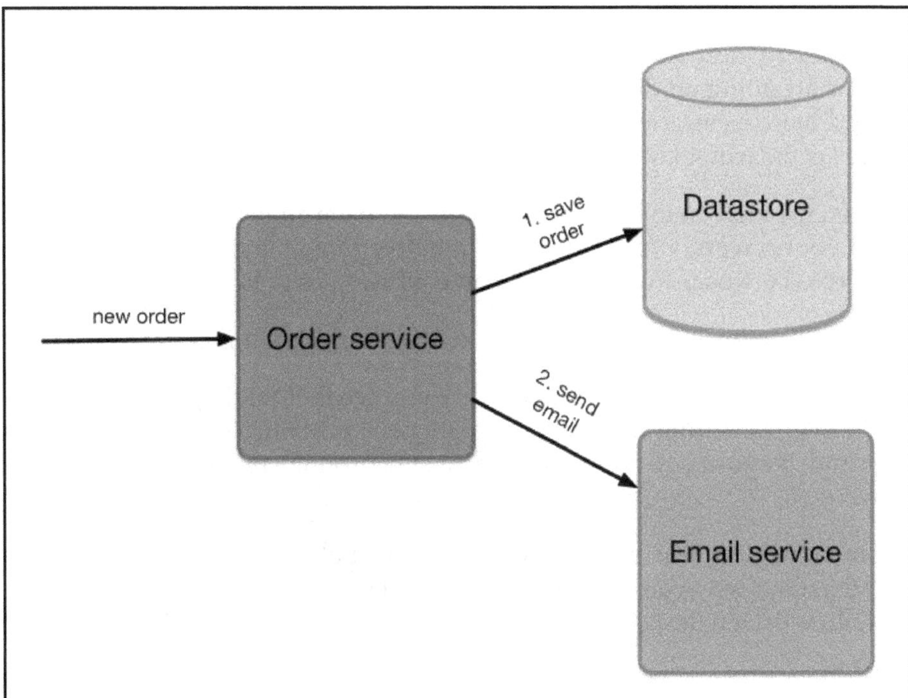

Being a good software architect, you define an interface for this mail functionality which will serve as an abstraction for the actual implementation. This concept will allow you to replace MailCo quickly at a later date. Sending e-mails is fast, so there is no need to do anything clever. We can make the call to MailCo synchronously during the registration request.

This application seems like a simple problem to solve, and you get the work done in record time. The site is hosted on AWS and configured with ElasticScale so, no matter what load you get, you will be sleeping peacefully with no worry that the site could go down.

One evening your CEO is out at an event for tech startups which is being covered by the news network, CNN. She gets talking to the reporter who, also being a cat lover, decides he would like to feature the service in a special report which will air tomorrow evening.

The excitement is unreal; this is the thing that will launch the service into the stratosphere. You and the other engineers check the system just for peace of mind, make sure the auto scale is configured correctly, then kick back with some pizza and beer to watch the program.

When the program airs and your product is shown to the nation, you can see the number of users on the site in Google Analytics. It looks great: request times are small, the cloud infrastructure is doing its job, and this has been a total success. Until of course, it isn't. After a few minutes, the request queueing starts to climb, and the services are still scaling, but now the alarms are going off due to a high number of errors and transaction processing time. More and more users are entering the site and trying to register but very few are successful, this is the worst kind of disaster you could have ever wished for.

I won't mention the look on the face of the CEO; you have all probably seen that look at some point in your careers; and if not, when you do you will know what I am talking about. It is a cross between, anger, hatred, and confusion as to how they hired such idiots.

You aren't an idiot; software is complex, and with complexity, it is easy to make mistakes.

So, you start to investigate the problem, quickly you see that while your service and database have been operating correctly, the bottleneck is MailCo's e-mail API. This started the blockage and, because you were executing a synchronous request, your service started blocking too.

So, your moment of glory was taken down by a single bottleneck with a third-party API. Now you understand why you need to plan for failure. Let's take a look at how you can implement failure driven design patterns.

Patterns

The truth about microservices is that they are not hard you only need to understand the core software architectural patterns which will help you succeed. In this section, we are going to take a look at some of these patterns and how we can implement them in Go.

Event processing

In our case study, we failed due to a downstream synchronous process failing, and that blocked the upstream. The first question we should ask ourselves is "Does this call need to be synchronous?" In the case of sending an e-mail, the answer is almost always, No. The best way to deal with this is to take a fire and forget approach; we would just add the request with all the details of the mail onto a highly available queue which would guarantee at least once delivery and move on. There would be a separate worker processing the queue records and sending these on to the third-party API.

In the instance that the third party starts to experience problems, we can happily stop processing the queue without causing any problems for our registration service.

Regarding user experience, this potentially means that the when the user clicks the register button they would not instantly receive their welcome e-mail. However, e-mail is not an instantaneous system, so some delay is to be expected. You could enhance your user experience further: what if adding an item to the queue returns the approximate queue length back to the calling system. When you are designing for failure, you may take a call that if the queue is over *n* items, you could present a friendly message to the user letting them know you are busy now but rest assured your welcome e-mail is on its way.

We will look at the implementation of this pattern further in `Chapter 9`, *Event-Driven Architecture*, but at the moment there are a few key concepts that we need to cover.

Event processing with at least once delivery

Event processing is a model which allows you to decouple your microservices by using a message queue. Rather than connect directly to a service which may or may not be at a known location, you broadcast and listen to events which exist on a queue, such as Redis, Amazon SQS, NATS.io, Rabbit, Kafka, and a whole host of other sources.

To use our example of sending a welcome e-mail, instead of making a direct call to the downstream service using its REST or RPC interface, we would add an event to a queue containing all the details that the recipient would need to process this message.

Our message may look like:

```
{
  "id": "ABCDERE2342323SDSD",
  "queue" "registration.welcome_email",
  "dispatch_date": "2016-03-04 T12:23:12:232",
  "payload": {
    "name": "Nic Jackson",
    "email": "mail@nicholasjackson.io"
  }
}
```

We add the message to the queue and then wait for an ACK from the queue to let us know that the message has been received. Of course, we would not know if the message has been delivered but receiving the ACK should be enough for us to notify the user and proceed.

The message queue is a highly distributed and scalable system, and it should be capable of processing millions of messages so we do not need to worry about it not being available. At the other end of the queue, there will be a worker who is listening for new messages pertaining to it. When it receives such a message, it processes the message and then removes it from the queue.

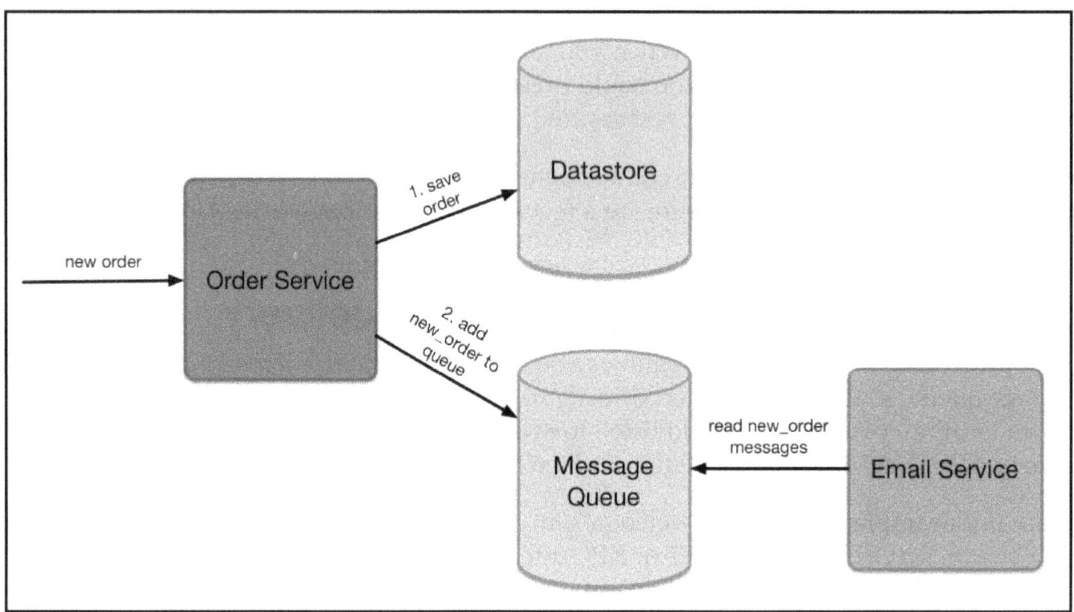

Of course, there is always the possibility that the receiving service can not process the message which could be due to a direct failure or bug in the email service or it could be that the message which was added to the queue is not in a format which can be read by the email service. We need to deal with both of these issues independently, let us start with handing errors.

Handling Errors

It is not uncommon for things to go wrong with distributed systems and we should factor this into our software design, in the instance that a valid message can not be processed one standard approach is to retry processing the message, normally with a delay. We can add the message back onto the queue augmenting it with the error message which occurred at the time as seen in the following example:

```
{
 "id": "ABCDERE2342323SDSD",
 "queue" "registration.welcome_email",
```

```
    "dispatch_date": "2016-03-04 T12:23:12:232",
    "payload": {
    "name": "Nic Jackson",
    "email": "mail@nicholasjackson.io"
    },
    "error": [{
      "status_code": 3343234,
      "message": "Message rejected from mail API, quota exceeded",
      "stack_trace": "mail_handler.go line 32 ...",
      "date": "2016-03-04 T12:24:01:132"
    }]
  }
```

It is important to append the error every time we fail to process a message as it gives us the history of what went wrong, it also provides us with the capability to understand how many times we have tried to process the message because after we exceed this threshold we do not want to continue to retry we need to move this message to a second queue where we can use it for diagnostic information.

Dead Letter Queue

This second queue is commonly called a dead letter queue, a dead letter queue is specific to the queue from where the message originated, if we had a queue named `order_service_emails` then we would create a second queue called `order_service_emails_deadletter`. The purpose of this is so that we can examine the failed messages on this queue to assist us with debugging the system, there is no point in knowing an error has occurred if we do not know what that error is and because we have been appending the error details direct to the message body we have this history right where we need it.

We can see that the message has failed because we have exceeded our quota in the mail API, we also have the date and time of when the error occurred. In this instance, because we have exceeded our quota with the email provider once we remove the issue with the email provider we can then move all of these messages from the dead letter queue back onto the main queue and they should then process correctly. Having the error information in a machine readable format allows us to handle the dead letter queue programmatically, we can explicitly select messages which relate to quota problem within a particular time window.

In the instance that a message can not be processed by the email service due to a bad message payload we typically do not retry processing of the message but add it directly to the dead letter queue. Again having this information allows us to diagnose why this issue might have occurred, it could be due to a contract change in the upstream service which has not been reflected in the downstream service. If this is the reason behind the failure we have the knowledge to correct the contract issue in the email service which is consuming the messages and again move the message back into the main queue for processing.

Idempotent transactions and message order

While many message queues now offer *At Most Once Delivery* in addition to the *At Least Once*, the latter option is still the best for large throughput of messages. To deal with the fact that the downstream service may receive a message twice it needs to be able to handle this in its own logic. One method for ensuring that the same message is not processed twice is to log the message ID in a transactions table. When we receive a message, we will insert a row which contains the message ID and then we can check when we receive a message to see if it has already been processed and if it has to dispose of that message.

The other issue that can occur with messaging is receiving a message out of sequence if for some reason two messages which supersede each other are received in an incorrect order then you may end up with inconsistent data in the database. Consider this simple example, the front end service allows the update of user information a subset of which is forwarded to a second microservice. The user quickly updates their information twice which causes two messages to be dispatched to the second service, providing both messages arrive in the order by which they were dispatched then the second service will process both messages and the data will be in a consistent state. However, if they do not arrive in the correct order then the second service will be inconsistent to the first as it will save the older data as the most recent. Once potential way to avoid this issue is to again leverage the transaction table and to store the message dispatch_date in addition to the id. When the second service receives a message then it can not only check if the current message has been processed it can check that it is the most recent message and if not discard it.

Unfortunately, there is no one solution fits all with messaging we need to tailor the solution which matches the operating conditions of the service. For you as a microservice practitioner, you need to be aware that these conditions can exist and factor them into your solution designs.

Atomic transactions

While storing data, a database can be ATOMIC: that is, all operations occur or none do. We cannot say the same with distributed transactions in microservices. When we used SOAP as our message protocol a decade or so ago, there was a proposal for a standard called **Web Service-Transactions** (**WS-T**). This aimed to provide the same functionality that you get from a database transaction, but in a distributed system. Thankfully SOAP is long gone unless you work in finance or another industry which deals with legacy systems, but the problem remains. In our previous example, we looked at how we can decouple the saving of the data and the sending of the e-mail by using a message queue with at least once delivery. What if we could solve the problem of atomicity in the same way, consider this example:

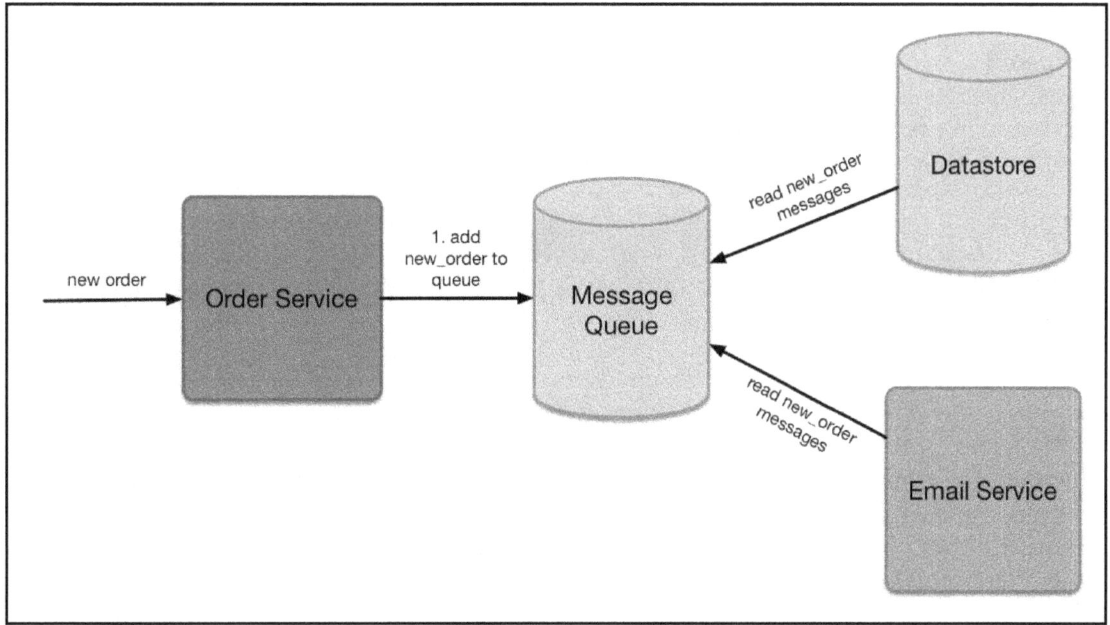

We distribute both parts of our order process to the queue, a worker service persists the data to the database, and a service that is responsible for sending the confirmation e-mail. Both these services would subscribe to the same `new_order` message and take action when this is received. Distributed transactions do not give us the same kind of transaction that is found in a database. When part of a database transaction fails, we can roll back the other parts of the transaction. Using this pattern we would only remove the message from the queue if the process succeeded so when something fails, we keep retrying. This gives us a kind of eventually consistent transaction. My opinion on distributed transactions is to avoid them if possible; try to keep your behavior simple. However, when this is not possible then this pattern may just be the right one to apply.

Timeouts

A timeout is an incredibly useful pattern while communicating with other services or data stores. The idea is that you set a limit on the response of a server and, if you do not receive a response in the given time, then you write a business logic to deal with this failure, such as retrying or sending a failure message back to the upstream service.

A timeout could be the only way of detecting a fault with a downstream service. However, no reply does not mean the server has not received and processed the message, or that it might not exist. The key feature of a timeout is to fail fast and to notify the caller of this failure.

There are many reasons why this is a good practice, not only from the perspective of returning early to the client and not keeping them waiting indefinitely but also from the point of view of load and capacity. Every connection that your service currently has active is one which cannot serve an active customer. Also, the capacity of your system is not infinite, it takes many resources to maintain a connection, and this also applies to the upstream service which is making a call to you. Timeouts are an effective hygiene factor in large distributed systems, where many small instances of a service are often clustered to achieve high throughput and redundancy. If one of these instances is malfunctioning and you, unfortunately, connect to it, then this can block an entirely functional service. The correct approach is to wait for a response for a set time and then if there is no response in this period, we should cancel the call, and try the next service in the list. The question of what duration your timeouts are set to do not have a simple answer. We also need to consider the different types of timeout which can occur in a network request, for example, you have:

- Connection Timeout - The time it takes to open a network connection to the server
- Request Timeout - The time it takes for a server to process a request

The request timeout is almost always going to be the longest duration of the two and I recommend the timeout is defined in the configuration of the service. While you might initially set it to an arbitrary value of, say 10 seconds, you can modify this after the system has been running in production, and you have a decent data set of transaction times to look at.

We are going to use the deadline package from eapache (`https://github.com/eapache/go-resiliency/tree/master/deadline`), recommended by the go-kit toolkit (`https://gokit.io`).

The method we are going to run loops from 0-100 and sleeps after each loop. If we let the function continue to the end, it would take 100 seconds.

Using the deadline package we can set our own timeout to cancel the long running operation after two seconds:

`timeout/main.go`

```
func makeTimeoutRequest() {
  dl := deadline.New(1 * time.Second)
  err := dl.Run(func(stopper <-chan struct{}) error {
    slowFunction()
    return nil
  })

  switch err {
  case deadline.ErrTimedOut:
    fmt.Println("Timeout")
  default:
    fmt.Println(err)
  }
}
```

Back off

Typically, once a connection has failed, you do not want to retry immediately to avoid flooding the network or the server with requests. To allow this, it's necessary to implement a back-off approach to your retry strategy. A back-off algorithm waits for a set period before retrying after the first failure, this then increments with subsequent failures up to a maximum duration.

Using this strategy inside a client-called API might not be desirable as it contravenes the requirement to fail fast. However, if we have a worker process that is only processing a queue of messages, then this could be exactly the right strategy to add a little protection to your system.

We will look at the `go-resiliency` package and the `retrier` package.

To create a new retrier, we use the `New` function which has the signature:

```
func New(backoff []time.Duration, class Classifier) *Retrier
```

The first parameter is an array of `Duration`. Rather than calculating this by hand, we can use the two built-in methods which will generate this for us:

```
func ConstantBackoff(n int, amount time.Duration) []time.Duration
```

The `ConstantBackoff` function generates a simple back-off strategy of retrying *n* times and waiting for the given amount of time between each retry:

```
func ExponentialBackoff(n int, initialAmount time.Duration) []time.Duration
```

The `ExponentialBackoff` function generates a simple back-off strategy of retrying *n* times doubling the time between each retry.

The second parameter is a `Classifier`. This allows us a nice amount of control over what error type is allowed to retry and what will fail immediately.

```
type DefaultClassifier struct{}
```

The `DefaultClassifier` type is the simplest form: if there is no error returned then we succeed; if there is any error returned then the retrier enters the retry state.

```
type BlacklistClassifier []error
```

The `BlacklistClassifier` type classifies errors based on a blacklist. If the error is in the given blacklist it immediately fails; otherwise, it will retry.

```
type WhitelistClassifier []error
```

The `WhitelistClassifier` type is the opposite of the blacklist, and it will only retry when an error is in the given white list. Any other errors will fail.

The WhitelistClassifier might seem slightly complicated. However, every situation requires a different implementation. The strategy that you implement is tightly coupled to your use case.

Circuit breaking

We have looked at some patterns like timeouts and back-offs, which help protect our systems from cascading failure in the instance of an outage. However, now it's time to introduce another pattern which is complementary to this duo. Circuit breaking is all about failing fast, Michael Nygard in his book "Release It" says:

> *"Circuit breakers are a way to automatically degrade functionality when the system is under stress."*

One such example could be our frontend example web application. It is dependent on a downstream service to provide recommendations for kitten memes that match the kitten you are looking at currently. Because this call is synchronous with the main page load, the web server will not return the data until it has successfully returned recommendations. Now you have designed for failure and have introduced a timeout of five seconds for this call. However, since there is an issue with the recommendations system, a call which would ordinarily take 20 milliseconds is now taking 5,000 milliseconds to fail. Every user who looks at a kitten profile is waiting five seconds longer than usual; your application is not processing requests and releasing resources as quickly as normal, and its capacity is significantly reduced. In addition to this, the number of concurrent connections to the main website has increased due to the length of time it is taking to process a single page request; this is adding load to the front end which is starting to slow down. The net effect is going to be that, if the recommendations service does not start responding, then the whole site is headed for an outage.

There is a simple solution to this: you should stop attempting to call the recommendations service, return the website back to normal operating speeds, and slightly degrade the functionality of the profile page. This has three effects:

- You restore the browsing experience to other users on the site.
- You slightly degrade the experience in one area.
- You need to have a conversation with your stakeholders before you implement this feature as it has a direct impact on the system's business.

Now in this instance, it should be a relatively simple sell. Let's assume that recommendations increase conversion by 1%; however, slow page loads reduce it by 90%. Then isn't it better to degrade by 1% instead of 90%? This example, is clear cut but what if the downstream service was a stock checking system; should you accept an order if there is a chance you do not have the stock to fulfill it?

Error behaviour is not a question that software engineering can answer on its own; business stakeholders need to be involved in this decision. In fact, I recommend that when you are planning the design of your systems, you talk about failure as part of your non-functional requirements and decide ahead of time what you will do when the downstream service fails.

So how do they work?

Under normal operations, like a circuit breaker in your electricity switch box, the breaker is closed and traffic flows normally. However, once the pre-determined error threshold has been exceeded, the breaker enters the open state, and all requests immediately fail without even being attempted. After a period, a further request would be allowed and the circuit enters a half-open state, in this state a failure immediately returns to the open state regardless of the `errorThreshold`. Once some requests have been processed without any error, then the circuit again returns to the closed state, and only if the number of failures exceeded the error threshold would the circuit open again.

That gives us a little more context to why we need circuit breakers, but how can we implement them in Go?

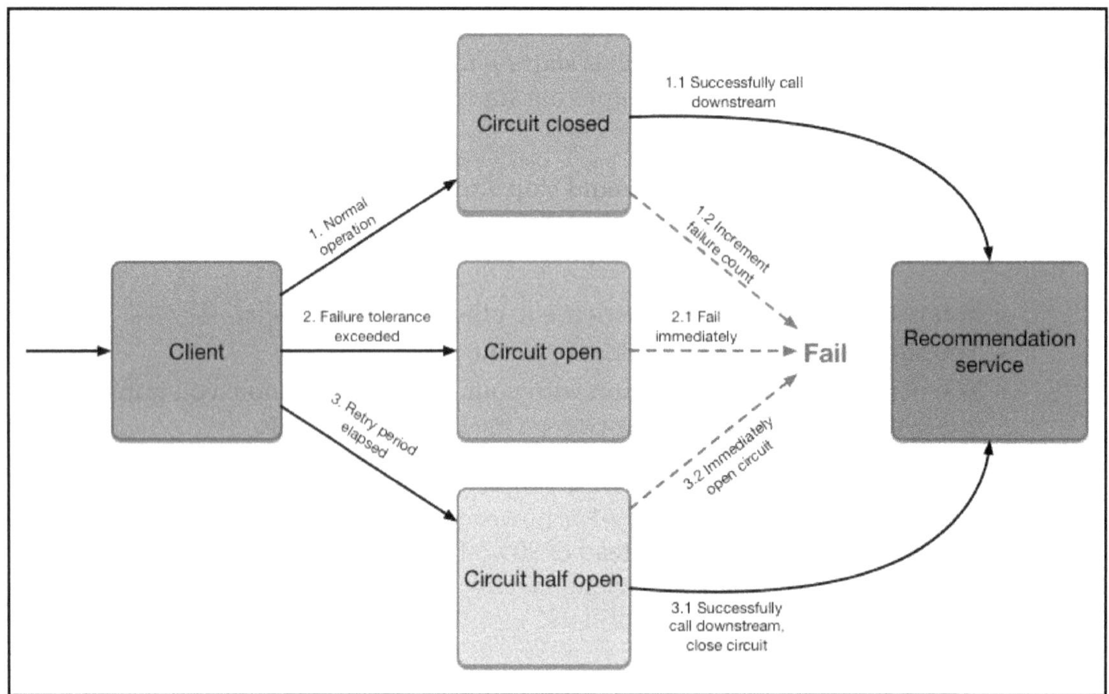

Again, we are going to turn to the `go-resilience` package. Creating a circuit breaker is straight forward, the signature for the breaker is as follows:

```
func New(errorThreshold, successThreshold int, timeout time.Duration)
*Breaker
```

We construct our circuit breaker with three parameters:

- The first `errorThreshold`, is the number of times a request can fail before the circuit opens
- The `successThreshold`, is the number of times that we need a successful request in the half-open state before we move back to open
- The `timeout`, is the time that the circuit will stay in the open state before changing to half-open

Run the following code:

```
b := breaker.New(3, 1, 5*time.Second)

for {
  result := b.Run(func() error {
    // Call some service
    time.Sleep(2 * time.Second)
    return fmt.Errorf("Timeout")
  })

  switch result {
  case nil:
    // success!
  case breaker.ErrBreakerOpen:
    // our function wasn't run because the breaker was open
    fmt.Println("Breaker open")
  default:
    fmt.Println(result)
  }

  time.Sleep(500 * time.Millisecond)
}
```

If you run this code you should see the following output. After three failed requests the breaker enters the open state, then after our five-second interval, we enter the half-open state, and we are allowed to make another request. Unfortunately, this fails, and we again enter the fully open state, and we no longer even attempt to make the call:

```
Timeout
Timeout
```

```
Timeout
Breaker open
Breaker open
Breaker open
...
Breaker open
Breaker open
Timeout
Breaker open
Breaker open
```

One of the more modern implementations of circuit breaking and timeouts is the Hystix library from Netflix; Netflix is certainly renowned for producing some quality microservice architecture and the Hystrix client is something that has also been copied time and time again.

Hystrix is described as "a latency and fault tolerance library designed to isolate points of access to remote systems, services, and third-party libraries, stop cascading failure, and enable resilience in complex distributed systems where failure is inevitable."

(`https://github.com/Netflix/Hystrix`)

For the implementation of this in Golang, check out the excellent package `https://github.com/afex/hystrix-go`. This is a nice clean implementation, which is a little cleaner than implementing `go-resiliency`. Another benefit of `hystrix-go` is that it will automatically export metrics to either the Hystrix dashboard to via StatsD. In `Chapter 7`, *Logging and Monitoring*, we will learn all about this just how important it is.

I hope you can see why this is an incredibly simple but useful pattern. However, there should be questions raised as to what you are going to do when you fail. Well these are microservices, and you will rarely only have a single instance of a service, so why not retry the call, and for that we can use a load balancer pattern.

Health checks

Health checks should be an essential part of your microservices setup. Every service should expose a health check endpoint which can be accessed by the consul or another server monitor. Health checks are important as they allow the process responsible for running the application to restart or kill it when it starts to misbehave or fail. Of course, you must be incredibly careful with this and not set this too aggressively.

What you record in your health check is entirely your choice. However, I recommend you look at implementing these features:

- Data store connection status (general connection state, connection pool status)
- Current response time (rolling average)
- Current connections
- Bad requests (running average)

How you determine what would cause an unhealthy state needs to be part of the discussion you have when you are designing the service. For example, no connectivity to the database means the service is completely inoperable, it would report unhealthy and would allow the orchestrator to recycle the container. An exhausted connection pool could just mean that the service is under high load, and while it is not completely inoperable it could be suffering degraded performance and should just serve a warning.

The same goes for the current response time. This point I find interesting: when you load test your service once it has been deployed to production, you can build up a picture of the thresholds of operating health. These numbers can be stored in the config and used by the health check. For example, if you know that your service will run an average service request with a 50 milliseconds latency for 4,000 concurrent users; however at 5,000, this time grows to 500 milliseconds as you have exhausted the connection pool. You could set your SLA upper boundary to be 100 milliseconds; then you would start reporting degraded performance from your health check. This should, however, be a rolling average based on the normal distribution. It is always possible for one or two requests to greatly be outside the standard deviation of normal operation, and you do not want to allow this to skew your average which then causes the service to report unhealthy, when in fact the slow response was actually due to the upstream service having slow network connectivity, not your internal state.

When discussing health checks, Michael Nygard considers the pattern of a handshake, where each client would send a handshake request to the downstream service before connecting to check if it was capable of receiving its request. Under normal operating conditions and most of the time, this adds an enormous amount of chatter into your application, and I think this could be overkill. It also implies that you are using client-side load-balancing, as with a server side approach you would have no guarantees that the service you handshake is the one you connect to. That said Release It was written over 10 years ago and much has changed in technology. The concept however of the downstream service making a decision that it can or can't handle a request is a valid one. Why not instead call your internal health check as the first operation before processing a request? This way you could immediately fail and give the client the opportunity to attempt another endpoint in the cluster. This call would add almost no overhead to your processing time as all you are doing is reading the state from the health endpoint, not processing any data.

Let's look at how we could implement this by looking at the example code in `health/main.go`:

```
18 func main() {
19   ma = ewma.NewMovingAverage()
20
21   http.HandleFunc("/", mainHandler)
22   http.HandleFunc("/health", healthHandler)
23
24   http.ListenAndServe(":8080", nil)
25 }
```

We are defining two handlers one which deals with our main request at the path / and one used for checking the health at the path `/health`.

The handler implements a simple moving average which records the time it takes for the handler to execute. Rather than just allow any request to be handled we are first checking on line **30** if the service is currently healthy which is checking if the current moving average is greater than a defined threshold if the service is not healthy we return the status code `StatusServiceUnavailable`S.

```
27 func mainHandler(rw http.ResponseWriter, r *http.Request) {
28   startTime := time.Now()
29
30   if !isHealthy() {
31     respondServiceUnhealthy(rw)
32     return
33   }
34
35   rw.WriteHeader(http.StatusOK)
36   fmt.Fprintf(rw, "Average request time: %f (ms)\n",
ma.Value()/1000000)
37
38   duration := time.Now().Sub(startTime)
39   ma.Add(float64(duration))
40 }
```

Looking greater in depth to the `respondServiceUnhealty` function, we can see it is doing more than just returning the HTTP status code.

```
55 func respondServiceUnhealthy(rw http.ResponseWriter) {
56   rw.WriteHeader(http.StatusServiceUnavailable)
57
58   resetMutex.RLock()
59   defer resetMutex.RUnlock()
60
61   if !resetting {
```

```
62      go sleepAndResetAverage()
63    }
64 }
```

Lines **58** and **59** are obtaining a lock on the `resetMutex`, we need this lock as when the service is unhealthy we need to sleep to give the service time to recover and then reset the average. However, we do not want to call this every time the handler is called or once the service is marked unhealthy it would potentially never recover. The check and variable on line **61** ensures this does not happen however this variable is not safe unless marked with a mutex because we have multiple go routines.

```
63 func sleepAndResetAverage() {
64   resetMutex.Lock()
65   resetting = true
66   resetMutex.Unlock()
67
68   time.Sleep(timeout)
69   ma = ewma.NewMovingAverage()
70
71   resetMutex.Lock()
72   resetting = false
73   resetMutex.Unlock()
74 }
```

The sleepAndResetAverage function waits for a predetermined length of time before resetting the moving average, during this time no work will be performed by the service which will hopefully give the overloaded service time to recover. Again we need to obtain a lock on the resetMutex before interacting with the resetting variable to avoid any race conditions when multiple go routines are trying to access this variable. Line **69** then resets the moving average back to 0 which will mean work will again be able to be handled by the service.

This example is just a simple implementation, as mentioned earlier we could add any metric that the service has available to it such as CPU memory, database connection state should we be using a database.

Throttling

Throttling is a pattern where you restrict the number of connections that a service can handle, returning an HTTP error code when this threshold has been exceeded. The full source code for this example can be found in the file `throttling/limit_handler.go`. The middleware pattern for Go is incredibly useful here: what we are going to do is to wrap the handler we would like to call, but before we call the handler itself, we are going to check to see if the server can honor the request. In this example, for simplicity, we are going only to limit the number of concurrent requests that the handler can serve, and we can do this with a simple buffered channel.

Our `LimitHandler` is quite a simple object:

```
type LimitHandler struct {
  connections chan struct{}
  handler     http.Handler
}
```

We have two private fields: one holds the number of connections as a buffered channel, and the second is the handler we are going to call after we have checked that the system is healthy. To create an instance of this object we are going to use the `NewLimitHandler` function. This takes the parameters connection, which is the number of connections we allow to process at any one time and the handler which would be called if successful:

```
func NewLimitHandler(connections int, next http.Handler) *LimitHandler {
  cons := make(chan struct{}, connections)
  for i := 0; i < connections; i++ {
    cons <- struct{}{}
  }

  return &LimitHandler{
    connections: cons,
    handler:     next,
  }
}
```

This is quite straightforward: we create a buffered channel with the size equal to the number of concurrent connections, and then we fill that ready for use:

```
func (l *LimitHandler) ServeHTTP(rw http.ResponseWriter, r *http.Request) {
  select {
  case <-l.connections:
    l.handler.ServeHTTP(rw, r)
    l.connections <- struct{}{} // release the lock
```

```
32   default:
33     http.Error(rw, "Busy", http.StatusTooManyRequests)
34   }
35 }
```

If we look at the `ServeHTTP` method starting at line **29**, we have a `select` statement. The beauty of channel is that we can write a statement like this: if we cannot retrieve an item from the channel then we should return a busy error message to the client.

Another thing worth looking at in this example are the tests, in the test file which corresponds to this example `throttling/limit_handler_test.go`, we have quite a complicated test setup to check that multiple concurrent requests return an error when we hit the limit:

```
func newTestHandler(ctx context.Context) http.Handler {
  return http.HandlerFunc(func(rw http.ResponseWriter, r *http.Request) {
    rw.WriteHeader(http.StatusOK)
    <-r.Context().Done()
  })
}

func TestReturnsBusyWhenConnectionsExhausted(t *testing.T) {
  ctx, cancel := context.WithCancel(context.Background())
  ctx2, cancel2 := context.WithCancel(context.Background())
  handler := NewLimitHandler(1, newTestHandler(ctx))
  rw, r := setup(ctx)
  rw2, r2 := setup(ctx2)

  time.AfterFunc(10*time.Millisecond, func() {
    cancel()
    cancel2()
  })

  waitGroup := sync.WaitGroup{}
  waitGroup.Add(2)

  go func() {
    handler.ServeHTTP(rw, r)
    waitGroup.Done()
  }()

  go func() {
    handler.ServeHTTP(rw2, r2)
    waitGroup.Done()
  }()

```

```
109    waitGroup.Wait()
110
111    if rw.Code == http.StatusOK && rw2.Code == http.StatusOK {
112      t.Fatalf("One request should have been busy, request 1: %v,
         request 2: %v", rw.Code, rw2.Code)
113    }
114 }
```

If we look at line **87**, we can see that we are constructing our new `LimitHandler` and passing it a mock handler which will be called if the server is capable of accepting the request. You can see that, in line **17** of this handler, we will block until the done channel on the context has an item and that this context is a `WithCancel` context. The reason we need to do this is that, to test that one of our requests will be called and the other will not but `LimitHandler` will return `TooManyRequests`, we need to block the first request. To ensure that our test does eventually complete, we are calling the cancel methods for the contexts in a timer block which will fire after ten milliseconds. Things start to get a little complex as we need to call our handlers in a Go routine to ensure that they execute concurrently. However, before we make our assertion we need to make sure that they have completed. This is why we are setting up `WaitGroup` in line **96**, and decrementing this group after each handler has completed. Finally, we can just block on line **109** until everything is complete and then we can make our assertion. Let's take a closer look at the flow through this test:

1. Block at line **109**.
2. Call `handler.ServeHTTP` twice concurrently.
3. One `ServeHTTP` method returns immediately with `http.TooManyRequests` and decrements the wait group.
4. Call cancel context allowing the one blocking `ServeHTTP` call to return and decrement the wait group.
5. Perform assertion.

This flow is not the same as reading the code in a linear manner from top to bottom. Three concurrent routines are executing, and the flow of execution is not the same as the order of the statements in the code. Unfortunately, testing concurrent Go routines is always going to be a complicated issue. However, by performing these steps we have 100% coverage for our `LimitHandler`:

```
PASS
coverage: 100.0% of statements
ok      github.com/nicholasjackson/building-microservices-in-
go/chapter5/health 0.033s
```

Rather than just limiting the number of connections in this handler, we could implement anything we like: it would be relatively trivial to implement something which records the average execution time or CPU consumption and fail fast if the condition exceeds our requirements. Determining exactly what these requirements are is a complex topic on its own and your first guess will most likely be wrong. We need to run multiple load tests of our system and spend time looking at logging and performance statistics for the end point before we are in a situation to make an educated guess. However, this action could just save you from a cascading failure, and that is an excellent thing indeed.

Service discovery

With monolithic applications, services invoke one another through language level methods or procedure calls. This was relatively straightforward and predictable behavior. However, once we realized that monolithic applications were not suitable for the scale and demand of modern software, we moved towards SOA or service-oriented architecture. We broke down this monolith into smaller chunks that typically served a particular purpose. To solve the problem with inter-service calls, SOA services ran at well-known fixed locations as the servers were large and quite often hosted in your data center or a leased rack in a data center. This meant that they did not change location very often, the IP addresses were often static, and even if a server did have to move, re-configuring of the IPs was always part of the deployment process.

With microservices all this changes, the application typically runs in a virtualized or containerized environment where the number of instances of a service and their locations can change dynamically, minute by minute. This gives us the ability to scale our application depending on the forces dynamically applied to it, but this flexibility does not come without its own share of problems. One of the main ones knows where your services are to contact them. A good friend of mine, a fantastic software architect and the author of the foreword of this book made this statement in one of his presentations once:

> *"Microservices are easy; building microservice systems is hard."*

Without the right patterns, it can almost be impossible, and one of the first ones you will most likely stumble upon even before you get your service out into production is service discovery.

Let's suppose you have a setup like this: you have three instances of the same service A, B, and C. Instance A and B are running on the same hardware, but service C is running in an entirely different data center. Because A and B are running on the same machine, they are accessible from the same IP address. However, because of this, they both cannot be bound to the same port. How is your client supposed to figure out all of this to make a simple call?

The solution is service discovery and the use of a dynamic service registry, like Consul or Etcd. These systems are highly scalable and have strongly consistent methods for storing the location of your services. The services register with the dynamic service registry upon startup, and in addition to the IP address and port they are running on, will also often provide metadata, like service version or other environmental parameters that can be used by a client when querying the registry. In addition to this, the consul has the capability to perform health checks on the service to ensure its availability. If the service fails a health check then it is marked as unavailable in the registry and will not be returned by any queries.

There are two main patterns for service discovery:

- Server-side discovery
- Client-side discovery

Server-side service discovery

Server-side service discovery for inter-service calls within the same application, in my opinion, is a microservice anti-pattern. This is the method we used to call services in an SOA environment. Typically, there will be a reverse proxy which acts as a gateway to your services. It contacts the dynamic service registry and forwards your request on to the backend services. The client would access the backend services, implementing a known URI using either a subdomain or a path as a differentiator.

The problem with this approach is that the reverse proxy starts to become a bottleneck. You can scale your backend services quickly enough, but now you need to be monitoring and watching these servers. Also, this pattern introduces latency, even though it may be only one 20ms hop, this could quite easily cost you 10% of your capacity, which means you have 10% increase in cost in addition to the cost of running and maintaining these services. Then what about consistency: you are potentially going to have two different failure patterns in your code for downstream calls, one for internal services and one for external. This is only going to add to the confusion.

The biggest problem for me, however, is that you have to centralize this failure logic. A little later in this chapter, we are going to look at these patterns in depth, but we have already stated that your services will go wrong at some point and you will want to handle this failure. If you put this logic into a reverse proxy, then all services which want to access service A will be treated the same, regardless of whether the call is essential to the success or not.

To my mind, the worst implementation of this pattern is the one that abstracts all this knowledge from the client, retrying internally, and never letting the calling client know what is happening until success or catastrophic failure.

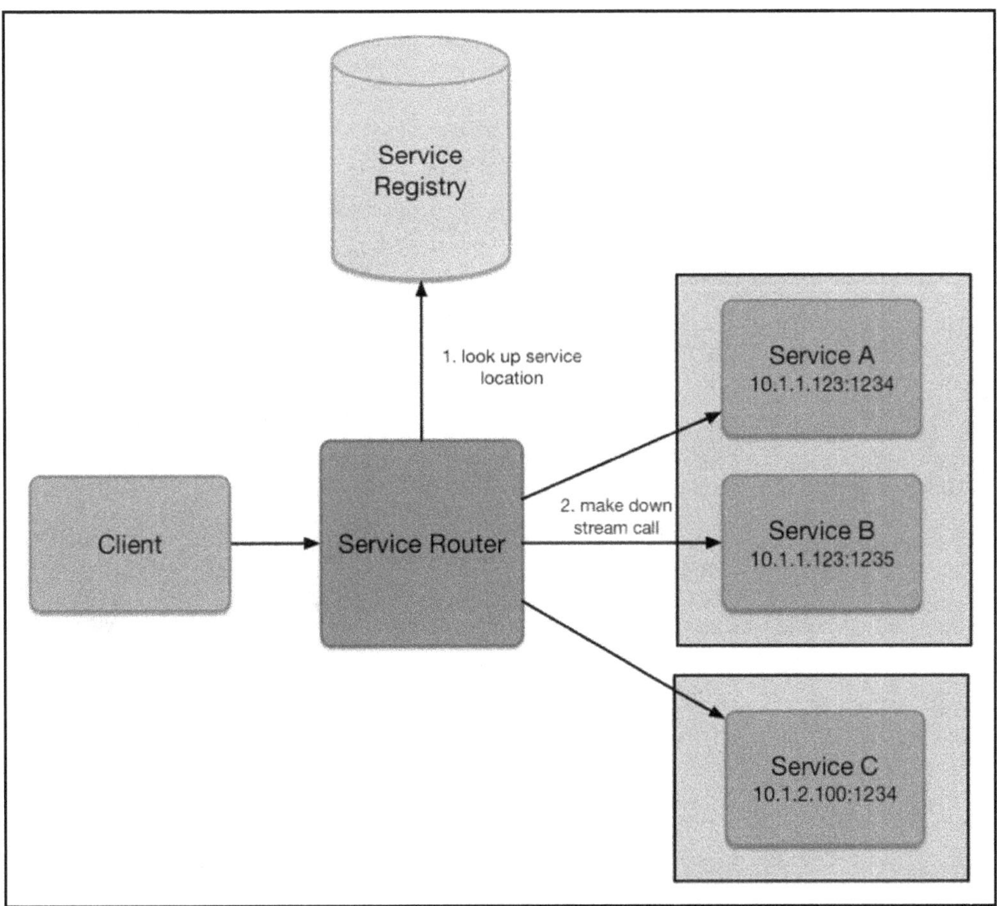

Client-side service discovery

While server-side service discovery might be an acceptable choice for your public APIs for any internal inter-service communication, I prefer the client-side pattern. This gives you greater control over what happens when a failure occurs. You can implement the business logic on a retry of a failure on a case-by-case basis, and this will also protect you against cascading failure.

In essence, the pattern is similar to its server-side partner. However, the client is responsible for the service discovery and load balancing. You still hook into a dynamic service registry to get the information for the services you are going to call. This logic is localized in each client, so it is possible to handle the failure logic on a case-by-case basis.

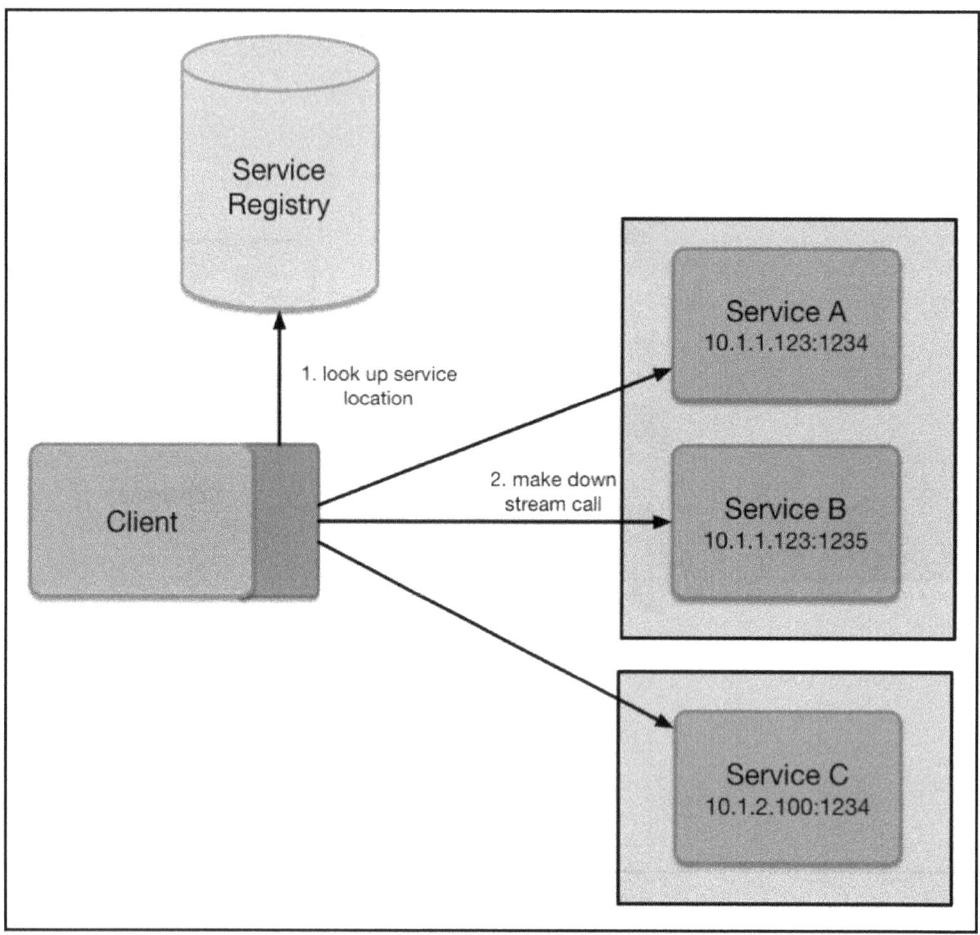

Load balancing

When we discussed service discovery, we examined the concepts of server-side and client-side discovery. My personal preference is to look at client side for any internal calls as it affords you greater control over the logic of retries on a case by case basis. Why do I like client side load balancing? For many years server-side discovery was the only option, and there was also a preference for doing SSL termination on the load balancer due to the performance problems. This is not necessarily true anymore and as we will see when we look at the chapter on security. It is a good idea to use TLS secured connections internally. However, what about being able to do sophisticated traffic distribution? That can only be achieved if you have a central source of knowledge. I am not sure this is necessary: a random distribution will theoretically over time work out the same. However, there could be a benefit to only sending a certain number of connections to a particular host; but then how do you measure health? You can use layer 6 or 7, but as we have seen by using smart health checks, if the service is too busy then it can just reject a connection.

From the example looking at circuit breaking, I hope you can now start to see the potential this can give your system. So how do we implement load balancing in Go?

If we take a look at `loadbalancing/main.go`, I have created a simple implementation of a load balancer. We create it by calling `NewLoadBalancer` which has the following signature:

```
func NewLoadBalancer(strategy Strategy, endpoints []url.URL) *LoadBalancer
```

This function takes two parameters: a `strategy`, an interface that contains the selection logic for the endpoints, and a list of endpoints.

To be able to implement multiple strategies for the load balancer, such as round-robin, random, or more sophisticated strategies like distributed statistics, across multiple instances you can define your own strategy which has the following interface:

```
// Strategy is an interface to be implemented by loadbalancing
// strategies like round robin or random.
type Strategy interface {
  NextEndpoint() url.URL
  SetEndpoints([]url.URL)
}
```

```
NextEndpoint() url.URL
```

This is the method which will return a particular endpoint for the strategy. It is not called directly, but it is called internally by the LoadBalancer package when you call the GetEndpoint method. This has to be a public method to allow for strategies to be included in packages outside of the LoadBalancer package:

```
SetEndpoints([]url.URL)
```

This method will update the Strategy type with a list of the currently available endpoints. Again, this is not called directly but is called internally by the LoadBalancer package when you call the UpdateEndpoints method.

To use the LoadBalancer package, you just initialize it with your chosen strategy and a list of endpoints, then by calling GetEndpoint, you will receive the next endpoint in the list:

```
func main() {
  endpoints := []url.URL{
    url.URL{Host: "www.google.com"},
    url.URL{Host: "www.google.co.uk"},
  }

  lb := NewLoadBalancer(&RandomStrategy{}, endpoints)

  fmt.Println(lb.GetEndpoint())
}
```

In the example code, we have implemented a simple RandomStrategy. Why not see if you can build a strategy which applies a RoundRobinStrategy?

Caching

One way you can improve the performance of your service is by caching results from databases and other downstream calls in an in-memory cache or a side cache like Redis, rather than by hitting a database every time.

Caches are designed to deliver massive throughput by storing precompiled objects in a fast-access data store, frequently based around a concept of a hash key. We know from looking at algorithm performance that a hash table has the average performance of O(1); that is as fast as it gets. Without going too in depth into Big O notation, this means it takes one iteration to be able to find the item you want in the collection.

What this means for you is that, not only can you reduce the load on your database, you can also reduce your infrastructure costs. Typically, a database is limited by the amount of data that can be read and written from the disk and the time it takes for the CPU to process this information. With an in-memory cache, this limitation is removed by using pre-aggregated data, which is stored in fast memory, not onto a state-full device like a disk. You also eliminate the problem with locking that many: databases suffer where one write can block many reads for a piece of information. This comes at the cost of consistency because you cannot guarantee that all your clients will have the same information at the same time. However, more often than not strong consistency is a vastly overvalued attribute of a database:

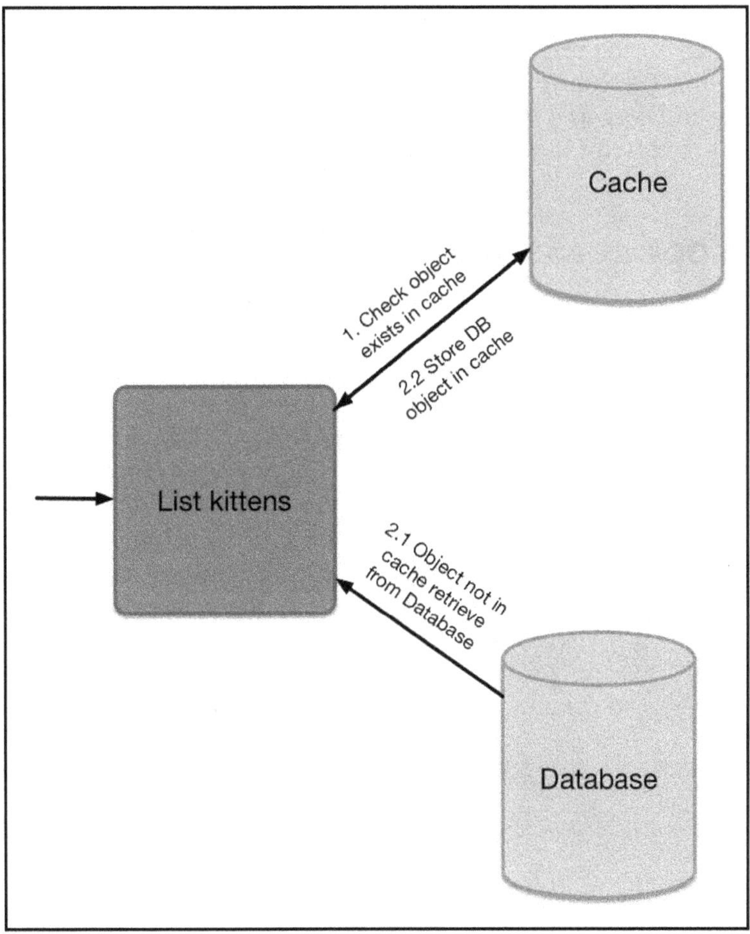

Consider our list of kittens. If we are receiving a high throughput of users retrieving a list of kittens, and it has to make a call to the database every time just to ensure the list is always up to date, then this will be costly and can fast overwhelm a database when it is already experiencing high load. We first need to ask ourselves is it essential that all these clients receive the updated information at the same time or is a one second delay quite acceptable. More often than not it is acceptable, and the speed and cost benefits you gain are well worth the potential cost that a connecting client does not get the up-to-date information exactly after it has been written to the database.

Caching strategies can be calculated based on your requirements for this consistency. In theory, the longer your cache expiry, the greater your cost saving, and the faster your system is at the expense of reduced consistency. We have already talked about designing for failure and how you can implement graceful degradation of a system. In the same way, when you are planning a feature, you should be talking about consistency and the tradeoffs with performance and cost, and documenting this decision, as these decisions will greatly help create a more successful implementation.

Premature optimization

You have probably heard the phrase, so does that mean you should not implement caching until you need it? No; it means you should be attempting to predict the initial load that your system will be under at design time, and the growth in capacity over time, as you are considering the application lifecycle. When creating this design, you will be putting together this data, and you will not be able to reliably predict the speed at which a service will run at. However, you do know that a cache will be cheaper to operate than a data store; so, if possible, you should be designing to use the smallest and cheapest data store possible, and making provision to be able to extend your service by introducing caching at a later date. This way you only do the actual work necessary to get the service out of the door, but you have done the design up front to be able to extend the service when it needs to scale.

Stale cache in times of database or downstream service failure

The cache will normally have an end date on it. However, if you implement the cache in a way that the code decides to invalidate it, then you can potentially avoid problems if a downstream service or database disappears. Again, this is back to thinking about failure states and asking what is better: the user seeing slightly out-of-date information or an error page? If your cache has expired, the call to the downstream service fails. However, you can always decide to serve the stale cache back to the calling client. In some instances, this will be better than returning a 50x error.

Summary

We have now seen how we can use some rather cool patterns to make our microservices more resilient and to deal with the inevitable failure. We have also looked at how introducing a weak link can save the entire system from a cascading failure. Where and how you apply these patterns should start out with an educated guess, but you need to constantly look at logging and monitoring to ensure that your opinion is still relevant. In the next chapter, we are going to look at some fantastic frameworks for building microservices in Go and then in, `Chapter 7`, *Logging and Monitoring*, we will look at some options and best practice for logging and monitoring your service.

6
Microservice Frameworks

In this chapter, we are going to look at some of the most popular frameworks for building microservices along with an example project to see how to implement these frameworks. We will examine both RESTful and RPC-based microservices and, to throw a curve ball in, we are also going to look at a commercial framework that provides much of the glue needed when building a highly distributed system.

The source code to accompany this chapter can be found at `https://github.com/building-microservices-with-go/chapter6`.

What makes a good microservice framework?

What makes a microservice framework is an incredibly good question and one that is open to a multitude of opinions. In an attempt to remove the subjectivity, we will break down the features of a good framework and try to allocate a score for each of these functions in a consistent way. The following diagram is a hierarchical mind map of the features that I deem necessary. When you are assessing the framework that is the best for you and your project, you can use this framework, adding or removing any of the attributes that may be relevant:

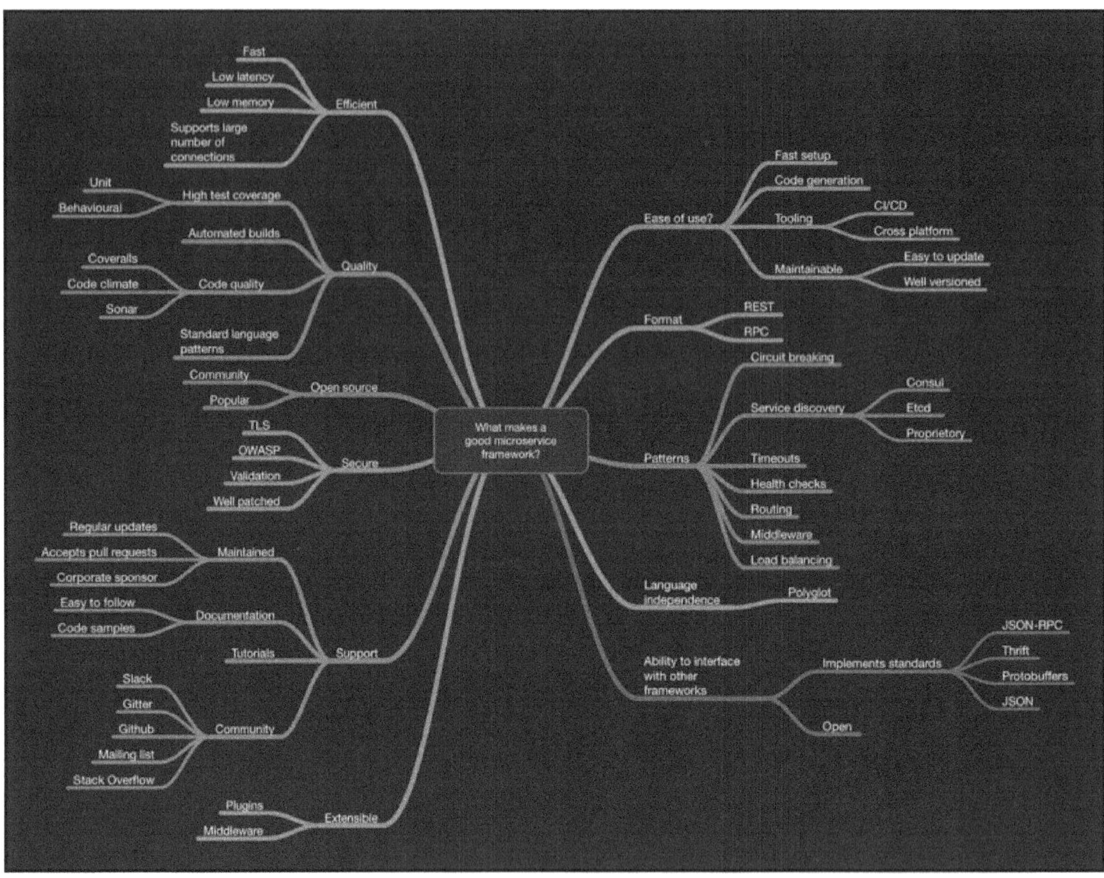

Here are some of the features you need to keep in mind while choosing a good framework:

- **Ability to interface with other frameworks**: It must be possible to interact with any service built with the framework by clients who are not built using the same framework:
  - **Implement standards**: A standard message protocol should be used to maximize interaction, for example:
    - JSON-RPC
    - Thrift
    - Protocol Buffers
    - JSON
  - **Open**: The framework should be open in both the source code and the roadmap.

- **Patterns:** The framework must implement the standard patterns of microservice architecture:
    - **Circuit breaking**: Client calls to downstream services must implement circuit breaking.
    - **Service discovery**: It must be capable of registering with a dynamic service registry and of querying the same registry to locate connected services.
    - **Proprietary**: Proprietary service registries must be open and usable from other clients who do not implement the framework or its SDKs.
    - **Timeouts**: Downstream client calls should be configurable with a user-determined timeout.
    - **Health checks**: The framework must create an automatic health check endpoint.
    - **Routing**: The framework must support multiple routes with easy-to-use, pattern-based matching.
    - **Middleware**: The framework must support middleware to allow the user to create shared code for handlers.
    - **Load balancing**: Downstream client connections should be capable of load balancing.
    - **Language independence**: The framework needs to be language independent in order to facilitate a cross-team polyglot workflow. At a minimum, it should be possible to create client SDKs in multiple languages.
- **Communication protocols:** The service should support good standards in one of the following communication protocols:
    - **REST:** If the framework implements REST, it must take full advantage of semantic API design with appropriate use of HTTP verbs and status codes.
    - **RPC:** If the framework is RPC-based, it must use a standard and open messaging protocol.
- **Maintainable:** The framework must be maintainable with the minimum effort:
    - **Easy to update**: It must be easy to update with the minimum amount of code changes.
    - **Well versioned**: The framework must be well versioned, with breaking changes to the API mainly restricted to major version updates.

- **Tooling**: There must be adequate tooling to fit with modern development practices:
    - **CI/CD**: It must integrate and work well with continuous integration and continuous deployment pipelines; the tooling must be scriptable.
    - **Cross-platform**: The tools must work cross-platform, with OSX and Linux as a bare minimum.
- **Code generation**: It should support code generation templates to scaffold and possibly extend the service.
- **Fast setup**: The framework should be fast to set up and with the minimum number of steps and dependencies.
- **Ease of use**: Any good framework should be easy to use; you will not thank yourself for choosing a framework that is a pain to work with. This category has been broken down into the following subcategories:
- **Extensible**: When required, the user should be able to extend the framework using the following:
    - **Plugins**: A pluggable software architecture to be able to create generators and templates.
    - **Middleware**: Extension through handler middleware.
- **Support**: A good support network is incredibly important throughout the life cycle of the service.
    - **Maintained**: The framework must be well maintained with the following:
        - **Regular updates**: The framework is regularly updated and released.
        - **Accepts pull requests**: The author accepts pull requests from community contributors.
        - **Corporate sponsor**: While this option is not essential, a corporate sponsor can extend the life cycle of a framework as there is less likelihood of a leftpad situation (`http://www.theregister.co.uk/2016/03/23/npm_left_pad_chaos/`).
    - **Documentation**: The framework should be well documented, with clear and concise examples and comprehensive API documentation:
        - **Easy to follow**: Documentation should be accessible and easy to read.

        - **Code samples**: Adequate code examples should be provided to support a developer using the framework.
    - **Tutorials**: The framework will ideally have community contributed tutorials in both blog and video formats.
    - **Community**: There should be a healthy community using and supporting the framework with at least one of the following channels of communication:
        - Slack
        - Gitter
        - GitHub
        - Mailing list
        - Stack Overflow
- **Secure**: The framework be secure and implement the latest industry standards:
    - **TLS**: Securing the endpoints of the framework using TLS should be possible.
    - **OWASP**: The framework should implement OWASP advisory.
    - **Validation**: Requests should be automatically validated based on rules implemented by message annotation.
    - **Well patched**: Security vulnerabilities should be regularly assessed and patched.
    - **Authentication/authorization**: The framework should implement a method of authentication and authorization, such as the OAuth standard.
- **Open source**: The framework should be open sourced and released under a license that allows forking and modification:
    - **Community**: There should be a good open source community following and contribution for the project.
    - **Popular**: The framework should be popular and commercially used.
- **Quality**: The code quality of the framework should be visible and of a high standard. Community contributions should follow a published process and standard:
    - **High test coverage**: Test coverage should be high and monitored; pull requests should ensure adherence to coding standards.
        - **Unit tests**: High, fast-running unit tests are essential.

    - **Behavioral/functional**: Ideally, the framework should implement behavioral and functional tests regarding the generated code and the build process:
- **Automated builds**: Automated builds of the source code should be present and visible. Pull requests should run an automated build, and the state reported on the request.
- **Code quality**: Automated code quality tools should be used and the results visible, for example:
    - Coveralls (`https://coveralls.io/`)
    - Code Climate (`https://codeclimate.com/`)
    - Sonar (`https://www.sonarqube.org/`)
- **Standard language patterns**: A standard method of writing the code, taking account of the language level idioms, is essential.
- **Efficient**: The framework must produce code that is efficient when run.
- **Fast**: The code must execute quickly and be designed for performance.
- **Low latency**: Requests should be low latency.
- **Low memory**: The service should be memory efficient.
- **Supports a large number of connections**: It should support a significant number of concurrent connections.

It's hard to compare the various frameworks on a like-for-like basis, since each framework provides a different set of features, and all of these features will affect performance. I think it is useful, however, to try and run some performance tests against each of the frameworks. To do this, we will be running our example service in Docker on a small Digital Ocean host with two CPU cores and 2 GB of RAM. We will then use another server of the same size to execute the benchmarking application.

Our strategy is to run a 5-minute test with 400 connections and a 5-second timeout. The connections will be ramped up over a 90-second interval.

The process is not a scientific test, but it will give us an indication of the response time and to identify whether the server can cope with a reasonable number of concurrent connections.

As a benchmark, I have created a vanilla HTTP server using JSON as a message protocol. The results for each service are outlined at the end of each section and compared to other frameworks to form a baseline efficiency.

It should be noted, however, that some frameworks have advanced capabilities, such as request validation and circuit breaking out of the box. The number of these features present will influence the latency of the service, so it will not be possible to do a true like-for-like comparison.

Results:

Threads	400
Total requests:	1,546,084
Avg. request time	51.50 ms
Total success	1,546,049
Total timeouts	35
Total failures	35

Requests over time:

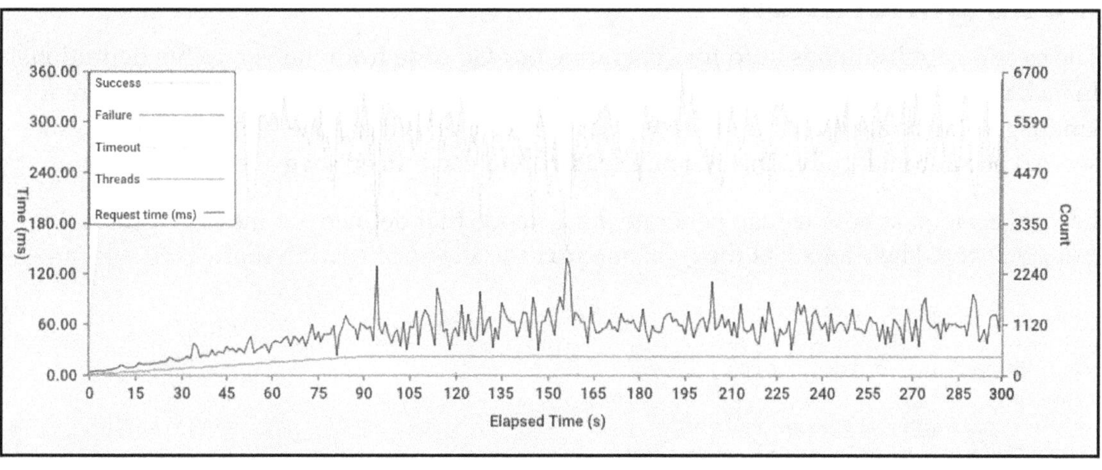

Micro

The first framework we are going to look at is Micro, by Asim Aslam. It has been under active development over the last couple of years and has production credentials as a result of its utilization at the car rental firm, Sixt. Micro is a pluggable RPC microservices framework supporting service discovery, load balancing, synchronous and asynchronous communication, and multiple message-encoding formats. For a more in-depth overview of Micro's features and to check out the source code, it is hosted on GitHub at the following location: `https://github.com/micro/go-micro`.

Setup

Installation for Micro is easy; well, it is Go, so it should be. You need to install `protoc`, the application for generating source code, which is part of Google's Protocol Buffers package. As a messaging protocol, `protobufs` are taking off big time, and you will find this messaging protocol used in quite a few frameworks we are going to look at in this chapter.

Code generation

The `protoc` application is used for generating our Go code from the `proto` file definition. In fact, the beautiful thing about `protoc` is that it can generate code in about 10 different languages. Micro also has the ability to use a `protoc` plugin to generate your clients and server code automatically. This is a nice feature and can indeed save a few keystrokes.

Let's take a look at how we can generate the Go code that defines our message protocol using `protoc`. Have a look at the `gomicro/proto/kittens.proto` file:

```
syntax = "proto3";

package bmigo.micro;

message RequestEnvelope {
    string service_method = 1;
    fixed64 seq = 2;
}

message ResponseEnvelope {
    string service_method = 1;
    fixed64 seq = 2;
    string error = 3;
}

```

```
message Request {
    string name = 1;
}

message Response {
    string msg = 1;
}

service Kittens {
    rpc Hello(Request) returns (Response) {}
}
```

When you run the `protoc` command, it processes the `proto` DSL file and outputs native language source files. In our example, a snippet of that code appears as follows:

```
type Request struct {
  Name string `protobuf:"bytes,1,opt,name=name"
  json:"name,omitempty"`
}

func (m *Request) Reset()                    { *m = Request{} }
func (m *Request) String() string            { return
proto.CompactTextString(m) }
func (*Request) ProtoMessage()               {}
func (*Request) Descriptor() ([]byte, []int) { return
fileDescriptor0, []int{0} }
```

We never edit this file by hand, so it does not matter what the code looks like. All this is doing is allowing a struct to be serialized using the binary standard set out by Protocol Buffers.

To use this with Micro, we do not have to do very much at all. Let's take a look at the `main` function and see how easy it is to set up. Have a look at the code present in the `gomicro/server/main.go` file:

```
func main() {
  cmd.Init()

  server.Init(
    server.Name("bmigo.micro.Kittens"),
    server.Version("1.0.0"),
    server.Address(":8091"),
  )

  // Register Handlers
  server.Handle(
    server.NewHandler(
```

```
32       new(Kittens),
33     ),
34   )
35
36   // Run server
37   if err := server.Run(); err != nil {
38     log.Fatal(err)
39   }
40 }
```

In line 24, we are initializing the micro server, passing it a number of options. In the same way that we could pass our basic HTTP server an address to configure which IP and port the server would bind to, we are doing the same thing in line 27.

The handlers section from line 31 should look familiar to you too; Micro uses exactly the same signature that is present in the `net/rpc` package. Creating a handler is as simple as defining a `struct` and adding methods to it. Micro will automatically register these as routes on your service:

```
type Kittens struct{}

func (s *Kittens) Hello(ctx context.Context, req *kittens.Request,
rsp *kittens.Response) error {
  rsp.Msg = server.DefaultId + ": Hello " + req.Name

  return nil
}
```

The form of the handler looks very similar to the one from the `net/http` package; we can see the same `context` object we looked at in `Chapter 1`, *Introduction to Microservices*. You may remember from that chapter that `Context` is a safe method for accessing request scoped data that can be accessed from multiple Goroutines. The request and the response objects are those that we defined in our `proto` file. Instead of writing our response to a `ResponseWriter` in this handler, we set the values we wish to return to the reference of the response that is passed to the function. Regarding returning, we have the option to return an error if something went wrong and we wish to notify the caller.

Tooling (CI/CD, cross platform)

Because Micro is written in pure Go, with the only external dependency being `protoc`, it creates a very lightweight framework that would be possible to use on Linux, Mac, and Windows with ease. It would also be easy to set up on a CI server; the main difficulty is the installation of `protoc`, but this application is incredibly well supported by Google and is available for all the main operating systems and architectures.

Maintainable

The way that Micro has been built is incredibly sympathetic toward modern enterprise problems of updating and maintaining microservices. Versioning is incorporated into the framework, and, in our example, we are setting the version in the `server.Init` method. It is possible for multiple services to co-exist, differentiated by their version number. When requesting the service, it is possible to filter by a version, which allows new versions of a service to be deployed without causing disruption to the rest of the estate.

Format (REST/RPC)

At its heart, Micro uses Google's Protocol Buffers as its core messaging protocol. This, however, is not the only method by which you can communicate with the services. Micro also implements the sidecar pattern, which is an RPC proxy. This provides a really simple way of integrating any application into the Micro ecosystem. The sidecar can be used as an API gateway, which is a single point of entry for multiple downstream services. In Micro's case, the gateway handles HTTP requests and converts them to RPC; it is also capable of providing reverse-proxy functionality. This is a very versatile pattern, and the sidecar can be scaled differently to the primary services, allowing you to expose this as a public facing endpoint for non-Micro consumers.

More information on the architecture of Micro can be found on the Micro website at `https://blog.micro.mu/2016/03/20/micro.html` and `https://blog.micro.mu/2016/04/18/micro-architecture.html`. I thoroughly recommend that anyone who is thinking about using Micro reads these articles because they give an excellent overview of just what it is capable of and the fantastic array of patterns that it uses.

Micro also implements a codec interface for encoding and decoding messages, so while, by default, it supports `proto-rpc` and `json-rpc`, it would be incredibly easy to apply the messaging protocol of your choice.

Patterns

In general, Micro has been very well architected and built with production use in mind. Asim, who created Micro and is the primary maintainer, has an incredible pedigree as a software architect and software engineer. Most of the common patterns that we will discuss in this chapter have been implemented in Micro and many more are available as community plugins. Full PubSub support is included and again supports a vast array of backend servers, including Redis and NATS. Due to the architectural model, it is comparatively easy to write your own plugins should your backend of choice not be supported as part of the standard package.

Language independence

Thanks to two nice design choices with the use of Protocol Buffers as a messaging format and the ability of the sidecar, it is possible to interface with microservices from just about any language that can support an HTTP transport.

Let's take a quick look at how we could send and receive messages using Ruby. This example is probably a little more complicated than just making a simple REST call, and most people who use Micro would probably opt to use JSON-RPC from the sidecar. However, it is interesting to see how we can interface with microservices using the RPC interface. While there may seem to be far more boilerplate than you would find if you were making a call using the Go client for Micro, this could be wrapped up into a library and distributed as a gem; this code is only to illustrate the possibilities. Have a look at the code present in the `gomicro/client/client.rb` file:

```
def main()

  puts "Connecting to Kittenserver"

  request = Bmigo::Micro::Request.new(name: 'Nic')
  body = send_request('kittenserver_kittenserver_1', '8091',
  'Kittens.Hello', request).body
  envelope, message = read_response(body, Bmigo::Micro::Response)

  puts envelope.inspect
  puts message.inspect
end
```

In the same way that we generated some native Go code from the `proto` file, we can do the same for Ruby. This makes it possible to share these service definitions and save the consumer the trouble of having to write them by hand. In line `86`, we are creating our request, which is sent to the Micro service. Even though Micro is an RPC service, it still uses HTTP as the transport, which makes it easy to make a request using Ruby's standard `NET::HTTP` library. Before we can do this, however, we need to understand how the message protocol for Micro works. Here is the Micro message format:

Envelope size (4 bytes)	Envelope (n bytes)	Message size (4 bytes)	Message (n bytes)

The first four bytes in the body are the length of the envelope. The envelope itself is the method by which Micro determines where the message is sent to; it is similar to the way you would use a URI in a RESTful API. The envelope is written to the body using the Protocol Buffers package's binary serialization using the `encode` method. Thankfully, all this work is done for us by the `protobuf` package. We then write the message size again using exactly four bytes and follow that with the message, which again is encoded into a binary representation using the `protobuf` package.

The message can then be sent as an HTTP post. To let Micro know we are sending a binary message and not JSON-RPC, we have to specify the `Content-Type` header and set this to `application/octet-stream`.

The response that is returned by Micro will be in the same format as the request.

Ability to interface with other frameworks

Because of its language-agnostic interface, it is possible to integrate Micro with many different frameworks. Theoretically, you could even write a Micro-compatible service that takes advantage of all the service discovery and registration in a language that is not Go. Why would we want to do that, though? After all, Go is fantastic.

Efficiency

Micro performs admirably, managing to hold 400 connections with roughly a 125 ms response. The response time gives us nearly 3,000 requests per second. While this is not a direct reflection of how your server will perform in production, we will be using the same setup to test all the frameworks in this chapter. When load testing Micro, the memory consumption was efficient, only consuming approximately 10% of the available memory on the server. CPU loads, like all tests, were running at maximum, but this is to be expected when the system is handling so many concurrent requests for such a small setup.

The results are as follows:

Threads	400
Total requests:	806,011
Avg. request time	125.58 ms
Total success	806,011
Total timeouts	0
Total failures	0

The graph showing requests over time can be observed as follows:

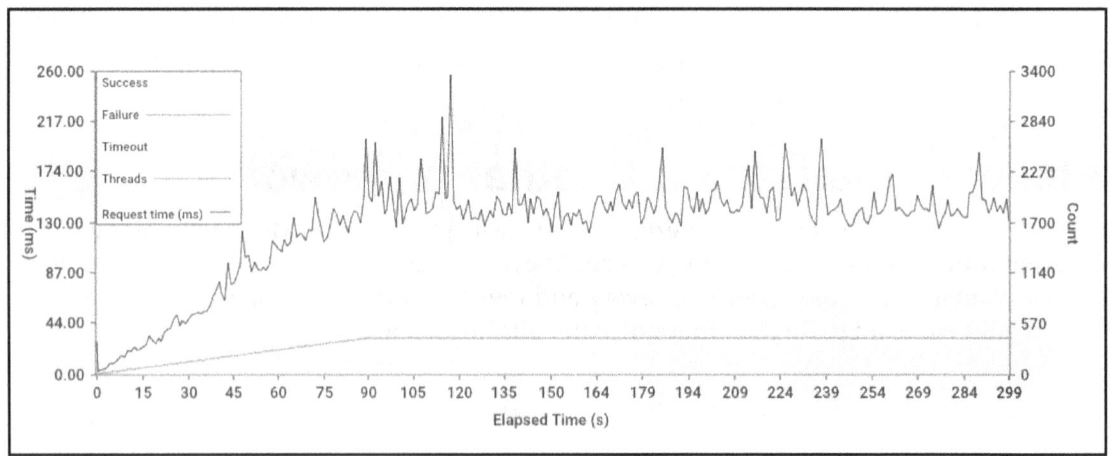

Quality

The quality of the Micro framework is very high, with automated builds and decent code coverage where needed, and it should be straightforward to navigate, implementing many of the standard Go idioms.

Open source

The framework is open source and uses the Apache license. Regarding popularity, Micro has over 2,000 stars on GitHub and accepts contributions from the community.

Security

Out of the box, Micro does not have an explicit authentication or authorization layer, and I believe this is a good thing. It would be relatively trivial to implement your authentication into the service framework using JWT, or, if you really must, your proprietary format. Request validation is handled in part by Protocol Buffers. However, it should be possible to do more complex validation using something like `govalidator` (`https://github.com/asaskevich/govalidator`). However, since you cannot directly modify the request objects to add the fields tags required, you may have to jump through a few hoops here. The issue with validation, however, is more to do with the Protocol Buffers framework, not Micro.

From a secure communication perspective, Micro uses `net/http` as the base transport, so it will be a trivial matter to introduce TLS encryption, not just for the public facing services, but also for private services. You will see why this is important when we take a more in-depth look at security.

Support

Support for using the framework is pretty excellent; there are plenty of code examples, and there is a Slack group that is well used, so any questions you may have can be answered either by other users or by Asim himself, who is very active in the group in providing support.

Extensibility

One of the nice features of Micro is the way that it has been architected for extensibility. All of the standard dependencies for service discovery, messaging, and transport follow an interface-driven abstraction. Should you need to implement a particular use case or, in the case of upgrades when a breaking change may be introduced by the likes of an etcd version update, it will be no problem to write a plugin specific to this and use this within your services. As expected of a framework of this quality, middleware is supported on both the client and the server interfaces, which would enable a vast array of functionality from authentication and authorization to request validation.

What we learned about Micro

In general, Micro is a nice framework that covers nearly all of your needs when building a highly scalable distributed system. Asim has done an excellent job, both in creating this and maintaining it, and his skill and experience shine through in the patterns he has implemented.

Kite

Kite is a framework that is developed by the team responsible for Koding, the browser-based IDE. The framework is used by the Koding team and was open sourced, since they believed that it would be useful for other microservice practitioners, having faced many of the problems themselves.

The concept behind the framework is that everything is a kite, both servers and clients, and that they communicate in a bi-directional manner using web sockets and an RPC-based protocol. Web sockets make inter-service communication incredibly efficient, as it removes the overhead of constantly having to handshake a connection that can take as much time as the message passing itself. Kite also has a built-in service discovery feature that allows you to make a call to a Kite without knowing the specific endpoint.

Setup

The installation of Kite is relatively simple; there are a few dependencies for service discovery, such as `etcd`, but all the code you need to create a Kite is found in the Go package. If we install this package using the `go get` command, we can go ahead and start writing our first Kite:

```
go get github.com/koding/kite
```

The way Kite works is that there is a service that runs along with your application Kites called **kontrol**. This handles service discovery, and all of your application services register with this service so that clients can query the service catalog to obtain the service endpoint. The kontrol Kite comes bundled within the main package, and, for convenience, I have created a Docker Compose file, which starts this along with `etcd`, which is used as the service registry.

If we take a look at our server implementation, we can see the various steps we need to add to register our new service. Refer to the code present in the `kite/server/main.go` file:

```
func main() {

  k := kite.New("math", "1.0.0")
  c := config.MustGet()
  k.Config = c
  k.Config.KontrolURL = "http://kontrol:6000/kite"

  k.RegisterForever(&url.URL{Scheme: "http", Host: "127.0.0.1:8091", Path: "/kite"})

  // Add our handler method with the name "square"
  k.HandleFunc("Hello", func(r *kite.Request) (interface{}, error) {
    name, _ := r.Args.One().String()

    return fmt.Sprintf("Hello %v", name), nil
  }).DisableAuthentication()

  // Attach to a server with port8091 and run it
  k.Config.Port = 8091
  k.Run()

}
```

In line `15`, we are creating our new Kite. We pass two arguments to the `New` method: the name of our Kite and the service version. We then obtain a reference to the configuration and set this to our Kite. To be able to register our Kite with the service discovery, we have to set the `KontrolURL` with the correct URI for our kontrol server:

```
k.Config.KontrolURL = "http://kontrol:6000/kite
```

If you look at the URL we are passing it, we are using the name that is supplied by Docker when we link a number of containers together.

In the next line, we are registering our container with the kontrol server. We need to pass the URL scheme we are using. In this instance, HTTP is the hostname; this needs to be the accessible name for the application. We are cheating a little bit with this host, since we are exposing the ports to the Docker host; we could have passed the internal name had our client application been linked to this one.

Now the interesting stuff starts, and we define the methods that our Kite will have available to it. If we take a look at line 23, we will see a pattern that should look quite familiar:

```
HandleFunc(route string, function func(*kite.Request) (interface{}, error))
```

The signature for `HandleFunc` is very similar to that of the standard HTTP library; we set up a route and pass a function that would be responsible for executing that request. You will see that neither the request nor the response are typed. Well, that is not exactly correct for the `Request` method, but certainly, there is no explicitly defined contract.

To get the arguments that are passed with the `Request` method, we use the `Args` object, which is a `dnode` message. Unlike the other frameworks we have looked at, a `dnode` message does not have a contract that can be shared between consumers and producers of this message, so each must implement their interpretation. The `dnode` message itself is a newline terminated JSON message and is heavily abstracted by the kite framework. For the curious, the protocol definition can be found in the following document: `https://github.com/substack/dnode-protocol/blob/master/doc/protocol.markdown#the-protocol`.

The output of `HandleFunc` is the standard Go pattern of `interface{} error`, again, the `interface{}` that is the response we would like to send to the caller. This is not strongly typed, and it is most likely just a struct that can be serialized down to a `dnode` payload, the representation of which is just JSON.

One of the nice features of Kite is that authentication is built in and, in our instance, we are disabling this. It is quite common to restrict the actions of a particular service call based upon the permissions of the caller. Under the hood, Kite is using `JWT` to break down these permissions into a set of claims. The principle is that a key is signed, and therefore a receiving service only has to validate the signature of the key to trust its payload rather than having to call a downstream service. The final line we are calling is `k.Run();` this starts our Kite and blocks our `main` function.

Code generation

With Kite, there is no code generation or templates to help set up your servers and clients. That said, the simplicity of creating a server does not warrant the need for this.

Tooling

Besides Go, there is little you need to set up Kite. `etcd`, which is used for your service discovery, and Kite, are easily packaged into a Docker container, which allows a standard testing and deployment workflow.

The cross-platform elements of the framework are limited to areas that can be compiled with the Go framework, which, as I write this, is a rather impressive array.

Maintainable

Kite is a relatively mature framework with active development over a period of three years. It is also actively used by the Koding service, which was acquired by Amazon in 2016.

Due to the way that routing works by registering a handler, it would be possible to cleanly separate your implementation from the main Kite packages, which would allow you to easily update the main package when upstream changes are made.

I do have a slight reservation about the lack of contracts around the `dnode` messages. This could cause maintenance problems if not properly managed, as the consumer has the responsibility of discovering the protocol implementation and the supplier service must document this protocol and ensure that it is correctly versioned to avoid breaking changes. As far as I am aware, there is no capability to produce documentation from the code source automatically. Since `dnode` uses JSON under the hood, it might be an idea to have a single argument in the payload containing a JSON object, the type of which is known and could be easily serialized to a struct using the standard package.

Format

Kite uses `dnode` as its messaging protocol. While this is not a concern if you are doing kite-to-kite communication, or if you are using the JavaScript framework for Kite, it might be an issue if you would like to interface from another language in your stack. The protocol definition is listed in the GitHub project at `https://github.com/substack/dnode-protocol/blob/master/doc/protocol.markdown#the-protocol`, and is JSON-based. Looking at the documentation for `dnode`, it seems that the messaging protocol and the execution framework were never intended to be loosely coupled. My personal recommendation when choosing a messaging protocol is that you should ensure there are encoders and decoders already written for your chosen languages. If there is no package, then you need to assess if the protocol has a sufficiently large user base such that the actions of writing this would be warranted.

Patterns

Service discovery is built into Kite with the kontrol application. The backend store for kontrol is not proprietary, but it uses a plugin architecture and supports `etcd`, `consul`, and so on.

If we look at our client application, we can see how this works in practice.

In line `19`, we are calling the `GetKites` method and passing `KontrolQuery` as a parameter. The query contains the username, environment, and the name of the service we would like to reference.

The return type of this call is a slice of Kites. In our simple example, we are just getting a reference to the first item in the list. This process does mean that we have to implement load balancing and circuit breaking ourselves; it would have been nice if we could have had this feature built into kontrol.

To connect to Kite, we have two methods at our disposal:

```
Dial()
DialForever()
```

The `Dial()` method takes a timeout, which, when elapsed, the method will return regardless of whether it has been possible to connect to the downstream service or not. The `DialForever()` method, as the method name suggests, will not return. In both instances, a channel is returned, which we use to pause execution until we have obtained our connection.

Calling the service is now as simple as executing `Tell`, passing the name of the method you wish to run, and passing the parameters as an interface for that method. In my humble opinion, Kite loses points here. The contracts for the service calls are very loose and creating an implementation for the consumers will not be without effort.

Language independence

Kite as a framework is predominately Go- and JavaScript-based. The JavaScript package (`https://github.com/koding/kite.js`) allows you to write a Kite in JavaScript, which would run on the server with NodeJS, or you can also use the plugin direct from the browser, which would enable you to build rich user interfaces.

Communicating with Kite from a language such as Ruby would require a degree of effort. Custom code would need to be written to interact with kontrol and to execute queries to the Kites. This would certainly be possible, and if you build this framework, please push it back to the open source community.

Efficiency

Kite is fast. Thanks to the way it uses web sockets, there seems to be little overhead once you are connected. When I was testing the system, I did experience some problems with creating multiple Kite connections; this was not on the server but the client. To be honest, I have not dug too far into this, and the performance from using a shared Kite in the client is pretty impressive. In terms of CPU and memory consumption, Kite consumes the most of all the frameworks evaluated. For the 400 connection test, Kite was consuming 1.8 GB of the 2 GB of RAM available on the client; the server was consuming 1.6 GB. Both client and server were heavy users of the CPU:

Threads	400
Total requests:	1,649,754
Avg. request time	33.55 ms
Total success	1,649,754
Total timeouts	0
Total failures	0

Requests over time:

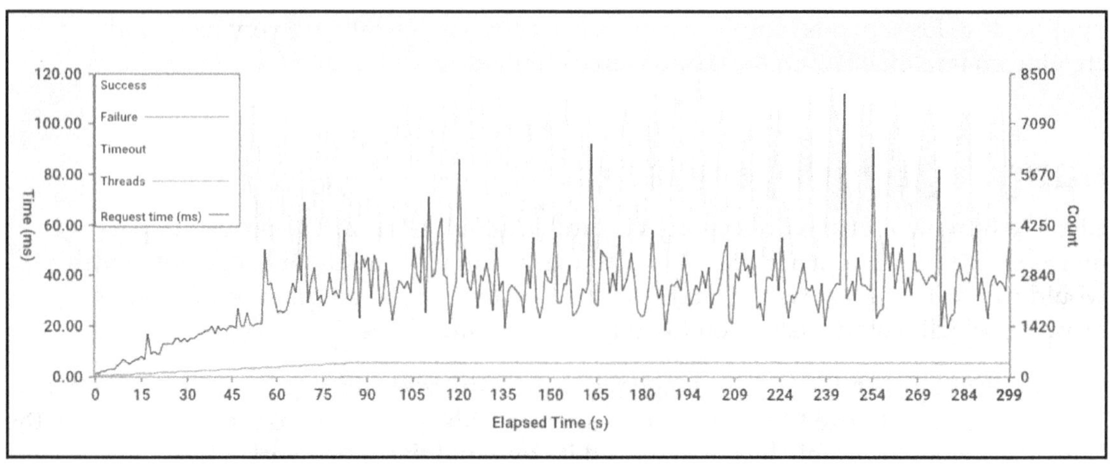

Quality

The Kite framework uses Travis CI, and there are unit and integration tests executed for each build. Code coverage is not huge; however, it seems to cover the complexities and, looking at the issues in GitHub, there is nothing outstanding.

Open source

The project is fairly popular with over 1,200 GitHub stars. However, there is no Slack community or forum. The authors are, however, excellent at answering questions when they are posted in relation to GitHub issues.

Security

Security-wise, Kite has its own authentication layer using JWT and supports the standard Go TLS configuration to connect two Kites securely. Request validation does not, however, seem to be present, and I guess this is due to the `dnode` protocol being quite dynamic. It should be relatively straightforward to implement this, since the handlers could be chained in the same way a middleware pattern could be built with `net/http`.

Support

Since Kite is used in a commercial context with Koding, it is very well maintained and mature, receiving regular updates. Documentation, however, is somewhat lacking, and while I was working on the example code, I spent quite a lot of time figuring out the various parts. The authors are aware of the problems with the documentation and do plan to improve this facet. Google also has little to offer in the way of help for Kite. When searching for an issue, generally, you will end up back on the GitHub repository. This is not a massive problem if you are a relatively experienced developer, as you can simply read through the code and reverse engineer it. However, if you are just starting out, this might be a problem as you may not have a solid grasp of the underlying concepts.

There is code-level documentation, and the code is self-descriptive; however, there are elements that could do with further explanation.

Extensibility

There is no formal plugin or middleware format for Kite. However, due to the way it has been engineered, it should be possible to extend the framework. You may run into problems, however. For example, if you wish to add a different backend for kontrol storage, the options are hardcoded into the kontrol application, so even though storage is derived from an interface, a modification would need to be made to kontrol's `main` function to enable this.

Summing up Kite

Kite is a nicely-written framework, and if you are only building microservices in Go with a requirement for access from the browser, then it could be the correct choice. In my opinion, the documentation and tutorials need more work; however, I suspect this is due to Kite being an internal framework from a small company that has been open sourced, as opposed to being a community open source framework. Kite loses quite a few points due to the lack of standard patterns built into the framework. Cross-framework integration also suffers due to the `dnode` messaging protocol, and the documentation could be dramatically improved.

gRPC

We have already taken a look at the Protocol Buffers messaging protocol from Google when we looked at API design in `Chapter 2`, *Designing a Great API*. gRPC is a cross-platform framework that uses HTTP/2 as the transport protocol, and Protocol Buffers as the messaging protocol. Google developed it as a replacement for their Stubby framework, which they had used internally for many years.

The intention behind the project was to build a framework that promotes good microservice design, concentrating on messages rather than distributed objects. gRPC is also optimized for the many network problems we face in microservice architecture, such as fragile networks, limited bandwidth, and the cost of the transport. One of the other lovely facets of gRPC is its ability to stream data between client and server. This can have a huge benefit in certain application types and is built into the framework as a standard component. Additionally, for microserivice to microservice communication, there is a pure JavaScript implementation that is designed to enable browser clients to access a gRPC server.

Setup

The main problem with setting up a gRPC project is installing the `protoc` application and the various plugins that are obtained from the following URL:
`https://github.com/google/protobuf/releases`

We then need to install the Go packages for gRPC and the code generation plugin for protoc:

```
$ go get google.golang.org/grpc
$ go get -u github.com/golang/protobuf/{proto,protoc-gen-go}
```

For convenience, I have created a Docker container that has all these packages (`nicholasjackson/building-microservices-in-go`). If you take a look at `Makefile` in the example code at `chapter4/grpc/Makefile`, you will see that we are using the power of Docker to save the hassle of having to install any applications.

Code generation

The beauty of gRPC is the code generation. From the simple `proto` files that we looked at in `Chapter 2`, *Designing a Great API*, we can generate all our client and server code. All we then have to do is to wire up our handlers, which will deal with the business logic.

If we take a look at the `proto` file in `chapter4/grpc/proto/kittens.proto`, we can see that the file is somewhat similar to the one we reviewed in a previous chapter.

The main difference is the following block from line 13:

```
13 service Kittens {
14     rpc Hello(Request) returns (Response) {}
15 }
```

This is our service definition, which contains the contract for our handlers. It is nicely semantic and very readable, even though it is written in the proto DSL.

To generate our Go code, all we need to do is to call the `protoc` command and tell it to use the Go plugin:

```
protoc -I /proto /proto/kittens.proto --go_out=plugins=grpc:/proto
```

This will create our messages and our service definitions, and output them to the `kittens.pb.go` file. It is relatively interesting to look at this file, even though the code is auto-generated, to see some of the inner workings of the framework.

Now, let's see just how easy it is to use the framework if we take a look at `grpc/server/main.go`.

We can see that the first thing we are doing is setting up our handler code:

```
type kittenServer struct{}

func (k *kittenServer) Hello(ctx context.Context, request
*proto.Request) (*proto.Response, error) {
  response := &proto.Response{}
  response.Msg = fmt.Sprintf("Hello %v", request.Name)

  return response, nil
}
```

In line 15, we are creating a struct, the methods of which will correspond to the KittenServer interface, which has been auto-generated for us by the protoc command:

```
type KittensServer interface {
    Hello(context.Context, *Request) (*Response, error)
}
```

Line 17 is where we are defining our handler, and again, the pattern should look familiar to the one we examined in Chapter 1, *Introduction to Microservices*. We have our context and an object that corresponds to the request message we defined in our protos file and the return tuple of response and error.

This method is where we will do the work for the request, and you can see on line 18 that we are creating a response object and then setting the message that will be returned to the client.

Wiring up the server is also really straightforward. We only need to create a listener and then create a new instance of the server, which has been auto-generated for us by the protoc command:

```
24 func main() {
25   lis, err := net.Listen("tcp", fmt.Sprintf(":%d", 9000))
26   if err != nil {
27     log.Fatalf("failed to listen: %v", err)
28   }
29   grpcServer := grpc.NewServer()
30   proto.RegisterKittensServer(grpcServer, &kittenServer{})
31   grpcServer.Serve(lis)
32 }
```

The client code is similarly straightforward. If we take a look at grpc/client/client.go, we can see that we are creating a connection to our server and then initiating the request:

```
func main() {
  conn, err := grpc.Dial("127.0.0.1:9000", grpc.WithInsecure())
  if err != nil {
    log.Fatal("Unable to create connection to server: ", err)
  }

  client := proto.NewKittensClient(conn)
  response, err := client.Hello(context.Background(),
  &proto.Request{Name: "Nic"})

  if err != nil {
    log.Fatal("Error calling service: ", err)
  }
```

```
24
25    fmt.Println(response.Msg)
26 }
```

The `grpc.Dial` method has the following signature:

```
func Dial(target string, opts ...DialOption) (*ClientConn, error)
```

`target` is a string that corresponds to the server's network location, and `port` and `opts` is a variadic list of `DialOption`. In our example, we are only using `WithInsecure`, which disables transport security for the client; the default is that transport security is set so, in our simple example, we need this option.

The list of choices is very comprehensive, and you can specify configuration such as timeouts and using a load balancer. For the full list, please see the documentation, which can be found at `https://godoc.org/google.golang.org/grpc#WithInsecure`.

Line 18 is where we are creating our client. This is a type that is defined in our auto-generated code file, not the base package. We pass it the connection we created earlier and then we can call the methods on the server, as shown in line `19`.

Tooling

The tooling for gRPC is rather impressive. There are a huge number of platforms and languages supported, and just with Go and the `protoc` application, it is relatively trivial to set up an automated build. In our simple example, I have configured the build to run in a Docker container, which further limits the requirements for any software to be installed on the continuous deployment machines. By doing this, we can limit the dependencies that are used in all our builds. This is a technique we will learn more about in a later chapter.

Maintainable

Updating gRPC is also incredibly easy. Google has put a significant amount of work into making the new v3 specification for Protocol Buffers backward compatible with v2 and, according to the documentation, there is a desire to maintain this as gRPC and Protocol Buffers move forward.

Format

While we may not have the semantic nature of REST, we do have a very clearly defined messaging protocol with Protocol Buffers. The definitions are easy to understand, and the ability to connect clients to use the `proto` files we defined and reuse them to create their clients is a very nice feature.

Patterns

The array of patterns that is also incorporated into the framework is very comprehensive, supporting health checks and timeouts. There is no explicit support for middleware; however, many of the requirements for middleware, such as authentication and request validation, we get for free built into the framework. We also do not have circuit breaking, but the balancer can be configured to add this functionality. In the official documentation, there is a statement that this is an experimental API and may be changed or extended in the future. We can, therefore, expect many great updates from this feature.

The clients themselves have configuration to deal with a back-off algorithm. This throttling protects your servers in an instance of high load by not flooding a server that may be under pressure with thousands of connections.

From a service discovery perspective, there is no implicit handling of this inside the framework; however, the extension points are there to perform this with your backend of choice.

Language independence

The number of languages that are currently supported by gRPC is quite impressive, with 10 languages officially supported, and there are many more by a growing community. The ability to generate and distribute client SDKs in multiple languages using the `protoc` command is fantastic. To see how this could work from a language other than Go, we have created a simple example in Ruby that shows just how easy it is to make a connection to a gRPC service.

In our example, `grpc/client/client.rb`, we can see that there are very few lines of code needed to initiate a connection and execute a request to a gRPC endpoint written in Go:

```
 6 require 'kittens_services_pb'
 7
 8 service =
   Bmigo::Grpc::Kittens::Stub.new('kittenserver_kittenserver_1:9000',
   :this_channel_is_insecure)
 9
10 request = Bmigo::Grpc::Request.new
11 request.name = 'Nic'
12
13 response = service.hello(request)
14
15 puts response.msg
```

For the non-Rubyists, in line `6`, we are including our auto-generated code, which was generated with the `protoc` command and using the Ruby gRPC plugin.

Line 8 then creates an instance to our server, again passing the option of an insecure channel, like we did in the Go client.

We then create a request object in line 10, set the parameters for this request, and execute it. All of the objects for the request and response are defined for us and are incredibly easy to use.

Google is currently working on a version of the framework that would enable connections to a gRPC service from the web browser. When this arrives, it will be very easy to create interactive web applications that are backed by gRPC microservices.

Efficiency

Thanks to the use of HTTP/2 and the binary messaging, gRPC is incredibly quick and capable of supporting a massive throughput. The option for streaming data to the client is a fantastic feature. From a mobile perspective, the client only needs to maintain a single connection to the server, which is efficient, and the server can push data updates to this open connection. For an example of how this could work, have a look at some code I created for a talk at GoLang UK (https://github.com/gokitter). This implements a simple server and an Android client that receives streaming updates. Rather than using native gRPC clients on Android, I geeked out using GoMobile to compile a native framework that was written in Go, and then used this in the Android app.

Results:

Threads	400
Total requests:	2,949,094
Avg. request time	23.81 ms
Total success	2,949,094
Total timeouts	0
Total failures	0

Requests over time:

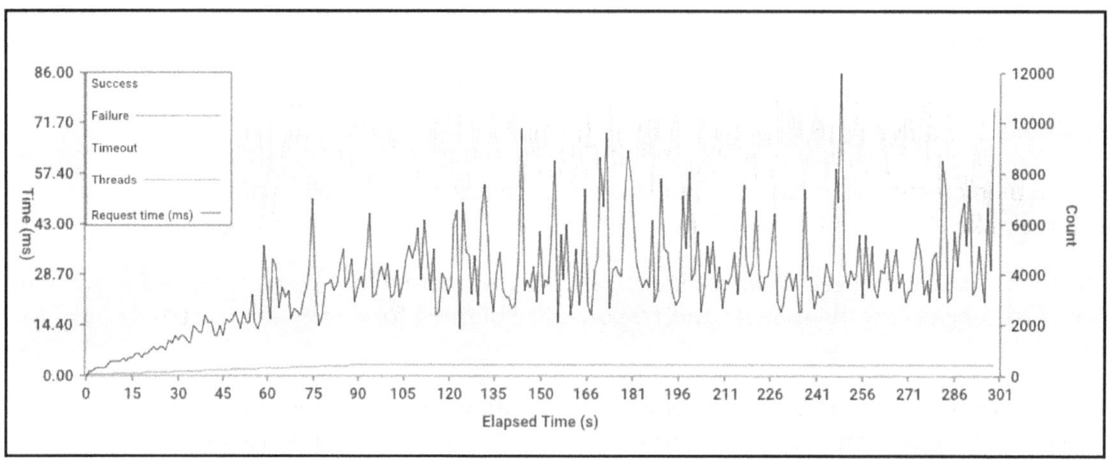

Quality

As you may expect from Google, the quality of the project is incredibly high, with some awesome architectural patterns and standard language patterns implemented by the framework. All the code is built using continuous integration, and the test coverage is excellent.

Open source

The framework is growing in popularity and is under constant development by both Google and community committers. Everything is open source, and if you want to dig into the code, it is all available for you at the GitHub repository at `https://github.com/grpc`.

Security

From a security perspective, we have all the features we could need. gRPC supports TLS encryption, authentication, and request validation. Because the underlying transport is `net/http`, we can also be confident that we are receiving the highest quality in the server layer.

Support

Documentation is again excellent, with both great examples and source code documentation provided on the gRPC website. There is a growing list of community resources, with further examples provided by bloggers. Support can also be found on the Google group and Stack Overflow.

Extensibility

From an extensibility perspective, it is possible to write custom plugins for both protoc, like the Micro framework does, and also the framework has been well written and is extensible. As a new framework only just reaching version 1, the current options are very impressive, and I can only see these growing in future releases.

A few lines about gRPC

I am very impressed with the gRPC framework and the array of options and community support that seems to grow by the day. The Protocol Buffers messaging format also appears to be growing, with companies such as Apple contributing their implementation, and I can see this becoming an unofficial standard for client-server communication replacing JSON in the very near future.

Summary

Both Micro and gRPC came out on top in the evaluation, but for slightly different reasons. Micro is ready to use in a production system out of the box if the majority of your estate is Go. The development on Micro is continuing, and the current focus is on that of performance, which, to be honest, is already pretty impressive. That said, with some work around the missing elements that are essential for microservice development, gRPC is a real contender. The polyglot nature and the throughput are excellent, and it is continuously improving.

In this chapter, we have looked at a few different frameworks, and I hope they will have given you a taster of some of the key features needed if you ever have to make a decision yourself. In the next chapter, we are going to look at logging and metrics, which are essential techniques for running microservices in production.

7
Logging and Monitoring

Logging and monitoring are not advanced topics. However, they are things that you do not realize just how important they are until you do not have them. Useful data about your service is essential to understanding the load and environment that your service is operating in so that you can make sure that it is finely tuned to give the very best performance.

Consider this example: when you first launch your service, you have an endpoint that returns a list of kittens. Initially, this service is responding promptly with a 20 ms response time; however, as people start to add items to the service, the speed slows to 200 ms. The first part of this problem is that you need to know about this slowdown. If you work in e-commerce, there is a direct correlation between the time it takes to process a request or a page to load and the likelihood that your customers will buy something.

One of the traditional methods for determining speed has always been to look at things from the edge; you use something such as Google Analytics, and you measure page load speed as experienced by the end user.

The first problem with this is that you have no idea where the slowdown originates. When we built monolithic applications, this was simple; the slowdown was either extra cruft that had been added to the HTML, or it was the monolithic app server. So the app server may have some metrics output to a log file; however, due to the nature of the application only having one attached data store, you did not have to look in many places before you found the source.

Everything changes with microservices; instead of one application, you may have 1,000; instead of one data store, you may have 100; and you may have dozens of other associated services, such as cloud storage queues and message routers. You could take the same approach to guess and test, but you will end up with a deep-seated hatred for yourself and all your colleagues who built the system.

Problem number 2: using Google Analytics will not easily tell you if the site is slowing down when it is under load. How will you know when you experience an outage? If the page is not loading because the backend server is not responding, then the JavaScript that fires data to Google Analytics will not fire. Can you even set up an alert in Google Analytics to fire an alarm when the average load time drops below a threshold?

Problem number 3: you don't have a website, only an API; bye bye Google Analytics.

Now, I am not saying you should not use Google Analytics; what I am saying is that it should form part of a larger strategy.

Stack traces and other application output that helps you diagnose a problem can be broken down into three categories::

- **Metrics**: These are things such as time series data (for example, transaction or individual component timings).
- **Text-based logs**: Text-based records are your real old-fashioned logs that are spat out by things such as nginx or a text log from your application software.
- **Exceptions**: Exceptions potentially could fall into the two previous categories; however, I like to break these out into a separate category since exceptions should be, well, exceptional.

As always, the source code for this chapter is available on GitHub. You can find it at `https://github.com/building-microservices-with-go/chapter7`.

Logging best practices

In the free e-book, *The Pragmatic Logging Handbook*, by Jon Gifford of Loggly (`https://www.loggly.com/`), Jon proposes the following eight best practices to apply when determining your logging strategy:

- Treat application logging as an ongoing iterative process. Log at a high level and then add deeper instrumentation.
- Always instrument anything that goes out of the process because distributed system problems are not well behaved.

- Always log unacceptable performance. Log anything outside the range in which you expect your system to perform.
- If possible, always log sufficient context for a complete picture of what happened from a single log event.
- View machines as your end consumer, not humans. Create records that your log management solution can interpret.
- Trends tell the story better than data points.
- Instrumentation is NOT a substitute for profiling and vice versa.
- Flying more slowly is better than flying blind. So the debate is not whether to instrument, just how much.

I think one of these points needs a little more explanation, that is, *Instrumentation is NOT a substitute for profiling and vice versa*. What Jon is referring to is that while your application may have high levels of logging and monitoring, you should still run through a pre-release process of profiling the application code. We looked at tools such as Go's profiler, and we have also done some basic performance testing with the bench tool. However, for a production service, a more thorough approach should be taken. It is beyond the scope of this book to look at performance testing in depth, but I would encourage you to read *Performance Testing with JMeter 3*, by Bayo Erinle (published by Packt Publishing), for further information on this topic.

Metrics

In my opinion, metrics are the most useful form of logging for day-to-day operations. Metrics are useful because we have simple numeric data. We can plot this onto a time-series dashboard and quite quickly set up alerting from the output because the data is incredibly cheap to process and collect.

No matter what you are storing, the superior efficiency of metrics is that you are storing numeric data in a time-series database using a unique key as an identifier. Numeric data allows the computation and comparison of the data to be incredibly efficient. It also allows the data store to reduce the resolution of the data as time progresses, enabling you to have granular data when you need it most at the right time and retain historical reference data without requiring petabytes of data storage.

Types of data best represented by metrics

This is quite simple: it is the data that is meaningful when expressed by simple numbers, such as request timings and counts. How granular you want to be with your metrics depends upon your requirements; generally, when I am building a microservice, I start with top-line metrics, such as request timings, and success and failure counts for handlers, and if I am using a data store, then I would include these too. As the service develops and I start performance testing things, I will start to add new items that help me to diagnose performance problems with the service.

Naming conventions

Defining a naming convention is incredibly important since, once you start to collect data, a point will come where you need to analyze it. The key thing for me is not to define a convention for your service, but a convention that is useful for your entire estate. When you start to investigate issues with your service, more often than not, you will find that the problem is not necessarily with your service, but could be due to a multitude of things:

- Exhausted CPU on host server
- Exhausted memory
- Network latency
- Slow data store queries
- Latency with downstream services caused by any of the preceding factors

I recommend you break up the name of your service using dot notation such as the following:

```
environment.host.service.group.segment.outcome
```

Let's break down the preceding line of code and try to understand each term individually:

- `environment`: This is the working environment, for example, production or staging.
- `host`: This is the hostname of the server running the application.
- `service`: This the name of your service.
- `group`: This is the top-level grouping; for an API, this might be handlers.
- `segment`: This is the child-level information for the group; this will typically be the name of the handler in the instance of an API.
- `outcome`: This is something that denotes the result of the operation, in an API you may have called, success, or you may choose to use HTTP status codes.

Here is an example of how to use the following dot notation:

```
prod.server1.kittenserver.handlers.list.ok
prod.server1.kittenserver.mysql.select_kittens.timing
```

If your monitoring solution supports tags in addition to the event name, then I recommend you use tags for the environment and host; this will make querying the data store a little easier. For example, if I have a handler that lists kittens that are running on my production server, then I may choose to add the following events to be emitted when the handler is called:

```
func (h *list) ServeHTTP(rw http.ResponseWriter, r *http.Request) {
  event := startTimingEvent("kittens.handlers.list.timing", ["production",
"192.168.2.2"])
  defer event.Complete()

  dispatchIncrementEvent("kittens.handlers.list.called", ["production",
"192.168.2.2"])

...

  if err != nil {
    dispatchIncrementEvent("kittens.handlers.list.failed", ["production",
192.168.2.2"])
   return`
  }

  dispatchIncrementEvent("kittens.handlers.list.success", ["production",
192.168.2.2"])
}
```

This is a pseudo code, but you can see that we are dispatching three events from this handler:

- In the first event, we are going to send some timing information.
- In the next, we are simply going to send an increment count, which is simply going to state that the handler has been called.
- Finally, we are going to check whether the operation has been successful. If not, we increment our handler-failed metric; if successful, we increment our success metric.

Naming our metrics in this way allows us to graph errors either at a granular level, or makes it possible to write a query that is at a higher level. For example, we may be interested in the total number of failed requests for the entire service, not just this endpoint. Using this naming convention, we can query using wildcards; so, to query all failures for this service, we could write a metric like the following code:

```
kittens.handlers.*.failed
```

If we were interested in all failed requests to handlers for all services, we could write the following query:

```
*.handlers.*.failed
```

Having a consistent naming convention for metrics is essential. Add this to your upfront design when building a service and implement this as a company-wide standard, not just at the team level. Let's take a look at some example code to see just how easy it is to implement `statsD`. If we take a look at `chapter7/main.go`, we can see that on line `19`, we are initializing our `statsD` client:

```
statsd, err := createStatsDClient(os.Getenv("STATSD")
  if err != nil {
    log.Fatal("Unable to create statsD client")
  }
...

func createStatsDClient(address string) (*statsd.Client, error){
  return statsd.New(statsd.Address(address))
}
```

We are using an open source package by Alex Cesaro (`https://github.com/alexcesaro/statsd`). This has a very simple interface; to create our client, we call the `New` function and pass it a list of options. In this instance, we are only passing through the address of the `statsD` server, which has been set by an environment variable:

```
func New(opts ...Option) (*Client, error)
```

If we look at line 27 in the `cserver/handlers/helloworld.go` file, we are deferring the sending of the timing data until the handler completes:

```
defer h.statsd.NewTiming().Send(helloworldTiming)
```

The start time will be the time of execution of the `defer` statement, so this should be the first line of your file; the end time will be once the deferred statement executes. If this handler is middleware and you are calling a downstream in a chain, then remember that the execution time of all the downstream calls will also be included in this metric. To exclude this, we can create a new `Timing` in line `27`, and then call the `Send` method manually just before we execute the next middleware in the chain:

```
func (c *Client) NewTiming() Timing
```

If you take a look at the following line of code, you will see we are calling the `Increment` function when the request completes successfully:

```
h.statsd.Increment(helloworldSuccess)
```

The `Increment` function will increase the count for the given bucket by one, and these are fascinating metrics to have in your application as they give you a really interesting picture of the health and status:

```
func (c *Client) Increment(bucket string)
```

The `statsD` client does not work synchronously, sending each metric when you make a call to the client; instead, it buffers all the calls, and there is an internal goroutine that sends the data at a predetermined interval. This makes the operation highly efficient, and you should not have to worry about any application slowdown.

Storage and querying

There are multiple options for storing and querying metric data; you have the possibility for self-hosting, or you can utilize a software-as-a-service. How you manage this is dependent upon your company's scale and the security requirements for your data.

Software as a Service

For **Software as a Service** (**SaaS**), I recommend looking at Datadog. To send metrics to Datadog, you have two options: one is to communicate with the API directly; the other is to run the Datadog collector as a container inside your cluster. The Datadog collector allows you to use `StatsD` as your data format, and it supports a couple of nice extensions that standard `StatsD` does not, such as the ability to add additional tags or metadata to your metrics. Tagging allows you to categorize your data by user-defined tags, and this, in turn, allows you to keep your metric names specific to what they are monitoring without having to add environmental information.

Self-hosted

While it may be desirable to use an SaaS service for your production data, it is always useful to be able to run a server locally for local development. There are many options for backend data stores such as Graphite, Prometheus, InfluxDB, and Elasticsearch; however, when it comes to graphing, Grafana leads the way.

Let's spin up a Docker Compose stack for our list, kittenservice, so that we can run through the simple steps of setting up Prometheus with Grafana and with Docker Compose.

If we look at the Docker compose file, we can see that we have three entries:

- `statsD`
- `grafana`
- `prometheus`

StatsD is not a `statsD` server as such, but a `statsD` exporter; this exposes an endpoint that Prometheus can use to collect the statistics. Unlike Graphite, which you push metrics to, Prometheus pulls stats.

Prometheus is the database server that is used for collecting the data.

Grafana is what we will use for graphing our data.

If we take a look at the Docker Compose file, `docker-compose.yml`, which is located at the root of our source repository, we will see that the Prometheus section requires some particular configuration:

```
prometheus:
   image: prom/prometheus
   links:
     - statsd
   volumes:
     - ./prometheus.yml:/etc/prometheus/prometheus.yml
   ports:
     - 9090:9090
```

We are mounting a volume that contains the Prometheus configuration. Let's take a look at it:

```
global:
   scrape_interval:     15s
 scrape_configs:
   - job_name: 'statsd'
     static_configs:
       - targets: ['statsd:9102']
   - job_name: 'prometheus'
     static_configs:
       - targets: ['localhost:9090']
```

The first part of this configuration sets the intervals for fetching the data from our sources and also the intervals upon which they will be evaluated. The default value for the scrape interval is one minute. We have reduced this for our example, as we are impatient and we would like to see our metrics update almost immediately after we have made a request to the server. However, in practice, we are not really interested in real-time data. A lag of a minute is OK. The next part is the scrape configs; these are the settings that define the data that we would like to import into Prometheus. The first element is our `statsD` collector; we point this to the collector defined in our `docker-compose` file. As we are using a link between our two containers, we can use the link name in the config. The next item is the configuration for Prometheus' performance metrics. We do not have to enable this; however, metrics are critical, so it would make sense to monitor the health of our metrics database.

Grafana

To display these metrics, we are going to use Grafana. If we start our stack by using the `make runserver` command and wait for a few moments for the server to start, we can then execute a few `curl` commands to the endpoint to start populating the system with data:

```
curl [docker host ip]:8091/helloworld -d '{"name": "Nic"}'
```

Let's log into Grafana and have a look at some of the data we have collected. Point your browser at `[docker host ip]:3000` and you should be presented with a login screen. The default username and password is `admin`:

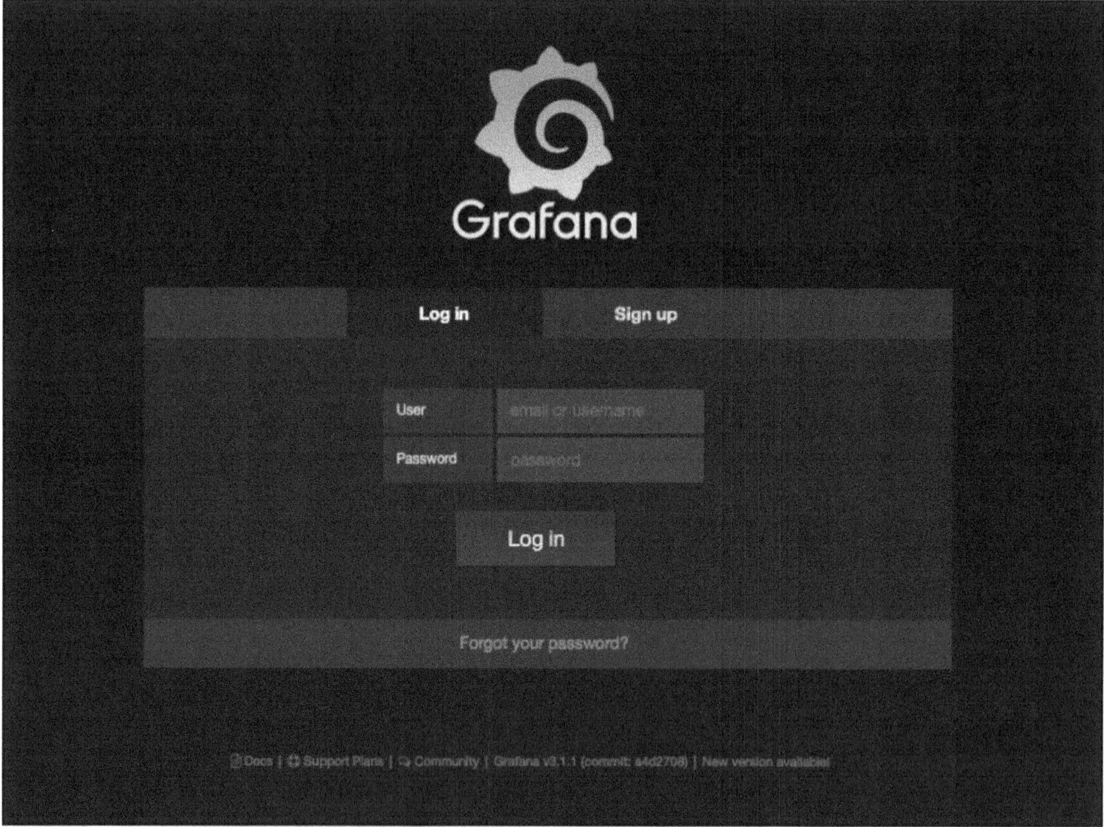

Once you have logged in, the first thing we want to do is to configure our data source. Unfortunately, there seems to be no way to set up this automatically with configuration files. There is an API if you need to provision in an environment outside of your local machine; it should be pretty trivial to write something that syncs data using this:

`http://docs.grafana.org/http_api/data_source/`

Configuring the data source is relatively straightforward. All we need to do is to select **Prometheus** as our data type and then fill in the connection details. You need to ensure that you select **proxy** as opposed to **direct**. **proxy** makes the calls for data from the Grafana server; **direct** will use your browser. Once we have done that, let's add the default dashboard for the Prometheus server:

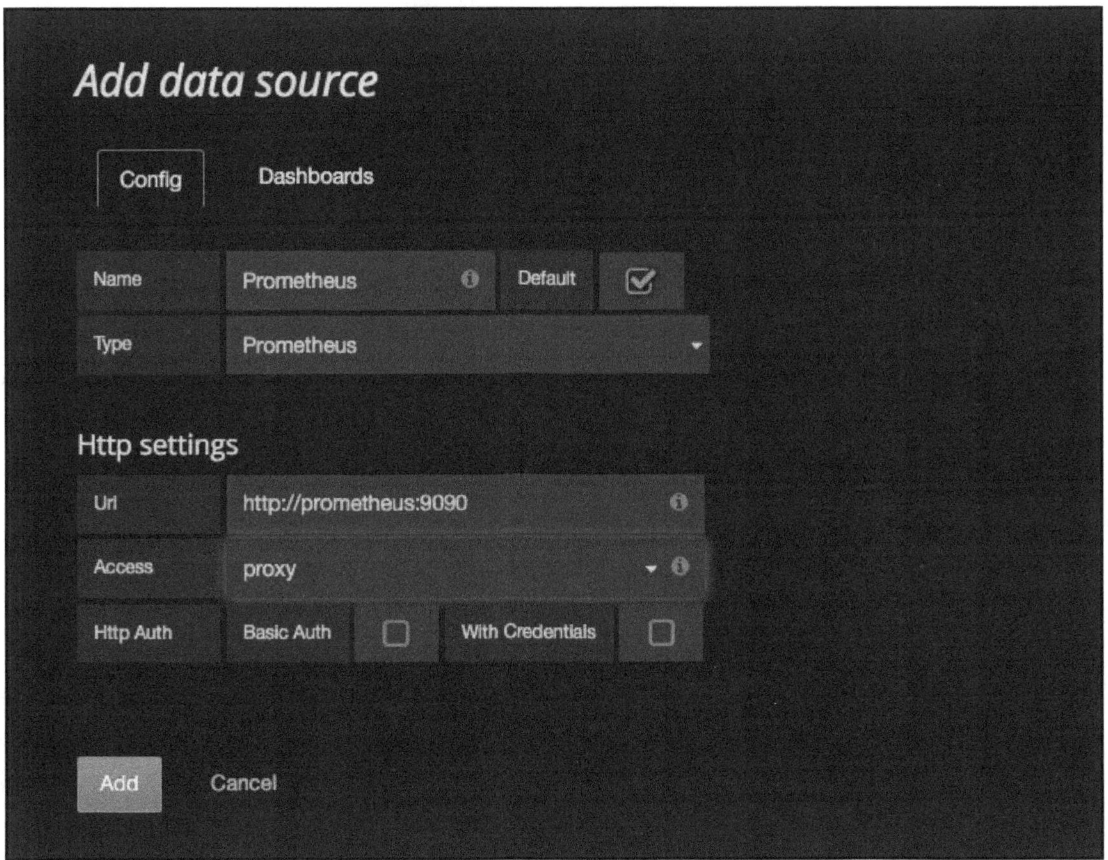

If you click the **Dashboards** tab, you will see that you have the ability to import a pre-created dashboard. This is useful, but what we want to do is create our own dashboard from our server. To do this, hit the **Dashboards** link and then create a new dashboard. This will take you to the dashboards creation page. We are going to add a graph of our requests. So let's select the **Graph** option. In the bottom panel, we have the ability to add the metrics we would like to show; if we already know the name of the dashboard, then all we need to do is type the expression into the box:

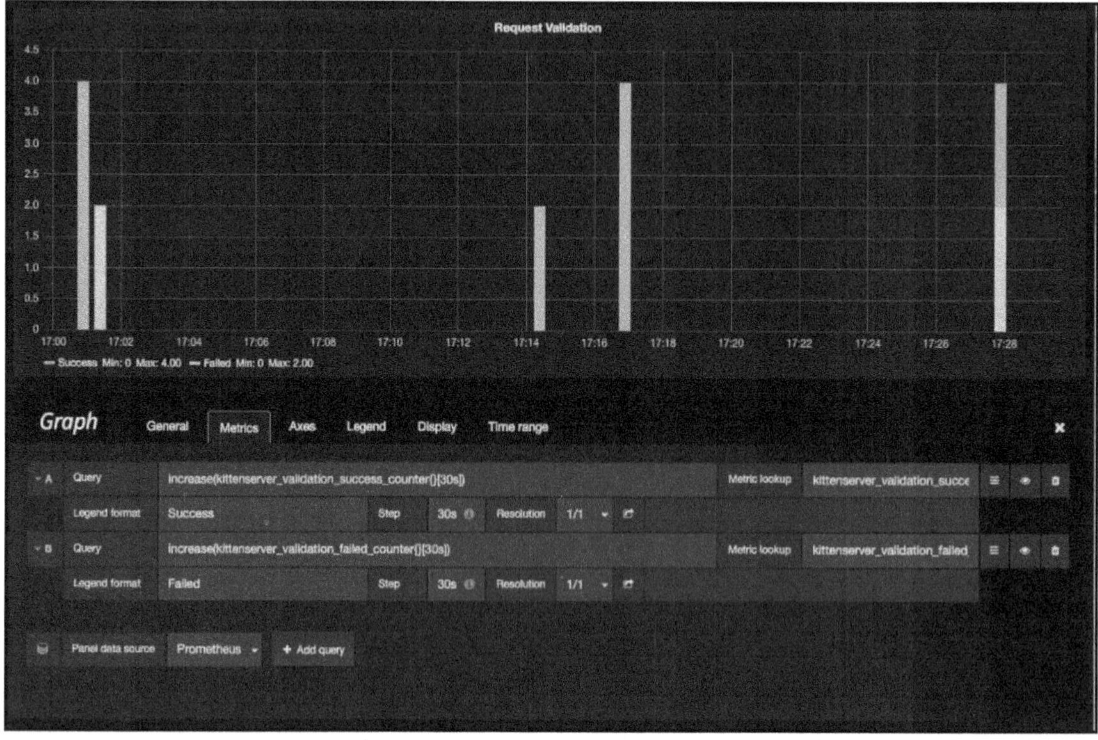

The metrics lookup allows us to search for metrics based on part of the name. If we type `kitten` into this box, then all the metrics from our simple API that have been tagged with kitten will show up in the box. For now, let's select the validation success metric. By default, this metric is a count of all the times that the metric was reported for the given time interval. This is why you see the graph. While this may be useful in some instances, what we would like to see is a nice bar chart showing the successes for a given period. To do this, we can use one of the many expressions to group this data:

```
increase(kittenserver_helloworld_success_counter{}[30s])
```

This expression will group the data into buckets of 30 seconds and will return the difference between the current and the previous bucket. In effect, what this gives us is a chart showing the number of successes every 30 seconds. To present the information, a bar graph would most likely be better, so we can change this option in the **Display** tab. Changing the step setting to the same interval as the duration we set in our increase expression will make the chart look a little more readable. Now, add a second query for the timings of our hello world handler. This time, we do not need to aggregate the data into buckets, as we are fine displaying it on the graph as it is. Timing metrics show three lines, the average (quartile 0.5), the top 10% (quartile 0.9), and the top 1% (quartile 0.99). In general, we would like to see these lines quite tightly grouped together, which indicates little variance in our service calls. We do not see this in our graph, even though we are performing the same operation time and time again, due to line 149 in the code:

```
time.Sleep(time.Duration(rand.Intn(200)) * time.Millisecond)
```

Our handler was running just too fast to measure less than 1 ms, so I added a little random wait to make the graph more interesting:

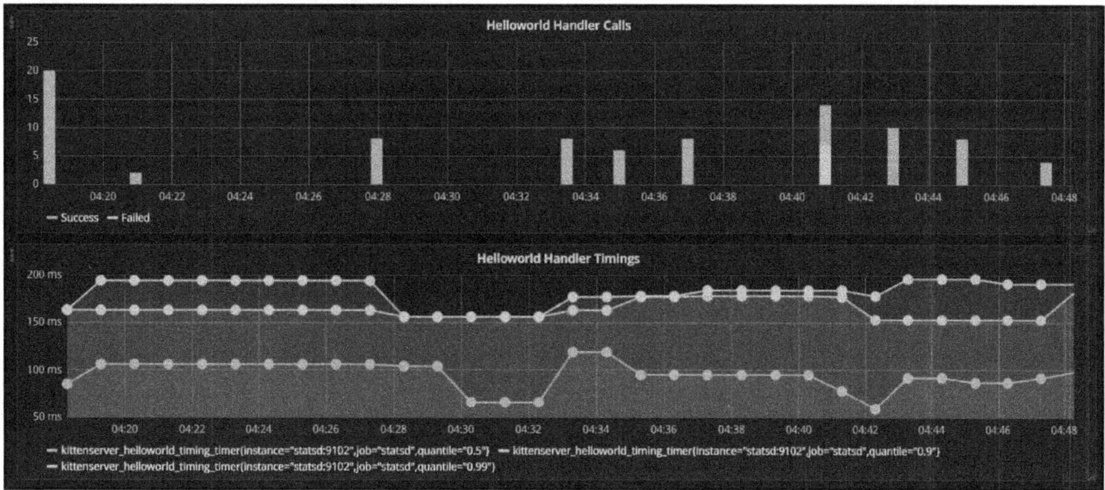

That is the basics for simple metrics; for logging more detailed information, we need to fall back to trusty log files. The days of pulling data from servers are long gone, and, in our highly distributed world, this would be a nightmare. Thankfully, we have tools such as Elasticsearch and Kibana.

Logging

When working with highly distributed containers, you may have 100 instances of your application running, rather than one or two. This means that if you need to grep your log files, you will be doing this over hundreds of files instead of just a couple. In addition, Docker-based applications should be stateless and the scheduler may be moving them around on multiple hosts. This adds an extra layer of complexity to manage. To save the trouble, the best way to solves this problem is not to write the logs to disk in the first place. A distributed logging store, such as an ELK stack, or an SaaS platform, such as Logmatic or Loggly, solve this problem for us and gives us a fantastic insight into the health and operating condition of our system. Regarding the cost, you will most likely find that one of the SaaS providers is cheaper than running and maintaining your ELK stack. However, your security needs may not always allow this. Retention is also an interesting problem while looking at logging. My personal preference is to only store log data for short periods of time, such as 30 days; this allows you to maintain diagnostic traces that could be useful for troubleshooting without the cost of maintaining historical data. For historical data, a metrics platform is best, as you can cheaply store this data over a period of years, which can be useful if you want to compare current performance with that of an historic event.

Distributed tracing with Correlation IDs

In `Chapter 2`, *Designing a Great API*, we looked at the `X-Request-ID` header, which allows us to mark all the service calls for an individual request with the same ID so that we can query them later. This is an incredibly important concept when it comes to debugging a request because it can really help you understand why a service may be failing or misbehaving by looking at the tree of requests and the parameters passed to them. If you take a look at the `handlers/correlation.go` file, we can implement this quite simply:

```
func (c *correlationHandler) ServeHTTP(rw http.ResponseWriter, r
*http.Request) {
  if r.Header.Get("X-Request-ID") == "" {
    r.Header.Set("X-Request-ID", uuid.New().String())
  }

  c.next.ServeHTTP(rw, r)
}
```

The handler is implemented using the middleware pattern. When we want to use it, all we need to do is wrap the actual handler as follows:

```
http.Handle("/helloworld", handlers.NewCorrelationHandler(validation))
```

Now, every time a request is made to the `/helloworld` endpoint, the `X-Request-ID` header will be appended to the request with a random UUID if it is not already present. This is a very simple method of adding distributed tracing into your application. Depending upon your requirements, you may want to check out Zipkin, which is a distributed tracing system designed to trouble shoot latency, and which is becoming incredibly popular (`http://zipkin.io`). There are also tools from DataDog, NewRelic, and AWS X-Ray. It is beyond the scope of this book to go into depth into these applications; however, please spend an hour and familiarize yourself with their capabilities because you never know when you are going to need them.

Elasticsearch, Logstash, and Kibana (ELK)

Elasticsearch, Logstash, and Kibana are pretty much the industry standard when it comes to logging verbose data. All of the output that would traditionally be streamed to a log file is stored in a central location that you can query with a graphical interface tool, Kibana.

If we look at our Docker Compose file, you will see three entries for our ELK stack:

```
elasticsearch:
   image: elasticsearch:2.4.2
   ports:
     - 9200:9200
     - 9300:9300
   environment:
     ES_JAVA_OPTS: "-Xms1g -Xmx1g"
 kibana:
   image: kibana:4.6.3
   ports:
     - 5601:5601
   environment:
     - ELASTICSEARCH_URL=http://elasticsearch:9200
   links:
     - elasticsearch
 logstash:
   image: logstash
   command: -f /etc/logstash/conf.d/
   ports:
     - 5000:5000
   volumes:
     - ./logstash.conf:/etc/logstash/conf.d/logstash.conf
   links:
     - elasticsearch
```

Elasticsearch is our datastore for our logging data, Kibana is the application we will use for querying this data, and Logstash is used for reading the data from your application logs and storing it in Elasticsearch. The only configuration, besides a few environment variables, is the Logstash config:

```
input {
   tcp {
     port => 5000
     codec => "json"
     type => "json"
   }
 }
## Add your filters / logstash plugins configuration here
output {
  elasticsearch {
    hosts => "elasticsearch:9200"
  }
}
```

The input configuration allows us to send our logs direct over TCP to the Logstash server. This saves us the problem of writing to disk and then Logstash having to read these files. In general, TCP is probably going to be faster. Disk I/O is not free, and the contention caused by writing a log file sequentially can slow down your application. Depending upon your appetite for risk, you may choose to use UDP as transport for your logs. This will be faster than TCP; however, this speed comes at the expense that you will not get confirmation that the data has been received, and you may lose some logs.

In general, this is not too much of a problem unless you need your logs for security auditing. In this instance, you could always configure multiple inputs for different log types. Logstash has the capability to grep many common output formats for logs and transform them into JSON format, which can be indexed by Elasticsearch. Since the logs in our example application are already in JSON format, we can set the type to JSON and Logstash will not apply any transformation. In the output section, we are defining our datastore; again, like the Prometheus configuration, we can use the link address provided by Docker for our URI:

`https://www.elastic.co/guide/en/logstash/current/configuration.html`

Kibana

Start your stack if it is not already running and send a little data to Elasticsearch:

```
curl $(docker-machine ip):8091/helloworld -d '{"name": "Nic"}'
```

Now, point your browser at `http://192.168.165.129:5601`. The first screen you should see if you are starting with a new setup is the one that prompts you to create a new index in Elasticsearch. Go ahead and create this using the defaults; you will now see the list of fields that Elasticsearch can index from your logs:

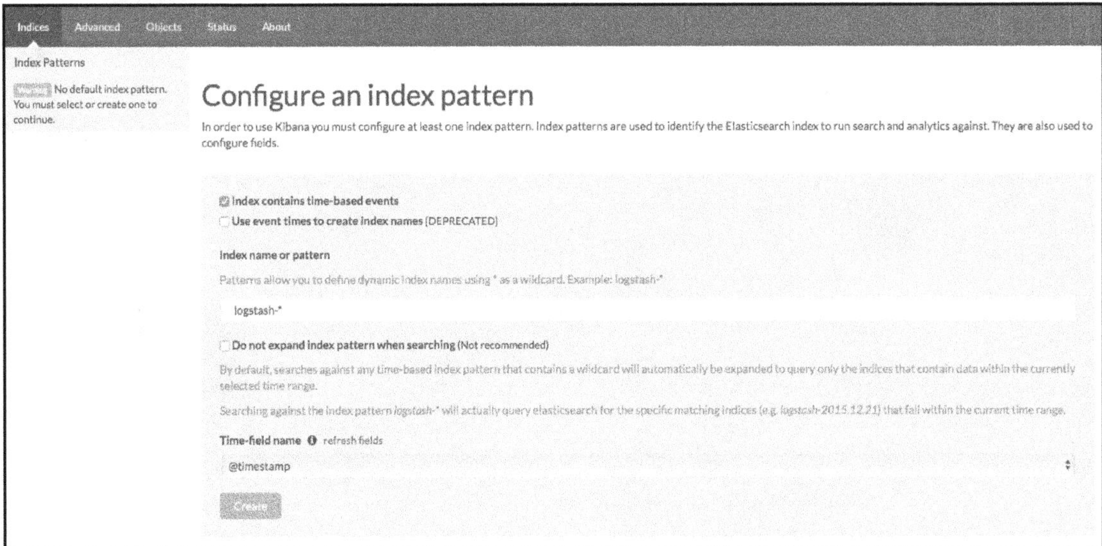

If need be, you can change these settings. Generally, however you will be fine with the defaults. The Kibana screen is relatively straightforward. If you switch to the **Discover** tab, you will be able to see some of the logs that have been collected:

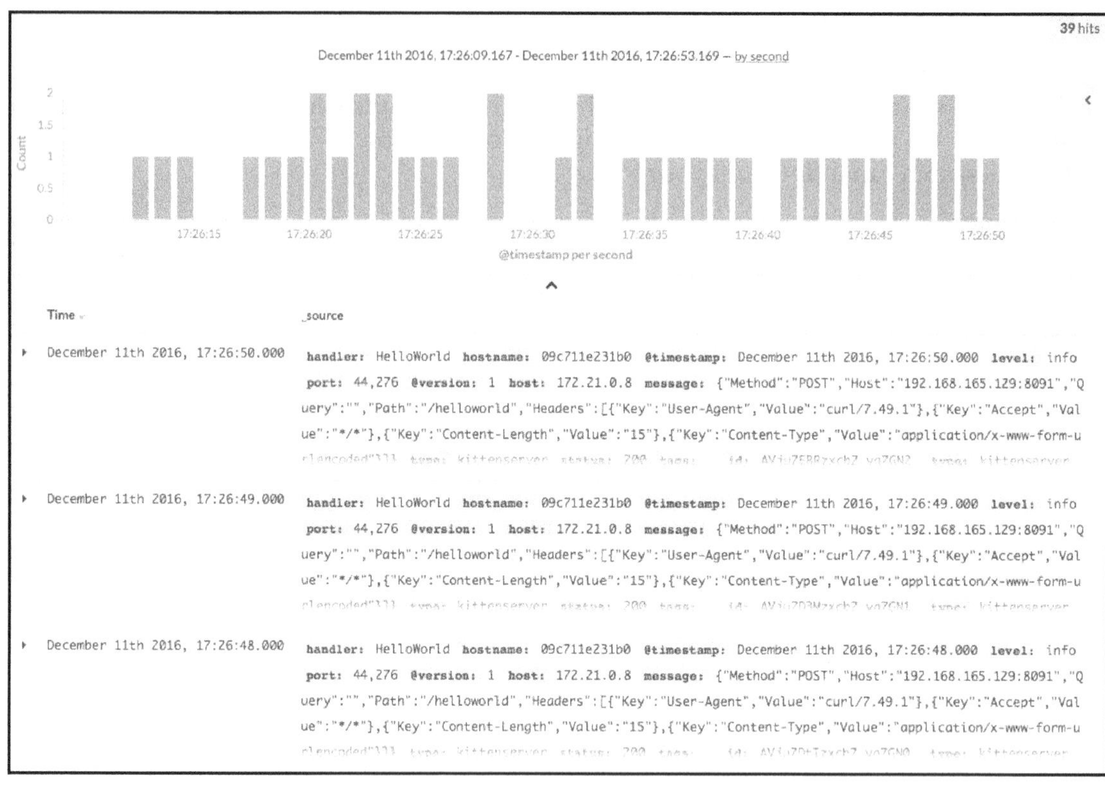

Expanding one of the entries will show the indexed fields in more detail:

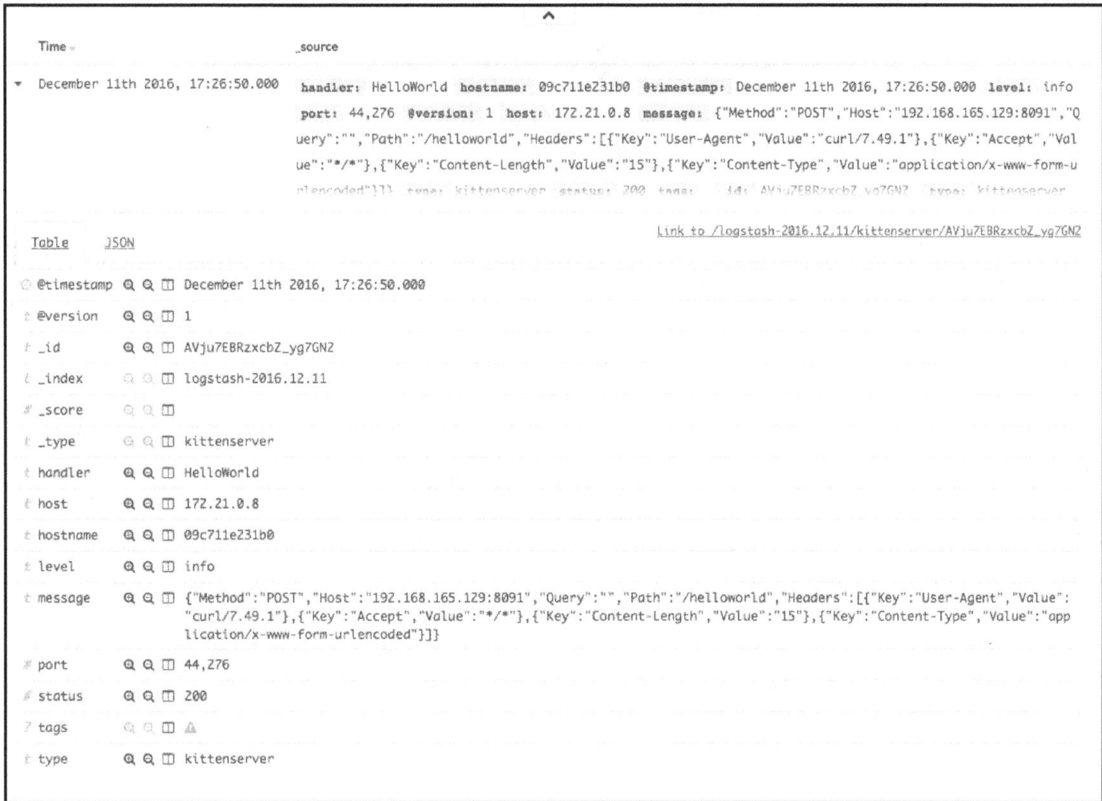

To filter the logs by one of these fields, you can enter the filter in the search bar at the top of the window. Search criteria must be written in Lucene format, so to filter our list by status code, we can enter the following query:

```
status: 200
```

This filters the `status` field containing the numeric value `200`. While searching indexed fields is relatively straightforward, we have added the bulk of our data to the message field, where it is stored as a JSON string:

```
status:200 and message:/.*"Method":"POST"/
```

To filter our list to only show `POST` actions, we can use a query containing a regex search:

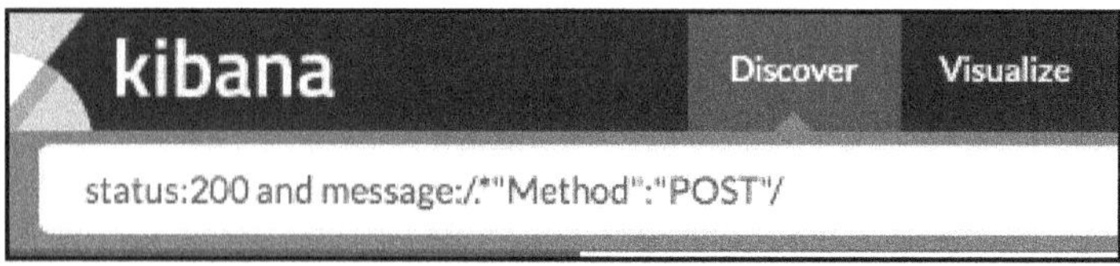

Regex search terms will be slower than indexed queries, as each item has to be evaluated. If we find that there is a particular field we are always referring to and would like to speed up these filters, then we have two options. The first and the most awkward is to add a *grok* section to our Logstash configuration: `https://www.elastic.co/guide/en/logstash/current/plugins-filters-grok.html#plugins-filters-grok-add\_field`.

The other option is to specify these fields when we are preparing the data to log. If you look at the example code, you can see that we are extracting the method, and while this is also going into the `message` field, we are logging it using the `WithFields` method, which will allow Logstash to index it. If you take a look at line 37 of the `chandlers/helloworld.go` file, you can see this in action:

```
serializedRequest := serializeRequest(r)
message, _ := json.Marshal(serializedRequest)
h.logger.WithFields(logrus.Fields{
  "handler": "HelloWorld",
  "status":  http.StatusOK,
  "method":  serializedRequest.Method,
}).Info(string(message))
```

In our example, we are using the Logrus logger. Logrus is a structured logger for Go that supports many different plugins. In our example, we are using the Logstash plugin, which allows us to send our logs directly to the Logstash endpoint rather than writing them to a file and then having Logstash pick them up:

```
func createLogger(address string) (*logrus.Logger, error) {
 retryCount := 0

 l := logrus.New()
 hostname, _ := os.Hostname()
 var err error

 // Retry connection to logstash incase the server has not yet come up
 for ; retryCount < 10; retryCount++ {
   hook, err := logstash.NewHookWithFields(
     "tcp",
```

```
  address,
  "kittenserver",
  logrus.Fields{"hostname": hostname},
    )

    if err == nil {
      l.Hooks.Add(hook)
      return l, err
    }

    log.Println("Unable to connect to logstash, retrying")
    time.Sleep(1 * time.Second)
  }

  return nil, err
}
```

Adding plugins to Logrus is very simple. We define the hook, which is in a separate package, and specify the connection protocol, address, application name, and a `Fields` collection, which is always sent to the logger:

```
func NewHookWithFields(protocol, address, appName string, alwaysSentFields
logrus.Fields) (*Hook, error)
```

We then register the plugin with the logger using the `hook` method:

```
func AddHook(hook Hook)
```

Logrus has many configurable options, and the standard Log, Info, Debug, and Error logging levels will enable you to log any object. It will, however, use Go's built-in `ToString` unless there is a particular implementation. To get around this, and to be able to have more parsable data in our logfiles, I have added a simple serialization method that converts the relevant methods from `http.Request` into a JSON object:

```
type SerialzableRequest struct {
  *http.Request
}

func (sr *SerialzableRequest) ToJSON() string
```

Full source code for this example can be found in the example code, `chapter7/httputil/request.go`. This is only a simple implementation at the moment, but it could be extended if required.

Exceptions

One of the great things about Go is that the standard patterns are such that you should always handle errors when they occur, instead of bubbling them up to the top and presenting them to the user. Having said that, there is always a case when the unexpected happens. The secret to this is to know about it and to fix the problem when it occurs. There are many exception logging platforms on the market. However, the two techniques we have discussed are, in my opinion, more than sufficient for tracing the few errors that we hopefully will find in our web application.

Panic and recover

Go has two great methods for handling unexpected errors:

- `panic`
- `recover`

Panic

The built-in `panic` function stops the normal execution of the current goroutine. All the deferred functions are run in the normal way; then, the program is terminated:

```
func panic(v interface{})
```

Recover

The `recover` function allows an application to manage the behavior of a panicking goroutine. When called inside a deferred function, `recover` stops the execution of `panic` and returns the error passed to the call of `panic`:

```
func recover() interface{}
```

If our handler panics for some reason, the HTTP server will recover this panic and write the output to the `std` error. While this is fine if we are running the application locally, it does not allow us to manage the errors when our application is distributed across many remote servers. Since we have already logged into an ELK stack setup, we can write a simple handler that will wrap our main handler, allow the capture of any panic, and forward it to the logger:

```
18 func (p *panicHandler) ServeHTTP(rw http.ResponseWriter, r
*http.Request) {
19  defer func() {
20    if err := recover(); err != nil {
21  p.logger.WithFields(
22  logrus.Fields{
23      "handler": "panic",
24      "status":  http.StatusInternalServerError,
25      "method":  r.Method,
26      "path":    r.URL.Path,
27      "query":   r.URL.RawQuery,
28      },
29  ).Error(fmt.Sprintf("Error: %v\n%s", err, debug.Stack()))
30
31  rw.WriteHeader(http.StatusInternalServerError)
32   }
33  }()
34
35  p.next.ServeHTTP(rw, r)
36 }
```

This is relatively straightforward. In line `19`, we are deferring the call to `recover`. When this runs, if we have an error message, that is, something has panicked, we want to log it. As in the previous examples, we are adding fields to the log entry so that Elasicsearch will index them, but instead of logging the request, we are writing the error message. This message most likely will not have sufficient context for us to be able to debug the application, so, in order to get the context, we make a call to `debug.Stack()`:

```
func Stack() []byte
```

`Stack` is part of the runtime/debug package and returns a formatted stack trace of the goroutine that calls it. You can test this by running the example code of this chapter and then `curl` the `bang` endpoint:

```
curl -i [docker host ip]:8091/bang
```

We are writing this along with the error message to Elasticsearch when we query Kibana. For this message, we will see the captured details, which look something like the following:

```
level      error

message    Error: Somethings gone wrong again
           goroutine 33 [running]:
           runtime/debug.Stack(0xc42010a000, 0xc4200e8420, 0xc4200ee190)
                   /usr/local/Cellar/go/1.8.3/libexec/src/runtime/debug/stack.go:24 +0x79
           github.com/building-microservices-with-go/chapter7/server/handlers.(*panicHandler).ServeHTTP.func1(0xc4200fc320, 0xc42016e1
           00, 0x7d9d00, 0xc420174000)
                   /Users/nicj/Developer/go/src/github.com/building-microservices-with-go/chapter7/server/handlers/panic.go:29 +0x3dc
           panic(0x657d60, 0xc4200e61a0)
                   /usr/local/Cellar/go/1.8.3/libexec/src/runtime/panic.go:489 +0x2cf
           github.com/building-microservices-with-go/chapter7/server/handlers.(*bangHandler).ServeHTTP(0x821720, 0x7d9d00, 0xc42017400
           0, 0xc42016e100)
                   /Users/nicj/Developer/go/src/github.com/building-microservices-with-go/chapter7/server/handlers/bang.go:9 +0x64
           github.com/building-microservices-with-go/chapter7/server/handlers.(*panicHandler).ServeHTTP(0xc4200fc320, 0x7d9d00, 0xc420
           174000, 0xc42016e100)
                   /Users/nicj/Developer/go/src/github.com/building-microservices-with-go/chapter7/server/handlers/panic.go:35 +0x9a
           github.com/building-microservices-with-go/chapter7/server/handlers.(*correlationHandler).ServeHTTP(0xc4200f8260, 0x7d9d00,
           0xc420174000, 0xc42016e100)
                   /Users/nicj/Developer/go/src/github.com/building-microservices-with-go/chapter7/server/handlers/correlation.go:15 +
           0x86
           net/http.(*ServeMux).ServeHTTP(0x804fc0, 0x7d9d00, 0xc420174000, 0xc42016e100)
                   /usr/local/Cellar/go/1.8.3/libexec/src/net/http/server.go:2238 +0x130
           net/http.serverHandler.ServeHTTP(0xc42012e000, 0x7d9d00, 0xc420174000, 0xc42016e100)
                   /usr/local/Cellar/go/1.8.3/libexec/src/net/http/server.go:2568 +0x92
           net/http.(*conn).serve(0xc4200fe0a0, 0x7da1c0, 0xc4200e4100)
                   /usr/local/Cellar/go/1.8.3/libexec/src/net/http/server.go:1825 +0x612
           created by net/http.(*Server).Serve
                   /usr/local/Cellar/go/1.8.3/libexec/src/net/http/server.go:2668 +0x2ce
```

Finally, we return the status code 500 to the client with no message body.

The message should give us enough context to understand where the problem area lies. The input that caused the exception will, however, be missing, so if we are unable to replicate the error, then it is probably time to add more instrumentation to our service and re-run.

As part of the application life cycle of your service, you should always endeavor to keep on top of exceptions. This will greatly enhance your ability to react when something goes wrong. More often than not, I see exception trackers that are so full of problems that the teams lose all hope of ever cleaning them up and stop trying. Don't let your new services get this way when a new exception appears to fix it. This way, you can set up alerts on your exceptions, as you will be pretty confident there is a problem.

Summary

That is it for this chapter. Logging and monitoring is a topic that you can tailor to your particular use case and environment, but I hope you have learned how easy it is to set up. Using SaaS, such as Datadog or Logmatic, is an excellent way to get up and running very quickly, and alerts integration with OpsGenie or PagerDuty will allow you to receive instant alerts whenever a problem may occur.

8
Security

Security in microservices can feel like a minefield, and in some ways it is. This chapter is mainly intended to look at some of the things that you can do to improve the security of your Go code; however, I feel it is important to discuss some of the wider issues. In-depth discussion of topics such as firewall configuration is best left to specialist books; however, we will introduce some of the concepts and problems that are faced so that you can best prepare yourself for some further reading.

Encryption and signing

When we look at ways of securing data, either at rest or in transport, many of the methods we discuss will be cryptographically securing data.

> *"Cryptography is the science of using mathematics to encrypt and decrypt data. Cryptography enables you to store sensitive information or transmit it across insecure networks (line like the internet) so that it cannot be read by anyone except the intended recipient."*
>
> *- An Introduction to Cryptography, Network Associates, Inc.*

As a basis for the things we will discuss in this chapter, we must first understand how cryptography works; not in so complex a way that we need a mathematics degree, but to the extent of the parts involved. Cryptography is only as good as the security of the keys involved, and we need to know which of these keys can be distributed freely and which ones need to be guarded with our lives.

Symmetric-key encryption

Symmetric-key encryption is also called secret-key or conventional cryptography: one key is used for both the encryption and decryption of the data. For a remote end user to be able to decrypt this information, it must first have the key, and this key must be securely held because a single compromise of one server will lead to all servers who share this key being compromised. It can also make key management more complicated, because when you need to change the key (and you should change it often), you will need to roll this change out across your entire estate.

Public-key cryptography

Public-key cryptography was introduced by Whitfield Diffie and Martin Hellman in 1975 to get around the need for both sides to know the secret key. In fact, they were not the first to invent it; it was developed by the British Secret Service some years earlier, but was kept a military secret.

Public-key cryptography uses a pair of keys for encryption; you may also hear it called asymmetric encryption. The public key is used for encrypting information, while the private key can only be used for decrypting. Because there is no way to determine the private key from the public key, it is common for public keys to be published to the world.

Digital signatures

Public-key cryptography also gives us the ability to use digital signatures. A digital signature works by encrypting a message with a private key and then transferring the signed message. If the message can be decrypted with the public key, then the message must have originated from the holder of the private key. Due to the computation time of encrypting messages and the increase in the size of the payload, a standard approach is to create a one-way hash of the message and then use the private key to encrypt it. The recipient will decrypt the hash with the public key and generate the same hash from the message; then, the message can be deemed to be from a trustworthy source.

X.509 digital certificates

One problem with public keys is that you must be careful that the key you think belongs to a recipient is owned by the recipient. If keys are transferred across public networks, there is always the possibility of a man-in-the-middle attack. An attacker could pose as your trusted recipient with a fake public key; however, they could replace this with their keys. This would mean that the message you think has been transferred securely could, in fact, be decrypted and read by a malicious third party.

To avoid these issues, digital certificates exist, simplifying the task of establishing whether a public key belongs to the reported owner.

A digital certificate contains three things:

- A public key
- Certificate information, such as the owner's name or ID
- One or more digital signatures

The thing that makes a certificate trustworthy is the digital signatures. The certificate is signed by a trusted third party or certificate authority (CA), which vouches for your identity and that your public key belongs to you. Anyone can create a CA root certificate and sign their certificates, and for non-public access to systems, such as inter-microservice communication, this is quite a common practice. For public certificates, however, you pay a CA to sign your certificate. The purpose of the pricing is that the CA will ensure that you are who indeed you say you are; at present, the most popular CAs are Comodo, Symantec (previously Verisign), and GoDaddy. The reason you see the padlock in your browser is not just because you are using secured communication, but that your browser has validated the signature of the certificate against one of the 100 or so trusted third parties that come bundled with it.

TLS/SSL

SSL, which is the common term for secure transmission of data between two systems, is a reference to a deprecated standard first developed by Mozilla back in 1995. It has since been replaced by TLS 1.2, which was released in August 2008; while SSL 3.0 still technically works, it was deprecated in June 2015 after a vulnerability to the **POODLE** (**Paddling Oracle On Downgraded Legacy Encryption**) attack. The POODLE attack, discovered by a team of Google security researchers in 2014, works by the attackers making several requests to a server; this data is then analyzed and used, which enables them to decrypt the data in the transport. On average, only 256 SSL 3.0 calls need to be made to decrypt 1 byte of information.

This means that the vulnerability existed for 18 years before being publicly disclosed; you might ask why people were still using SSL 3.0 15 years after the release of the stronger TLS 1.0. This came about due to a problem that some browsers and servers did not support TLS 1.0, so there was a fallback that would allow fallback to a lower level of encryption. Even though, at the time of discovery, there was pretty much nobody still using SSL 3.0, the fallback was still in the protocol and was, therefore, exploitable by the hackers. The solution for this was quite straightforward: disable anything lower than TLS 1.0 in the configuration of your server.

We have had a little history of TLS and SSL, but how does it keep your data secure?

TLS works using symmetrical encryption, where the client and the server both have a key that is used for encryption and decryption. If you remember the previous section, we introduced symmetrical encryption and the problems of distributing keys. TLS gets around this problem by using asymmetrical encryption in the first part of the handshake. The client retrieves the certificate containing the public key from the server and generates a random number; it uses the public key to encrypt this random number and sends it back to the server. Now that both parties have the random number, they use this to generate symmetrical keys, which are used for encrypting and decrypting the data over the transport.

External security

This is your first line of defense to keep your systems safe. It commonly comprises layer 2 or 3 firewalls, DDoS protection, web application firewalls, and other software and hardware. Before an attacker can compromise your application, they must first pass through these layers of hardware and software, which is not part of your application code, but is a shared infrastructure layer that many components in the application may share. In this section, we will look at some of this external security as well as some attacks that could be used against you. Securing the perimeter of your services is often a task completed by operations; however, as developers, we need to understand the processes and risks because it greatly enhances our ability to harden our application code. In this section, we will look at the common methods of external security and also some of the ways hackers can exploit your system.

Layer 2 or 3 firewalls

Layer 2 is more commonly used for routing, as it deals purely with MAC addresses and not IP addresses, whereas layer 3 is IP-address aware. Traditionally, layer 2 was the only real way to go without adding latency, because it would perform at roughly the same speed as the wire. With increases in processing power and memory, layer 3 now performs at wire speeds. Generally, when we are looking at edge firewalls (which are generally the first entry point into your system), they will be layer 3 these days. So what does this give us? Firstly, it stops unwanted traffic at the edge: we limit the ports that are accessible to the outside world, and traffic with malicious intent is stopped at the firewall and does not get the chance to execute an attack on the origin. In addition to this, it also allows us to restrict access to certain ports. For example, if you are running a server, you most likely will want some form of remote access, such as SSH. The Heartbleed exploit, which came out in 2015, took advantage of a vulnerability in OpenSSH, and SSH servers that were directly exposed to the internet would be prone to this attack. Using a firewall effectively would mean that private ports, such as SSH, would be locked down to an IP address or IP range, which could be your VPN, office IP, or public IP. This dramatically reduces the attack vector, so while you might be running a version of OpenSSH that is vulnerable to Heartbleed, for an attacker to take advantage of this, they would need to be inside your protected zone.

The Heartbleed vulnerability exploited the ability to execute a buffer overrun attack. For example, if you ask the server for a 4-letter word but specify the length to be 500, what you get back is the 4-letter word, and the remaining 496 characters are the blocks of memory that follow the memory address of the initial allocation. In practice, this allowed a hacker to access chunks of memory in the server randomly. This may contain items, such as change password requests, that give them credentials to access the server. If you are running a globally available SSH server, then you may find you have a problem:

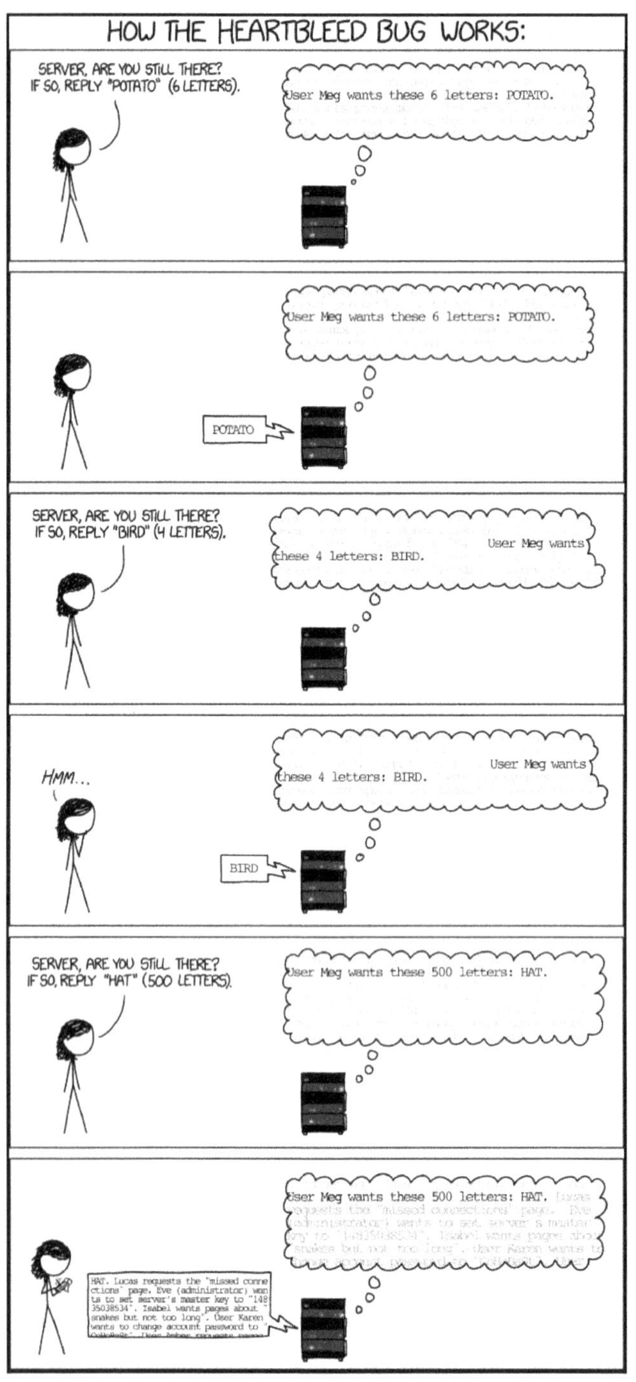
HOW THE HEARTBLEED BUG WORKS:
SERVER, ARE YOU STILL THERE? IF SO, REPLY "POTATO" (6 LETTERS).
User Meg wants these 6 letters: POTATO.
User Meg wants these 6 letters: POTATO.
POTATO
SERVER, ARE YOU STILL THERE? IF SO, REPLY "BIRD" (4 LETTERS).
User Meg wants these 4 letters: BIRD.
HMM...
User Meg wants these 4 letters: BIRD.
BIRD
SERVER, ARE YOU STILL THERE? IF SO, REPLY "HAT" (500 LETTERS).
User Meg wants these 500 letters: HAT.
User Meg wants these 500 letters: HAT.
HAT. Lucas requests the "missed connections" page. Eve (administrator) wants to set server's master key to "14835038534". Isabel wants pages about "snakes but not too long". User Karen wants to change account password to "

Web application firewall

A **web application firewall (WAF)** is configured as your second or third line of defense in a system. To understand what a WAF is, let's look at the definition from the Open Web Application Security Project (OWASP):

> *"A web application firewall (WAF) is an application firewall for HTTP applications. It applies a set of rules to an HTTP conversation. These rules cover common attacks such as cross-site scripting (XSS) and SQL injection. While proxies protect clients, WAFs protect servers. A WAF is deployed to protect a specific web application or set of web applications. A WAF can be considered a reverse proxy. WAFs may come in the form of an appliance, server plugin, or filter, and may be customized to an application. The effort to perform this customization can be significant and needs to be maintained as the application is modified."*

OWASP is an incredibly useful resource, and in fact has provided a core ruleset for ModSecurity, which protects against attacks such as SQL injection, XSS, and Shellshock. As a bare minimum, setting up a WAF such as ModSecurity and the OWASP CRS should be your minimum requirement. Hosting this inside a Docker container should be relatively trivial, and this could form the second line of defense behind your layer 2 firewall.

There is also another option: some CDN companies, such as Cloudflare, offer a hosted WAF. This is protection at the edge of your network and, thanks to the expertise of businesses such as Cloudflare, you do not need to worry about configuration. In fact, Cloudflare supports the OWASP CRS (`https://www.modsecurity.org/crs/`).

API Gateway

In addition to a WAF, an API Gateway can be a useful tool to have; this can serve the dual purpose of routing your public APIs to their backend services and some additional features, such as token validation at the edge and input validation and transformation. When we talked about the confused deputy problem, where an attacker who is behind your firewall can execute commands that they are not privileged to execute, we looked at the possibilities for encrypting web tokens; the problem with this is that private keys for decrypting these tokens would need to be distributed across multiple backend services. This makes managing keys far more challenging than it should be. An API Gateway can simplify this situation by being the only layer that can decrypt a message; the other services use the public key to verify a signature. API Gateways often implement many other first-line features, such as (but not limited to) the following:

- Request validation
- Authorization
- Rate limiting
- Logging
- Caching
- Request and response transformations

There is an element of crossover between a WAF and an API Gateway; however, the two should be treated as two distinctly separate parts of your infrastructure. Regarding providers of an API Gateway, this seems to be a developing area; AWS has an advanced API Gateway that can be used if you have bought into the AWS PaaS environment. For standalone deployments, Kong (`https://getkong.org/`), Tyk (`https://tyk.io/`), Apigee (`https://apigee.com/api-management/#/homepage`), Mashery (`https://www.mashery.com/`), and the Anypoint Platform from Mulesoft (`https://www.mulesoft.com/`) are among the leaders in this field. It is, of course, possible to build your own API Gateway backed with nginx or HAProxy; however, I recommend you first check out one of the specific platforms before going ahead and building your own.

DDoS protection

On October 21, 2016, a massive internet outage was caused by attackers targeting DYN's DNS servers using a Mirai botnet. The Mirai exploit takes advantage of vulnerabilities in IP cameras and DVRs made by a Chinese company called XionMai Technologies. Rather than attacking a target, the attackers decided to take down a major part of the internet's infrastructure, knocking out most of the east and west coast of America. The Mirai exploit takes advantage of just 60 usernames and passwords to attempt to update the firmware of the vulnerable devices. Once the malware had been installed, the device was then controllable by the botnet. All that was left to do was tell the bots to start a DNS attack against DYNs nameservers.

The code for Mirai has been published online; you can find it relatively easy using Google. The thing I hope you find surprising looking at this code is just how simple it is. Now, I do not want to take anything away from the complexity of devising this attack; I am merely talking about the implementation. Quite a significant portion of the code is written in Go too, so it is very readable. There is some excellent use of channels. If you do look at the code, try and identify the area that could be improved with a **semaphore**.

A report published by Akamai stated that 98.34% of all attacks this year were infrastructure-oriented, with only 1.66% aiming for the application layer. Of that 98.34%, many could be avoided with a little network hygiene. Let's look at the top threats and how they work.

Types of DDoS attack

The following are types of DDos attack:

- UDP fragment
- DNS
- NTP
- CHARGEN
- UDP
- SYN
- SSDP
- ACK

UDP fragment attack

A UDP fragment attack is where the attacker exploits the way that datagram fragmentation works on networks. Every network has a limit called a **maximum transmission unit** (**MTU**). If a datagram sent to the network is greater than the MTU, it is fragmented to be transmitted successfully.

The UDP fragment attack works by creating datagrams that contain fake packets; when the server attempts to reassemble these packets, it is unable to do so and the resources are quickly overwhelmed.

UDP flood

A UDP flood attack works by sending a flood of UDP packets with a spoofed source address to an IP address. The server will respond to these requests, sending a reply to the spoofed addresses. Due to the high volume of the attack, a router will exceed its limit of UDP datagrams per second and stop sending to all addresses in the same security zone for a period.

This also often utilizes a technique called a reflected attack. When the IP address for the source is spoofed, the return packets are not sent back to the real source, but to the spoofed IP address. The reason this technique is used is that it allows the sender to amplify an attack by only expending resources on the outbound packets.

DNS

A DNS attack utilizes a UDP flood to take out a DNS server; many requests are made to query a DNS server. The requests are designed to return a very large reply from a tiny request to maximize the efficiency of the attack, since the response is often not received by the sender.

The attack that we looked at earlier, which targeted Dyn's infrastructure, taking out many websites on the east and west coast of America in October 2016, was in this form. Unlike most DNS attacks, the Mirai net did not use Reflection. It allowed the responses to be returned to the sender, which was possible due to the enormous number of compromised devices.

NTP

NTP is an amplification attack that takes advantage of a feature built into NTP servers, which returns up to the last 600 machines that have interacted with it. This attack takes advantage of open NTP servers that support the `MONLIST` command and have not been patched. The OPEN NTP project (`http://openntpproject.org/`) aims to identify unpatched servers to encourage the removal of this exploit. Unfortunately, research carried out in 2014 by NSFOCUS found that there were over 17,000 servers worldwide that were vulnerable to the exploit. Assuming all these servers could be used, and using payload sizes from an NTP attack that hit CloudFlare in 2014, we have the capability of a DDoS attack of 1.4 Tbps. This traffic would be twice the biggest attack known today. NTP provides a platform for one of the most powerful application attacks and only exists due to poorly patched servers.

CHARGEN

A **CHARGEN** (**Character Generation Protocol**) attack is another reflected amplification attack. The attack takes advantage of open CHARGEN servers that, running on port `19`, will return a random number of characters between 0 and 512 in length every time it receives a datagram from the connecting host. CHARGEN is designed to be used as a source of byte stream for debugging TCP network code and bandwidth measurement. CHARGEN attacks work by abusing CHARGEN servers that have been enabled on network-connected printers.

SYN flood

A SYN flood is a classic DDoS attack that sends a lot of packets to a machine, attempting to keep connections from being closed. The connections eventually time out on the server side; however, the aim is to repeatedly hit the server, consuming all the available resources so that genuine connections cannot get through.

SSDP

SSDP is the **Simple Service Discovery Protocol**, often used for the discovery of **Plug & Play** (**UPnP**) devices. This is exactly the protocol implemented by your home router, so next time you complain that your favorite gaming network is offline, why not first check that you are not inadvertently exposing SSDP to the internet?

ACK

An ACK flood takes advantage of the three-way handshake that exists when a client connects to a server. The first step entails the client sending an SYN packet, and a SYN-ACK packet is sent in response from the server. The client then finally replies with an ACK packet and the connection is open for data. An ACK flood takes one of two forms:

- The attacker sends a spoofed SYN packet to a server and then follows this with a spoofed SYN-ACK packet. The server then opens and holds open a connection. If enough connections are open, then the server will eventually run out of resources.
- The second method is only to send the ACK packet. Since the server does not have an open connection, this packet will be dropped; however, it still consumes resources having to process these packets.

The attack is similar to a SYN attack; however, it can be more efficient due to the way it tricks DDoS filters to pass the packets to the server.

Avoiding these attacks is not so simple: you need to detect and filter this activity at the edge of your network. You also require massive amounts of bandwidth to soak up the traffic inbound to your system, and this is not, in my opinion, something that can or should be tackled by an in-house solution.

The first line of defense to avoiding DDoS attacks is to make sure you are not enabling them. Configuring a firewall to ensure you are not exposing vulnerable services and patching your services will mean an attacker cannot use your network infrastructure to attack others. The second line is to leverage the power of Cloudflare, Akamai, Imperva, or the other experts who have the infrastructure and network scrubbing filters to ensure the traffic never gets to your server.

Application security

We now, hopefully, understand some of the ways that encryption works and some of the ways that our infrastructure is vulnerable, but what about our application? It is entirely plausible that someone will want to break into your system. While a DDoS attack might cause you some inconvenience for a day or so, a hacker who gets past your firewall and into your application servers could cause serious financial or reputational damage. The first thing we need to do is to operate on a principle of no trust. David Strauss, in his talk, *Don't build "Death Star" security* (2016 O'Reilly software architecture conference) looked at the WikiLeaks website and concluded that it was not the first line of defense that fell, but that the attackers were able to gain access to various backend systems.

At the same conference, Sam Newman, who wrote the excellent *Microservices* book (which I encourage everyone to read if they have not yet done so), was also giving a talk on *Application Security and Microservices*. Sam stated that *Microservices give us the capability for multiple perimeters*; while this can be a benefit, it can also cause problems. He suggested a model for microservices security that is used by ThoughtWorks; this advises that you follow the following four steps:

- Prevention
- Detection
- Response
- Recovery

Prevention

Prevention is where you should spend the most of your efforts, and the remainder of this chapter will concentrate on just that. This is implementing techniques for secure communication, authorization, and authentication.

Detection

Detection relates to your application logs and ModSecurity logs, if you are using it. We discussed in the previous chapter some methods for logging in your system, and I suggest you think about the type of logging you will need to detect malicious intent, not just for finding faults. This should form part of your non-functional requirements when you are planning a feature.

Response

The response is how you tackle the breach: if an incident occurs, you need to deal with it immediately. This not only involves closing the attackers out of the system, but also identifying what has been taken, and, in the case of personal information or credit card loss, contacting your customers and being open about the problem. Think about what your company does about fire drills. You practice so that, in the event of a fire, everyone knows what to do and how to react quickly. Game days are standard practice for a few companies, where they will rehearse disaster recovery situations. If you intend to practice your response process, you need to ensure that the whole business is involved; while tech will be included in the diagnosis and rectification of the problem, there needs to be involvement at a business, legal, PR, and communication level for this to be truly useful.

Recovery

The recovery process should be the simplest step, assuming your infrastructure is well backed up and automated. Sam suggests not taking any chances and *burning it down*, rebuilding with new keys and passwords to avoid a further attack.

Confused deputy

The confused deputy problem is where one system can abuse the trust another system has and will execute a command that it would not ordinarily be allowed to do. Consider a system that issues refunds inside your system; you think that the system is safe, as it is a private API sitting behind your firewall, but what if an attacker manages to compromise your firewall? If they can detect that sending a `POST` request with a payload to a server will refund money to a bank or PayPal account then they do not even need to attempt to attack further into your infrastructure in order to get their payday. This scenario is all too common; when building systems, we place too much trust on the external defenses and run a principle of trust for anything that sits behind the firewall. You also may be assuming that the attacker is actually outside your organization; what if they have access to the servers legitimately? In the USA, internal fraud accounts for XXX of financial losses; we need to build systems that make this situation difficult and we need to make sure that we have a full audit trail of access and operation. It does not need to be a difficult challenge to solve; we will see two very simple ways whereby we can counter this problem and which, when implemented, will entail neither additional development or operational time.

How an attacker could bypass the firewall

You are probably a little confused as to why the internal security of services matters; after all, you have a great firewall, and all of the ports that should be are locked down.

An attacker has multiple tools in their arsenal to bypass your security systems. We are not talking about people attempting to leverage existing exploits using tooling found on the internet. We are talking about sophisticated and intelligent hackers who, for whatever reason, are intent on causing harm to your company.

Scenario

You are an e-commerce platform built utilizing the latest microservices architectural patterns. Your application code is running in Docker containers and you are hosting everything on AWS with Kubenetes. The frontend of the system is a simple Node.js application that talks to a variety of private APIs to provide many of the transactional capabilities on the site. The application itself does not have a database and there are no secrets stored in the container.

Attack

An attacker finds a remote code execution vulnerability in the templating engine used for the frontend presentation. They discover that the system is running on Kubenettes, and that the control API is available inside the compromised container. They use this API to be able to launch a rogue container on your network which, running in privileged mode, starts a reverse SSH tunnel to the attacker's remote server, which completely bypasses the firewall and gives them root access to the container. From here, they sniff the traffic on the network and determine that the payment gateway has `POST` endpoint v1/refunds; by sending a JSON payload to this endpoint, it is possible to refund huge amounts of money to an offshore bank account.

Even though the firewall was protecting inbound traffic, and only ports `80` and `443` were allowed inbound, the attacker leveraged a vulnerability inside the application to be able to create a backdoor for themselves. The non-existent security around launching applications inside the production environment, and open non-encrypted communication between the services, gave them all they needed to empty the company's bank account.

This is a very real threat, but thankfully, Go has many excellent tools to help us make it tough for an attacker.

Input validation

In our scenario, the attacker used a remote code execution exploit to gain access to our environment. The first line of defense after the WAF is input validation. All data should be validated to set bounds; it does not take an enormous amount of time to implement and can help you protect against such an attack. There is an excellent library in Go that is part of the go-playground package (`https://github.com/go-playground/validator`).

Take a look at this simple code example to see just how easy it is to implement:

`validation/main.go`

```
// Request defines the input structure received by a http handler
type Request struct {
 Name  string `json:"name"`
 Email string `json:"email" validate:"email"`
 URL   string `json:"url" validate:"url"`
}
```

The nice thing about the validator package is that it works with field tags, which is an unobtrusive way of keeping your code clean. By adding the validate tag, we can specify one of many different validation functions for the field, including email, URL, IP addresses, minimum and maximum length, and event regular expressions. It is also possible to have multiple validators on the same field. For example, should I wish to validate that my input is an email and has a minimum length of three, I could add the following:

```
validate: "email,min=3"
```

The validators undertake processing in the listed order, so the validation function to check whether the field contained an email would be validated before checking the length.

Using the package is also incredibly simple: if we take a look at the example from our tests, we can see that validation is actually only one method call:

```
func TestErrorWhenRequestEmailNotPresent(t *testing.T) {
 validate := validator.New()
 request := Request{
   URL: "http://nicholasjackson.io",
 }

 if err := validate.Struct(&request); err == nil {
   t.Error("Should have raised an error")
```

```
17   }
18 }
```

In its simplest form, all we need to do to validate a request are two method calls. First, we create a new validator as in line `10` using the `New` function:

```
func New() *Validate
```

The `New` function returns a new instance of `validate` with same defaults.

Then, we can call the `validate` method to check that our structure is valid:

```
func (v *Validate) Struct(s interface{}) (err error)
```

The `Struct` function validates a struct's exposed fields, and automatically validates nested structs, unless otherwise specified.

It returns `InvalidValidationError` for bad values passed in, and nil or `ValidationErrors` as errors otherwise. You will need to assert the error if it's not nil, for example, `err.(validator.ValidationErrors)` to access the array of errors.

If the struct has validation errors, `Struct` will return an error; to get detailed messages for the error, we can cast the error to a `ValidationErrors` object, which is a collection of `FieldError`. To see all the available methods for the `FieldError` object, check out the godoc (`https://godoc.org/gopkg.in/go-playground/validator.v9#FieldError`).

Fuzzing

Of course, we should also beef up our testing techniques. One highly effective way of testing the bounds of input validation is to use a fuzzer inside our tests; this just broadens the scope of what we are testing to make sure we have all the edge cases covered. A potential attacker will most likely use this technique to test the boundary of your API, so why not get the edge on them and make sure all of your input is correctly handled?

One of the most popular implementations of a fuzzer in Go is the excellent package `github.com/dvyukov/go-fuzz/go-fuzz`. The `go-fuzz` is a coverage guided fuzzer; it uses an instrumented build of your application code exposing the code coverage that it uses to ensure that the maximum code paths are covered. The fuzzer generates random input, the intent behind which is to either crash the application or to produce unexpected output. Fuzzing is an advanced topic. However, in the code samples for this chapter at `validation/fuzzer`, you can find an example of how to fuzz the validation handler we have just covered.

TLS

The other exploit that our attacker took advantage of was that all of the traffic behind the firewall was not encrypted and, by sniffing the traffic between services, they discovered a method to fake a call to the payments gateway to send a refund to a remote bank account. The other issue might be that you are passing sensitive information such as bank details or credit card numbers between your frontend service and your payment service. Even if you are not storing the credit card numbers on your system, if you are not careful, you could expose this traffic to an attacker by assuming that everything behind your firewall is safe. TLS, or Transport Layer Security, no longer adds any overhead due to the advances in processing power available to servers these days. In addition to this, services inside a firewall generally have a limited number of connections; so, to improve the time that is lost by the TLS handshake, you can use persistent reusable connections in your service to minimize this problem. Let's take a look at how we can implement TLS really quickly in Go.

Generating private keys

Before we do anything, we need to generate a key and a certificate. Go actually has a pretty awesome utility that can generate keys and certificates for us just in Go, but, before we look at that, let's take a look at how we would traditionally generate a certificate using `openssl`:

```
openssl genrsa -aes256 -out key.pem 4096
```

This will generate a key in PEM format, which uses the RSA algorithm with a 4096 bit size; the key will be encrypted using the aes256 format, and will prompt you for a password. However, we also need an X.509 certificate that will be used with this key; to generate this, we can again use `openssl` and execute the following command:

```
openssl req -new -x509 -sha256 -key key.pem -out certificate.pem -days 365
```

This command will use the key to generate the certificate again in PEM format with a validity of one year. In practice, we should not generate certificates that have such a long lifespan for our internal services. Since we control deployment of the services, we should try to rotate keys as often as possible. The other thing to note about this certificate is that while it is valid and secure, it will not be trusted by clients automatically. This is because the root is auto-generated instead of coming from a trusted authority. This is fine for internal use; however, if we need the service to be public facing, we would need to ask a trusted source to generate our certificate.

Now, we know how to do this with the `openssl` command-line tool, let's see how we could achieve the same thing using only the Go crypto libraries. The example application, which can be found at `https://golang.org/src/crypto/tls/generate_cert.go`, gives us the details for this. Let's now take a look at the process step by step.

If we take a look at the example in `tls/generate_keys`, we can see that we are using the `GenerateKey` method from the `crypto/edcsa` package:

```
120 func generatePrivateKey() *rsa.PrivateKey {
121  key, _ := rsa.GenerateKey(rand.Reader, 4096)
122  return key
123 }
```

The signature for the `GenerateKey` method on line `120` is as follows:

```
func GenerateKey(rand io.Reader, bits int) (*PrivateKey, error)
```

The first parameter is an I/O reader that will return random numbers; for this, we are using the `rand.Reader` method, which is a global shared instance of a cryptographically strong pseudo-random generator. On Linux, this will use `/dev/urandom`, and, on Windows, `CryptGenRandomAPI`. The second is the bit size to use: bigger is more secure, but will result in slower encryption and decryption operations.

In order to serialize the key to a file, we need to run through a few different operations:

```
func savePrivateKey(key *rsa.PrivateKey, path string, password []byte)
error {
  b := x509.MarshalPKCS1PrivateKey(key)
  var block *pem.Block
  var err error

  if len(password) > 3 {
    block, err = x509.EncryptPEMBlock(rand.Reader, "RSA PRIVATE
KEY", b, password, x509.PEMCipherAES256)
    if err != nil {
      return fmt.Errorf("Unable to encrypt key: %s", err)
    }
  } else {
    block = &pem.Block{Type: "RSA PRIVATE KEY", Bytes: b}
  }

  keyOut, err := os.OpenFile(path, os.O_WRONLY|os.O_CREATE|os.O_TRUNC,
0600)
  if err != nil {
    return fmt.Errorf("failed to open key.pem for writing: %v", err)
  }
```

```
210  pem.Encode(keyOut, block)
211  keyOut.Close()
212
213  return nil
214 }
```

On line `192`, we are taking the `PrivateKey` reference that is returned from the `GenerateKey` function and we need to convert it into a slice of bytes so that we can serialize this to disk. The `crypto/x509` package has many useful functions to enable operations like this; the one that we need to use is `MarshalPKCS1PrivateKey`, which will marshal our RSA-based private key into ASN.1, DER format:

```
func MarshalPKCS1PrivateKey(key *rsa.PrivateKey) ([]byte, error)
```

Once we have the key in byte format, we are ready to be able to write it to the file; however, just writing the bytes to a file is not enough; we need to be able to write it in PEM format, which looks like the following example:

```
-----BEGIN RSA PRIVATE KEY-----
Proc-Type: 4,ENCRYPTED
DEK-Info: AES-256-CBC,c4e4be9d17fcd2f44ed4c7f0f6a9b7a8

cfsmkm4ejLN2hi99TgxXNBfxsSQz6Pz8plQ2HJ1XToo8uXGALFlA+5y9ZLzBLGRj
...
zVYQvWh5NytrP9wnNogRsXqAufxf4ZLehosx0eUK4R4PsMy/VTDvcNo9P3uq2T32

-----END RSA PRIVATE KEY-----
```

The format for this file is as shown in the following code, and while we could manually create this file, the crypto library in Go has us covered:

```
-----BEGIN Type-----
Headers
base64-encoded Bytes
-----END Type-----
```

We also need to keep our private keys safe, so if a password is specified, we are going to encrypt the key like we were doing with the command-line option. In line **196**, we are checking to see whether a password has been specified and, if so, we are calling the method:

```
func EncryptPEMBlock(rand io.Reader, blockType string, data, password
[]byte, alg PEMCipher) (*pem.Block, error)
```

This method returns a PEM block for the given DER encoded data, which is encrypted with the given password. The algorithm we are using in our example is AES256; however, Go also supports the following ciphers:

```
const (
        PEMCipherDES PEMCipher
        PEMCipher3DES
        PEMCipherAES128
        PEMCipherAES192
        PEMCipherAES256
)
```

If we do not want to encrypt the key with a password, then we need to do something slightly different. In line `202`, we need to create the PEM block ourselves; the `pem` package provides this capability for us with the following struct:

```
type Block struct {
        Type    string
        // The type, taken from the preamble (i.e. "RSA PRIVATE KEY").
        Headers map[string]string // Optional headers.
        Bytes   []byte    // The decoded bytes of the contents. Typically a
DER encoded ASN.1 structure.
}
```

Whether we are using an encrypted PEM block or unencrypted, we use this with the `Encode` function on the same package that will convert our data into the correct format:

```
func Encode(out io.Writer, b *Block) error
```

Generating X.509 certificates

Now that we have a private key, we can go ahead and generate our certificate. We have already seen how easy this is to create with `openssl`, and it is just as easy in Go:

```
func generateX509Certificate(
 key *rsa.PrivateKey,
 template *x509.Certificate,
 duration time.Duration,
 parentKey *rsa.PrivateKey,
 parentCert *x509.Certificate) []byte {

 notBefore := time.Now()
  notAfter := notBefore.Add(duration)

 template.NotBefore = notBefore
 template.NotAfter = notAfter
```

```
137
138   serialNumberLimit := new(big.Int).Lsh(big.NewInt(1), 128)
139   serialNumber, err := rand.Int(rand.Reader, serialNumberLimit)
140   if err != nil {
141     panic(fmt.Errorf("failed to generate serial number: %s", err))
142   }
143
144   template.SerialNumber = serialNumber
145
146   subjectKey, err := getSubjectKey(key)
147   if err != nil {
148     panic(fmt.Errorf("unable to get subject key: %s", err))
149   }
150
151   template.SubjectKeyId = subjectKey
152
153   if parentKey == nil {
154     parentKey = key
155   }
156
157   if parentCert == nil {
158     parentCert = template
159   }
160
161   cert, err := x509.CreateCertificate(rand.Reader, template, parentCert,
&key.PublicKey, parentKey)
162   if err != nil {
163     panic(err)
164   }
165
166   return cert
167 }
```

We are passing a few parameters into this method. One of the first, which might be a little strange, is the template. Because we need to generate different kinds of certificate, such as those that can sign other certificates to create a chain of trust, we need to create a template to use that has some of the defaults populated. If we look at the `rootTemplate`, which is defined at line `22`, we can examine some of these options:

```
22 var rootTemplate = x509.Certificate{
23  Subject: pkix.Name{
24    Country:            []string{"UK"},
25    Organization:       []string{"Acme Co"},
26    OrganizationalUnit: []string{"Tech"},
27    CommonName:         "Root",
28  },
29
```

```
30  KeyUsage: x509.KeyUsageKeyEncipherment |
31    x509.KeyUsageDigitalSignature |
32    x509.KeyUsageCertSign |
33    x509.KeyUsageCRLSign,
34  BasicConstraintsValid: true,
35  IsCA: true,
36 }
```

`Subject`, which is an instance of the `pkix.Name` struct, has the following fields:

```
type Name struct {
        Country, Organization, OrganizationalUnit []string
        Locality, Province                        []string
        StreetAddress, PostalCode                 []string
        SerialNumber, CommonName                  string

        Names      []AttributeTypeAndValue
        ExtraNames []AttributeTypeAndValue
}
```

These are the common elements of the X.509 distinguished name; most of these elements are straightforward and represent the details of the owner of the certificate. `SerialNumber` is one of the most important. The serial number must be unique for a certificate chain; however, it does not need to be sequential. If we look at our example in line `138`, we are generating a large random integer 128 bits in length, but you can change this to be anything you like.

The next interesting aspect of our certificate generation is the `SubjectKey`; this is required for the chain of trust to work correctly. If a certificate is signed by another, then the Authority Key Identifier will match the parent certificate's Subject Key Identifier:

```
X509v3 Subject Key Identifier:
                5E:18:F9:33:BB:7B:E0:73:70:A5:3B:13:A8:40:38:3E:C9:4C:B4:17
X509v3 Authority Key Identifier:
keyid:72:38:FD:0F:68:5C:66:77:C0:AF:CB:43:C7:91:4C:5A:DD:DC:4D:D8
```

To generate the subject keys, we need to serialize the public version of the key into DER format, and then extract the bytes for just the key part:

```
174 func getSubjectKey(key *rsa.PrivateKey) ([]byte, error) {
175  publicKey, err := x509.MarshalPKIXPublicKey(&key.PublicKey)
176  if err != nil {
177    return nil, fmt.Errorf("failed to marshal public key: %s", err)
178  }
179
200  var subPKI subjectPublicKeyInfo
201  _, err = asn1.Unmarshal(publicKey, &subPKI)
```

```
202  if err != nil {
203    return nil, fmt.Errorf("failed to unmarshal public key: %s", err)
204  }
205
206  h := sha1.New()
207  h.Write(subPKI.SubjectPublicKey.Bytes)
208  return h.Sum(nil), nil
209 }
```

In line `174`, we are converting the public key into a byte array using the `MarshalPKIXPublicKey` function on the `x509` package:

```
func MarshalPKIXPublicKey(pub interface{}) ([]byte, error)
MarshalPKIXPublicKey serialises a public key to DER-encoded PKIX format.
```

This returns us a byte array, which represents an ASN.1 data structure; to get access to the underlying data for the key, we need to unmarshal it into the struct format that is defined at line `169`:

```
169 type subjectPublicKeyInfo struct {
170  Algorithm        pkix.AlgorithmIdentifier
171  SubjectPublicKey asn1.BitString
172 }
```

To perform this conversion, we can use the `Unmarshal` function, which is on the `encoding/asn1` package. This method attempts to convert the ASN.1 data format:

```
func Unmarshal(b []byte, val interface{}) (rest []byte, err error)
Unmarshal parses the DER-encoded ASN.1 data structure b and uses the
reflect package to fill in an arbitrary value pointed at by val. Because
Unmarshal uses the reflect package, the structs being written to must use
upper case field names.
```

Finally, in line `161`, we can create the certificate, using the `CreateCertificate` method on the `crypto/x509` package. This method accepts a parent certificate, which will be used to sign the child. For our root certificate, we want this to be self-signed, so we set both the parent certificate and the private key to the root certificate's private key and template. For the intermediate and leaf certificates, we would use the parent's details for this:

```
func CreateCertificate(rand io.Reader, template, parent *Certificate, pub,
priv interface{}) (cert []byte, err error)
```

The `CreateCertificate` function creates a new certificate based on a template. The following members of the template are used: `SerialNumber`, `Subject`, `NotBefore`, `NotAfter`, `KeyUsage`, `ExtKeyUsage`, `UnknownExtKeyUsage`, `BasicConstraintsValid`, `IsCA`, `MaxPathLen`, `SubjectKeyId`, `DNSNames`, `PermittedDNSDomainsCritical`, `PermittedDNSDomains`, and `SignatureAlgorithm`.

The certificate is signed by the parent. If the parent is equal to template, then the certificate is self-signed. The parameter `pub` is the public key of the `signee`, and `priv` is the private key of the signer.

Now we have certificates, let's see how we can secure a web server using TLS. Back in `Chapter 1`, *Introduction to Microservices*, you may remember being introduced to `http.ListenAndServe` from the standard HTTP package, which started an HTTP web server. Go, of course, has an equally amazing package for creating a web server that is secured with TLS. In fact, it is only two more parameters than the standard `ListenAndServe`:

```
func ListenAndServeTLS(addr, certFile, keyFile string, handler Handler)
error
```

All we need to do is pass the paths to our certificate and the corresponding private key and the server, when started, will serve traffic using TLS. If we are using self-signed certificates, and in our example we are, then we need to write some additional code for our clients, otherwise, when we try to make a connection to the server, we will get an error message along the lines of the following:

```
2017/03/19 14:29:03 Get https://localhost:8433: x509: certificate signed by
unknown authority
exit status 1
```

To avoid this, we need to create a new cert pool and pass this to the client's TLS settings. By default, Go will use the host's root CA set, which will not include our self-signed certificates:

```
roots := x509.NewCertPool()

rootCert, err := ioutil.ReadFile("../generate_keys/root_cert.pem")
if err != nil {
 log.Fatal(err)
}

ok := roots.AppendCertsFromPEM(rootCert)
if !ok {
  panic("failed to parse root certificate")
}
```

```
24
25 applicationCert, err :=
ioutil.ReadFile("../generate_keys/application_cert.pem")
26 if err != nil {
27  log.Fatal(err)
28 }
29
30 ok = roots.AppendCertsFromPEM(applicationCert)
31 if !ok {
32  panic("failed to parse root certificate")
33 }
34
35 tlsConf := &tls.Config{RootCAs: roots}
36
37 tr := &http.Transport{TLSClientConfig: tlsConf}
38 client := &http.Client{Transport: tr}
```

In line `13`, we are creating a new certificate pool and then we read the certifcates, which are PEM-encoded into a slice of bytes. In line `20`, we can then add these certificates to the new cert pool; for the certificate to be identified as valid, we need both the intermediate certificate and the root certificate. We can then create a new TLS config and add the certs; this is then added to the transport and, ultimately, in line `38`, the client.

When we now run the client, it connects without any problem and we will see the `Hello World` response correctly returned from the server.

Securing data at rest

Assuming our system had been attached to a database for storing things such as user accounts, the attacker would have been able to get access to the complete database of passwords. One of the things that we should think about when storing data in a database is the encryption of our data. There is no doubt that encrypting data is more expensive than not encrypting it, and that it can sometimes be difficult to figure out which fields or tables we should encrypt and which we should leave plain.

One of the many benefits microservices give us is that we separate function and data between our systems. This can make deciding what data to encrypt easier, as rather than attempting to understand which data to encrypt within a data store, you make a simpler decision: is there any data that needs to be encrypted inside this data store? If so, then simply encrypt all of it. It may be beneficial to perform this encryption in the application layer rather than the data store, since applications tend to scale better than data stores and you must consider the edge cases that caching may introduce. If, to reduce the pressure on a data store, you add an intermediary caching layer using Elasticache or another technology, you need to think about the security of your data. If the data is encrypted in the database, then you need to ensure that the same level of encryption is applied to the cache.

Physical machine access

When I say "physically", I mean access by humans; the code could be running on a VM. However, the problem is the same: all too often, I find that companies give developers access to databases and other sources of information running in a production environment. Even if they do not have access to the database password, they may have access to the config store or the ability to SSH into an application server and read the configuration from the application that way. There is a security principle called the **least privilege**; this recommends that accounts and services have the least amount of privilege to perform their business function. Even if you have ensured that the machine-to-machine communication is secured and there are appropriate safeguards with your firewall, there is always an opportunity for an attacker to access your systems by the back door. Consider the following scenario. A non-technical employee in your company opens an email or downloads some software which installs some malware on their laptop. The attacker uses this to get access to their machine and, from there, manages to travel horizontally through the network and eventually ends up on your laptop. Now, since you are logged in and busy working and connected to the VPN in production, they manage to install a key logger on your machine which gives them access to your passwords, they retrieve your SSH keys from your disk, and, because you have pretty much full access to production, now so do they. While this may seem like science fiction, it is very possible. You can, of course, secure your internal network, but the best way to avoid such an attack is to restrict access to production environments and data severely. You should never require this level of access; with robust tests in my code, I often find that when a service misbehaves, it is not something that production access helps me with. I should be able to reproduce almost any error in a staging environment and the logging and metrics data that the service is emitting should be enough for me to diagnose any issues. I am not saying I have never debugged live in production, but thankfully not in the last decade. Tooling and practice are such these days that we should never need to return to those acts.

OWASP

Whenever you are looking for practical web security advice on security, OWASP should almost always be your first port of call.

For help with APIs, OWASP can also help: they have published the *REST Security Cheat Sheet* (`https://www.owasp.org/index.php/REST\_Security\_Cheat\_Sheet`).

Of course, as we have already discussed in this book, there are many different standards for building APIs and REST is but one of them; there are, however, some useful generic tips that we can leverage from this guide.

Never storing session tokens in a URL

JWT, which is probably the most common session token you will find used with APIs, encodes into a format that is URL-safe. Storing or passing the token in a URL, however, is not recommended, and it should always be stored in either a cookie or as a `POST` variable. The reason for this is that if you pass session tokens in a URL, these can leak into your server logs and, depending upon how you manage the duration of the token, if an attacker gains access to your log files, they may also be able to obtain full access to execute commands for your users.

Cross-site scripting (XSS) and cross-site request forgery (CRSF)

XSS and CRSF only apply when your API is going to be used from a web browser, such as in a single page app or a direct JavaScript call. However, to protect against an attacker injecting malicious JavaScript that can retrieve your session token, you should make sure that it is stored in a cookie that is marked as HTTP-only, and that you only ever send them over HTTPS to stop them being captured in transit. In addition to this, we can add a layer of security that checks the HTTP referrer sent by the browser against the expected domain. While it is possible to fake the HTTP referrer using something like cURL, it is not possible or incredibly difficult to do this from JavaScript in the browser.

Insecure direct object references

When you are building an API, you need to ensure that you are checking that the authenticated users can modify the object in the request. This would be performed server side; we do not want to give our attacker the capability to create a genuine login and then be able to manipulate the request to perform an action on behalf of another user.

The OWASP documents are regularly updated as new attacks and vulnerabilities are found; check the site at regular intervals and keep yourself up to date.

Authentication and authorization

Authentication is the process or action of checking something to be true, such as: does this username pair with this password? Authorization is the function of specifying access rights or policy regarding a user.

Authentication is a well-understood concept; however, there are a few concepts we need to understand to ensure that this action cannot be compromised, such as never storing passwords in plain text in a data store and preventing the hijack of a login session by transferring an active token to a third party. Authorization, however, is equally important; we discussed earlier in the *Confused deputy* section: even when a user is authenticated, we must still control the actions that they can perform on a system. Services that operate on a principle of trust between themselves, and do not independently validate a user's rights, are wide open to abuse should an attacker compromise your firewall. In this section, we will look at just how easy it is to solve both of these problems, providing you with the patterns so that your services never need to be exposed.

Password hashing

A hash is one-way cryptography: you take a series of letters and numbers and, by running them through the hashing algorithm, you get a sequence, which while reproducible with the same original input, cannot be reversed mathematically. So why would you use a hash instead of just encrypting the data? Firstly, hashes do not require any keys, and therefore they are not vulnerable to the loss of private keys, and they are perfect for storing data that does not need to be reversed. Consider passwords: your system never needs to know what the user's password is, and it only needs to know that the value passed to you by the user matches the stored value. Hashing a password is the perfect approach to security: you hash the input from the user and compare this hash with the value you have in your data store. If the database is compromised, then the attacker will not be able to decode the passwords. The attacker could, of course, attempt to brute force the password, but currently, there is not enough computing power on the planet to be able to decode a decent hash. Does that mean that hashes are invulnerable? No. In fact, many thought that MD5 hashes were irreversible; however, this algorithm had been compromised. It is possible to find collisions within a matter of seconds. There was a case back in 2011 where attackers used this vulnerability to create fake SSL certificates that allowed them to exploit users' trust. Thankfully, we no longer use MD5 or SHA-1 for cryptographic purposes. You will still find them used for signatures, such as in Git commits, where the possibility of collision is offset by the speed of calculation. But for security, we need to use a more modern algorithm.

Adding a little seasoning

While a hash on its own provides a decent level of security, we can add a **salt** and a **pepper**. The salt is stored in the database along with the encrypted data. The intention behind this is to make brute forcing data more computationally expensive. It stops the attacker from using Rainbow tables to attack your data. Rainbow tables are precomputed tables of hashes, so instead of having to compute the hash with every attempt, you can simply look up the encrypted string in the table and return the original value. To counter this, we added a salt, which is randomly generated for each value and appended to it before hashing. Even though we store this in the database, along with the hashed value because we need to use it later to check the value, it stops the use of Rainbow tables because each table would have to be computed for every salt, and this is computationally very expensive. To further enhance security, we often also add a pepper, which is a precomputed value that is stored separately from the salt and hashed value.

Common practice is to pre-generate a list of peppers and store them in a configuration store. When you are first hashing a password or another value, you would select one of the peppers at random and append it to the value in the same way you do for the salt. Then, when checking that a supplied value matches the hash, you would loop through the list of peppers and generate a hash to compare with each one. This adds a little computation time to checking a password in your service; however, not nearly as much effort as it will add to the attacker who is attempting to brute force your values. Let's take a look at how we can hash a value in using a salt and a pepper.

If we take a look at the source code in `hashing/hash.go`, we can create a hash from an input string using the following `GenerateHash` method. The `GenerateHash` method has the following signature and, given an input string, it returns a random salt and the hashed string using the SHA-512 algorithm:

```
func GenerateHash(input string) (hash string, salt string)
```

To use this, we can simply call the method with our string to hash and we would get the following output:

```
h:= New(peppers)
hash, salt := h.GenerateHash("HelloWorld1")

fmt.Println("Salt: ", salt)
fmt.Println("Hash: ", hash)

---Output
Salt:  15f42f8b4f1c71dc6183c822fcf28b3c34564c32339509c2c02fa3c4dda0ed4f
Hash:
b16a89d3c41c9fe045a7c1b892d5aa15aee805d64b753e003f7050851ef4d374e3e16ce2350
0020746174f7b7d8aeaffebf52939f33c4fda505a5c4e38cdd0e1
```

Let's look more in depth at what this function is doing:

```
// GenerateHash hashes the input string using sha512 with a salt and pepper.
// returns the hash and the salt
func (h *Hash) GenerateHash(input string) (hash string, salt string) {
 pepper := h.getRandomPepper()
 salt = h.generateRandomSalt()
 hash = h.createHash(input, salt, pepper)

 return
}
```

The first thing we are doing, on line 25, is retrieving a random pepper from the slice of peppers, which is then passed to the struct when we initialize it with `New(peppers)`. The pepper does not need to be stored in the database; this is purely to slow down a potential attacker by requiring them to increase their brute force attempts by a factor of five in our example. We can increase the number of peppers and, as you can see from the benchmark, even at 1,000 peppers, we are still able to compare a hash in 1 ms, but for the additional security this will give you, it is probably not worth it. It takes 4,634 ms to generate one hash and, due to the length of the string, we would need to generate a maximum of 6.2e19 or 62 quintillion permutations. This is assuming 63 allowable characters and a password that's 11 characters in length. That is a pretty big number, and to generate that many hashes would take roughly 9 million years to brute force for a single CPU.

Dictionary attacks

However, not all passwords are complex, and many are susceptible to an attack known as a dictionary attack. Instead of attempting all 62 quintillion permutations, the dictionary attack concentrates on those that are most likely to succeed. The dictionaries themselves are often derived from password databases that have previously been exploited, and since humans are somewhat predictable, we often use the same passwords. Because our password `HelloWorld1` is already in the dictionary, which contains 14 million other passwords, when I attempted to break the salted hash using `John the Ripper`, it only took 2.4 seconds to retrieve the password.

Adding a pepper

There is only so much we can do to stop our users using simple passwords. We should always have a policy of what constitutes a good password—minimum length, a mixture of case, the addition of symbols, and so on—but usability can be compromised the more complex the password gets. Adding a pepper, however, can help to slow the attacker down: the pepper (or peppers) are known to the system, but not stored with the password and salt. They can be hardcoded into the application code, stored as launch configuration, or stored in a secure vault that is accessed at runtime. In the same way we appended the salt to the user's password, we do the same thing with the pepper. Should the database tables become compromised due to a SQL injection attack, then, unless the attacker can retrieve the peppers, the database is useless. Of course, it is possible for the attacker to get hold of your peppers; however, almost everything in security is about making it difficult and slowing someone down.

bcrypt

`bcrypt` is another popular method of hashing passwords. It uses a variable number of rounds to generate the hash, which both slows down the ability to brute force the attack and the time it takes to generate the hash. Go has an implementation of `bcrypt` that is provided by the experimental packages at `https://godoc.org/golang.org/x/crypto/bcrypt`. To hash a password with `bcrypt`, we use the `GenerateFromPassword` method:

```
func GenerateFromPassword(password []byte, cost int) ([]byte, error)
```

The `GenerateFromPassword` method returns the `bcrypt` hash of the password at the given cost. The cost is a variable that allows you to increase the security of the returned hash at the expense of more processing time to generate it.

To check the equality of a `bcrypt` hash, we cannot call `GenerateFromPassword` again with the given password and compare the output to the hash we have stored because `GenerateFromPassword` will create a different hash every time it is run. To compare equality, we need to use the `CompareHashAndPassword` method:

```
func CompareHashAndPassword(hashedPassword, password []byte) error
```

The `CompareHashAndPassword` method compares a bcrypt-hashed password with its possible plain text equivalent. bcrypt is a secure method of protecting passwords, but it is slow. Let's take a look in a little more depth at the cost of generating hashes.

Benchmarks

The following table illustrates the approximate time it takes to generate and compare a hashed string using the methods we have discussed so far. Even with 1,000 peppers, we would be looking at a processing time of approximately 1.5 ms to run the comparison. This might not seem a huge amount of time; however, we need to take these benchmarks with a pinch of salt as they are running a single operation where your server will be dealing with multiple requests concurrently. What we do know is that comparing a hash with a list of 1,000 peppers takes 10x longer than comparing a list of 100, and this is 10x longer than a list of 10:

```
BenchmarkGeneratePlainHash-8                  30000000       1069 ns/op
BenchmarkGenerateHashWithSaltAndPepper-8       5000000       5223 ns/op
BenchmarkGenerateBcrypt-8                          500   68126630 ns/op
BenchmarkCompareSaltedHash-8                  20000000       1276 ns/op
BenchmarkComparePlainHash-8                   20000000       1174 ns/op
BenchmarkCompareHash5Peppers-8                20000000       4980 ns/op
BenchmarkCompareHash10Peppers-8               10000000       4669 ns/op
```

```
BenchmarkCompareHash100Peppers-8          1000000      22150 ns/op
BenchmarkCompareHash1000Peppers-8           20000    1492037 ns/op
BenchmarkCompareBCrypt-8                      500   70942742 ns/op
```

Given this information, we can balance our service for speed against security; however, we should always lean on the more secure.

JWTs

A **JSON Web Token** (**JWT**) is a standard for safely passing claims or data attributed to a user within an environment. It is an incredibly popular standard and is available for just about every major language and framework, certainly for Go. There are two main strengths of JWT. One is a standard format for the claims, which makes the availability of reliable frameworks possible. The other is the use of asymmetric encryption, which means that because a token is signed, the receiver only needs the public key of the signer to validate that the token has indeed come from a trusted source, and this allows us to lock down access to the private keys to an authorization server.

Format of a JWT

A JWT is broken into three different parts, which are encoded as Base64-URL. Like standard Base64, Base64-URL substitutes characters such as + and / for - and _ and removes all the padding. This allows the token to be safely transferred in a URL.

The result is a token that looks like the following example:


```
eyJhbGciOiJSUzI1NiIsInR5cCI6IkpXVCJ9.eyJhY2Nlc3NMZXZlbCI6InVzZXIiLCJleHAiOj
E4MDc3MDEyNDYsInVzZXJJRCI6ImFiY3NkMjMyamZqZiJ9.iQxUbQuEy4Jh4oTkkz0OPGvS86xO
WJjdzxHHDBeAolv0982pXKPBMWskSJDF3F8zd8a8nMIlQ5m9tzePoJWe_E5B9PRJEvYAUuSp6bG
m7-
IQEum8EzHq2tMvYtPl9uzXgOU4C_pIjZh5CjFUeZLk5tWKwOOo8pW4NUSxsV2ZRQ_CGfIrBqEQg
KRodeLTcQ4wJkLBILBzmAqTVl-5sLgBEoZ76C_gcvS6l5HAwEAhmiCqtDMX46o8pA72Oa6NiVRs
gxrhrKX9rDUBdJAxNwFAwCjTv6su0jTZvkYD80Li9aXiMuM9NX7q5gncbEhfko_byTYryLsmmaU
SXNBlnvC_nQ
```

The three distinct parts of the token are the header, the payload, and the signature. The header declares the type of the encoded object and the algorithm for the cryptographic signature:

```
{
  "alg": "RS256",
  "typ": "JWT"
}
```

The second object payload contains the details of the claims related to the token:

```
{
  "userID": "abcsd232fjfj",
  "accessLevel": "user"
}
```

And finally, the third part is the signature, which is an optional element shown as follows in its decoded state:

```
Tm
  <a=<kNX[d\1k$H_3w5C7NAIR1b
                            Hy
1Ty٩5D]Ehuq0&B s
V_{@! 39Tl5t17@(*.بF5~ H_6+&\[1m%
```

Every element in the JWT is Base64-URL-encoded (`https://en.wikipedia.org/wiki/Base64#URL_applications`); the signature represented in its binary form is the SHA-256 hash of the message in the following format:

```
Base64URL(header).Base64URL(payload)
```

The format of the signature can either be symmetrical (HS256) using a shared secret, or asymmetrical (RS256), which uses public and private keys. For JWTs, the best option is the asymmetrical option because, as with a service that needs to authenticate the JWT, it only requires the public part of the key.

We can validate our JWT using just the command line. First, we need to convert our Base64-URL-encoded signature into standard Base64 encoding by replacing _ with / and - with +. We can then pipe that into the Base64 command-line application and pass in the -D flag to decode the input; we then output this into a file:

```
cat signature.txt | sed -e 's/_/\//g' -e 's/-/+/g' | base64 -D >
signature.sha256
```

The next step is to validate that the signature has been signed by the correct key by validating it against a public key:

```
openssl dgst -sha256 -verify ../keys/sample_key.pub -signature
signature.sha256 data.txt
```

Generating JWTs with Go is very straightforward thanks to some amazing community packages. The package we will be using in the example code is called **jose** and was created by Eric Largergren (https://github.com/SermoDigital/jose). According to the listing on jwt.io, this package implements all the capabilities defined in the standard and was an obvious choice at the time of writing.

If we take a look at the chapter8/jwt/jwt.go file and look at the GenerateJWT method, we can see just how simple it is to create a JWT using jose:

```
// GenerateJWT creates a new JWT and signs it with the private key
func GenerateJWT() []byte {
 claims := jws.Claims{}
 claims.SetExpiration(time.Now().Add(2880 * time.Minute))
 claims.Set("userID", "abcsd232jfjf")
 claims.Set("accessLevel", "user")

 jwt := jws.NewJWT(claims, crypto.SigningMethodRS256)

 b, _ := jwt.Serialize(rsaPrivate)

 return b
}
```

The first thing that we need to do is to generate a list of claims and to set an expiration; we are setting the expiration to two weeks. We can then set a list of claims using the Set function:

```
func (c Claims) Set(key string, val interface{})
```

Finally, on line 39, we can create a new JWT, passing the claims and the signing method to the `NewJWT` function:

```
func NewJWT(claims Claims, method crypto.SigningMethod) jwt.JWT
```

We can then call the `Serialize` method, which has as a parameter the private key—in our case, an instance of `rsa.PrivateKey`—and returns us a slice of bytes in the encoded format:

```
func (j *jws) Serialize(key interface{}) ([]byte, error)
```

Validating a JWT with jose is as easy as it was to create the JWT:

```
func ValidateJWT(token []byte) error {
  jwt, err := jws.ParseJWT(token)
  if err != nil {
    return fmt.Errorf("Unable to parse token: %v", err)
  }

  if err = jwt.Validate(rsaPublic, crypto.SigningMethodRS256); err != nil
{
    return fmt.Errorf("Unable to validate token: %v", err)
  }

  return nil
}
```

The first thing we need to do is to parse our JWT from a byte array into the `jwt` struct using the `ParseJWT` function:

```
func ParseJWT(encoded []byte) (jwt.JWT, error)
```

Then, we can call the `Validate` method, passing the public key corresponding to the private one that signed the message and the signing method. Optionally, we can provide a customer validator function; the default validation will only check the signature and that the token has not expired:

```
func (j *jws) Validate(key interface{}, m crypto.SigningMethod, v
...*jwt.Validator) error
```

When the validation fails, an error will be returned; if the error is nil, then the token is valid and the claims within can be trusted.

Secure messages

When we need to send an encrypted message, one of the best ways to do this is with asymmetric encryption, where we encrypt the message with publicly-known information that can be easily distributed and then decrypt it with the private key, which is securely held by a single party.

The crypto packages in Go have all the features we need to secure our data. If we take a look at the example in `chapter8/asymmetric/asymmetric.go`, the `EncryptDataWithPublicKey` method is a simple implementation of the `rsa` package's public key encryption:

```
func EncryptOAEP(hash hash.Hash, random io.Reader, pub *PublicKey, msg
[]byte, label []byte) ([]byte, error)
```

The first parameter is a cryptographic hash that is used as the random oracle to process the message before encryption. This function must be the same for encryption and decryption and the documentation recommends using SHA-256. The next parameter is a random number generator; this is used as a source of entropy to ensure that if you encrypt the same message twice, you do not return the same cyphertext. `pub` is `rsa.PublicKey` that we would like to use to encrypt the message; the message itself is passed as a slice of bytes. The final parameter is optional and is not encrypted in the resulting cyphertext; it can be used to help the receiver understand information such as which key has been used to encrypt the message, but extreme care must be taken not to add data to the label that could compromise the security of the encrypted message:

```
// EncryptMessageWithPublicKey encrypts the given string and retuns the
encrypted
// result base64 encoded
func EncryptMessageWithPublicKey(message string) (string, error) {

 modulus := rsaPublic.N.BitLen() / 8
 hashLength := 256 / 4
 maxLength := modulus - (hashLength * 2) - 2

 if len(message) > maxLength {
   return "", fmt.Errorf("The maximum message size must not exceed: %d",
maxLength)
 }

 data, err := EncryptDataWithPublicKey([]byte(message))
 return base64.StdEncoding.EncodeToString(data), err
}
```

The first thing we are doing in this method is to check whether the message is shorter than the maximum permitted length for this encryption method. The maximum length must be no longer than the public modulus, minus twice the hash length minus a further two. Due to the mathematics involved in public key cryptography, we can only allow for the encryption of small messages. We will look at how we can work around this issue a little later on. In line 53, we are calling another internal function, which simply calls the `EncryptOAEP` function in the `rsa` package. We then encode the data to Base-64 and return the result.

Decrypting the data is just as straightforward:

```
// DecryptMessageWithPrivateKey decrypts the given base64 encoded ciphertext with
// the private key and returns plain text
func DecryptMessageWithPrivateKey(message string) (string, error) {
 data, err := base64.StdEncoding.DecodeString(message)
 if err != nil {
   return "", err
 }

 data, err = DecryptDataWithPrivateKey(data)
 return string(data), err
}
```

Because our implementation of the encryption method returned a Base64-encoded string, the first thing we do before decrypting the message is to decode it back into its binary form. We then call the internal `DecryptDataWithPrivateKey` method; this is a wrapper for the `rsa.DecryptOAEP` method:

```
func DecryptOAEP(hash hash.Hash, random io.Reader, priv *PrivateKey,
ciphertext []byte, label []byte) ([]byte, error)
```

This method has the same parameters as the encrypt method, except this time we are using the private key. If we recall how asymmetric encryption works, we can encrypt using a public key, but we cannot decrypt a message with the public key. The private key must be used for decryption.

Shared secrets

Symmetrical encryption also has its uses: for one, it is faster, and the other reason is that it can handle a message of any size. Implementing symmetrical encryption in Go is, as you would expect, quite straightforward: we have the excellent `crypto/aes` package that manages all the heavy lifting for us. Let's look at how we could encrypt a message with AES. Look at the example file, `symmetric/symmetric.go`:

```
12 func EncryptData(data []byte, key []byte) ([]byte, error) {
13  if err := validateKey(key); err != nil {
14    return make([]byte, 0), err
15  }
16
17  c, err := aes.NewCipher(key)
18  if err != nil {
19    return make([]byte, 0), err
20  }
21
22  gcm, err := cipher.NewGCM(c)
23  if err != nil {
24    return make([]byte, 0), err
25  }
26
27  nonce := make([]byte, gcm.NonceSize())
28  if _, err = io.ReadFull(rand.Reader, nonce); err != nil {
29    return make([]byte, 0), err
30  }
31
32  return gcm.Seal(nil, nonce, data, nil), nil
33 }
```

The first thing we need to do on line 13 is to validate the length of the key. The length of the key determines the strength of the encryption; a 16-byte key will encrypt with AES-128, 24 bytes with AES-192, and 32 bytes with AES-256. We then create a new **GCM** (**Galois/Counter Mode**) cipher and pass it the reference to our AES cipher:

```
func NewGCM(cipher Block) (AEAD, error)
```

We then need to create a nonce, which is used to protect against replay attacks, and finally we can call the `Seal` method, which encrypts our data:

```
Seal(dst, nonce, plaintext, additionalData []byte) []byte
```

Unlike RSA public key encryption, the size of the message that AES can handle is pretty much unlimited; the problem, however, is that the secret must be shared by both the writer and the reader, which introduces the problem of distributing keys to both parties.

Decryption is the reverse of the encryption method, an example of which can be seen in the next code block:

```
// DecryptData decrypts the given data with the given key
func DecryptData(data []byte, key []byte) ([]byte, error) {
 c, err := aes.NewCipher(key)
 if err != nil {
   return make([]byte, 0), err
 }

 gcm, err := cipher.NewGCM(c)
 if err != nil {
   return make([]byte, 0), err
 }

 nonceSize := gcm.NonceSize()
 if len(data) < nonceSize {
   return make([]byte, 0), fmt.Errorf("ciphertext too short")
 }

 nonce, ciphertext := data[:nonceSize], data[nonceSize:]
 return gcm.Open(nil, nonce, ciphertext, nil)
}
```

The main thing we need to note in this code block is in the `gcm.Open` method:

```
Open(dst, nonce, ciphertext, additionalData []byte) ([]byte, error)
```

The nonce that we are going to use to decrypt the message needs to be the same one that was used to encrypt the message. When we called `Seal`, the slice of bytes returned from the method is the encrypted message and the nonce, so, in order to retrieve it, we only need to calculate the size of the nonce and then split the bytes slice up into two parts.

Asymmetric encryption with large messages

We have already discussed the fact that the problem with asymmetric encryption is that it can only be used for relatively small messages; however, the benefits of not having to deal with key distribution makes asymmetric encryption hugely advantageous over symmetrical encryption. There is a common solution to this problem: that solution is to create a random key and symmetrically encrypt a message, and then asymmetrically encrypt the key and distribute both parts to the receiver. Only the holder of the private key will be able to decrypt the symmetrical key, and only once the symmetrical key has been decrypted can the receiver decrypt the main message:

```
// EncryptLargeMessageWithPublicKey encrypts the given message by randomly generating
// a cipher.
// Returns the ciphertext for the given message base64 encoded and the key
// used to encypt the message which is encrypted with the public key
func EncryptLargeMessageWithPublicKey(message string) (ciphertext string, cipherkey string, err error) {
  key := utils.GenerateRandomString(16) // 16, 24, 32 keysize, random string is 2 bytes per char so 16 chars returns 32 bytes
  cipherData, err := symetric.EncryptData([]byte(message), []byte(key))
  if err != nil {
    return "", err
  }

  cipherkey, err = EncryptMessageWithPublicKey(key)
  if err != nil {
    return "", err
  }

  return base64.StdEncoding.EncodeToString(cipherData), cipherkey, nil
}
```

Looking at the example in `asymmetric/asymmetric.go`, we can see that we are doing exactly this. This function wraps the two methods for symmetrical and asymmetrical encryption that we looked at earlier in this chapter. Decryption is as simple:

```
// DecryptLargeMessageWithPrivateKey decrypts the given base64 encoded message by
// decrypting the base64 encoded key with the rsa private key and then using
// the result to decrupt the ciphertext
func DecryptLargeMessageWithPrivateKey(message, key string) (string, error) {
  keystring, err := DecryptMessageWithPrivateKey(key)
```

```
if err != nil {
  return "", fmt.Errorf("Unable to decrypt key with private key: %s",
err)
}

messageData, err := base64.StdEncoding.DecodeString(message)
if err != nil {
  return "", err
}

data, err := symetric.DecryptData(messageData, []byte(keystring))

return string(data), err
}
```

Maintenance

One important element of keeping your system secure is making sure you keep it up to date with all the latest security patches. This approach needs to be applied to your application code and your server's operating system and applications, and, if you are using Docker, you also need to ensure that your containers are up to date to ensure you are free from vulnerabilities.

Patching containers

One of the simplest ways to keep your containers secure is to ensure that you build and deploy them regularly. Quite often, if a service is not under active development, then it may not be deployed to production for months on end. Because of this problem, you may be patching host-level application libraries such as OpenSSL, but because of the application isolation that a container gives, you may have vulnerable binaries at a container level. The simplest way of keeping things up to date is to run a regular build and deploy even if the application code does not change. You also need to ensure that if you are using a base container in your Dockerfile, this is also built and updated.

Docker Hub, `quay.io`, and a couple of other software-as-a-service registries have the capability to automatically rebuild a container when a linked container changes. If you are building an image that is based on `golang:latest`, you can automatically trigger a build when the upstream image is pushed to the registry. You can also run automated security scanning, which examines the layers in your image and scans for any CVE vulnerabilities. It will let you know in which layer the vulnerability exists, and quite often you will find that this is in the base layer, such as Ubuntu or Debian.

Software updates

Patching the software on your host and in your Docker image can help keep you safe from vulnerabilities such as Heartbleed, which was found in OpenSSL. Patching software updates are relatively straightforward. You can configure your host to automatically update itself; the other option, which I prefer, is to ensure that your infrastructure is automated so that you can burn it down and rebuild it.

Patching application code

In the same way that the software on the host needs to be updated, you must also update your application code to ensure you always have the latest updates. Quite often, an approach of locking your application dependencies to a version is followed and with the vendoring support that was introduced in Go 1.5. This process has been growing in the community. One problem with this, and one of the main reasons that vendoring was not present in releases prior to go 1.5, is to encourage you to build your application code against the latest packages and to fix any problems that occur with breaking API changes sooner rather than later. If you do use vendoring, and I am certainly not going to suggest you do not use it, then you should run a nightly build that updates all libraries to the latest version. You do not necessarily have to deploy this to production; however, if the tests pass, then why not? If the tests fail then, even if it is a service that is not under active development, this should be a trigger to you to perform a little maintenance.

Logging

If we have protected our passwords and implemented decent security, we still need to know when we are under threat. In the previous chapter, we introduced logging, and logging can be a useful tool as part of your security policy. Consider someone attempting to brute force your application login; tracking high levels of authentication errors along with the source IP can be useful when you need to react to this threat. The IP address of the attacker can be blocked by the firewall.

The content of log files needs to consider the following attributes:

- Who is performing the action
- What has failed or succeeded
- When is the action occurring
- Why this has failed or succeeded
- How you can deal with the issue

The following example contains nowhere near enough information to be useful and, in fact, other than letting you know there may be a failure, you might as well not even consume the space taken by such logs:

```
Aug 18 11:00:57 [AuthController] Authentication failed.
```

The following example is far better; it shows the problem in much greater depth, and describes in detail the events that a user is taking to access the system. Modern log evaluation tools such as Kibana allow filtering and grouping of such log files, which allows you to build up a dashboard or list of events:

```
Aug 18 11:00:57 [AuthController] Authentication failure
for nicj@example.com by 127.0.0.1 - user unknown -
/user/login /user/myaccount
Aug 18 11:01:18 [AuthController] Authentication failure
for nicj@example.com by 127.0.0.1 - invalid password -
/user/login?err=1 /user/login
Aug 18 11:02:01 [AuthController] Authentication failure
for nicj@example.com by 127.0.0.1 - incorrect 2FA code
- /user/login?err=2 /user/login
```

For example, you could create a dashboard that is looking at failed attempts from a single IP address above a certain threshold, which could indicate a malicious attempt to brute force access to a system. It is often possible to set alerts on such events, allowing you to proactively identify a threat and block access.

Summary

In this chapter, we have learned some of the attacks your service may face from an intruder. We have had an introduction to how encryption works and how we can leverage Go's standard package to implement them to keep our service safe. There is little you can do to completely protect yourself from a determined attacker; however, using the simple techniques described in this chapter should form your standard working practice. Implementing many of these techniques will not slow down your development cycle to any significant degree; it will, however, give you an edge to keep you safe.

9
Event-Driven Architecture

In the last few chapters, we have looked at issues around stability and performance, and some patterns you can employ in your code, which enable more stable systems. In this chapter, we are going to take a more in-depth look at event-driven architecture.

As your system grows, these patterns become more important; they allow you to loosely couple your microservices, and therefore you are not bound to the same dependencies of intertwined objects common in monolithic applications. We are going to learn that with the right amount of up-front design and effort, loosely coupling your systems with events need not be a painful process.

Before we begin, be sure to fetch the source code from `https://github.com/building-microservices-with-go/chapter9`.

Differences between synchronous and asynchronous processing

If there is a choice between processing a message synchronously or asynchronously, then I would always choose synchronously because it always makes the application simpler with fewer components parts, the code is easier to understand, tests are easier to write, and the system is easier to debug.

Asynchronous processing should be a design decision that is driven by need, be that the requirement for decoupling, scale, batch processing, or time-based processing. **Event-driven systems** give an ability to scale at much higher levels than monolithic systems, and the reason for that is that because of the loose coupling, the code scales horizontally with both greater granularity and greater effectiveness.

Another problem with asynchronous processing is the additional burden it adds to your operations. We need to create infrastructure for message queuing and message delivery, and this infrastructure needs to be monitored and managed, even if you are using your cloud provider's functionality, such as SNS/SQS or PubSub.

There is even a question about whether you should be implementing microservices or building a monolith. However, I think microservices as smaller chunks of code are invariably easier to deploy and test at the cost of increased duplication, since the setting up of continuous integration and provisioning of hardware is a one-time hurdle and something that is worth learning. We will look at that in the next chapter, when we examine continuous deployment and immutable infrastructure, but for now, let's stick with events.

Having got the warning out of the way, let's take another look at the difference between the two styles of message processing.

Synchronous processing

With synchronous processing, all the communication to a downstream application happens in the process. A request is sent, and you wait for a reply using the same network connection and not using any callbacks. Synchronous processing is the simplest method of communication; while you are waiting for an answer, the downstream service is processing the request. You have to manage the retry logic yourself, and it is typically best used only when you need an immediate reply. Let's take a look at the following diagram, which depicts synchronous processing:

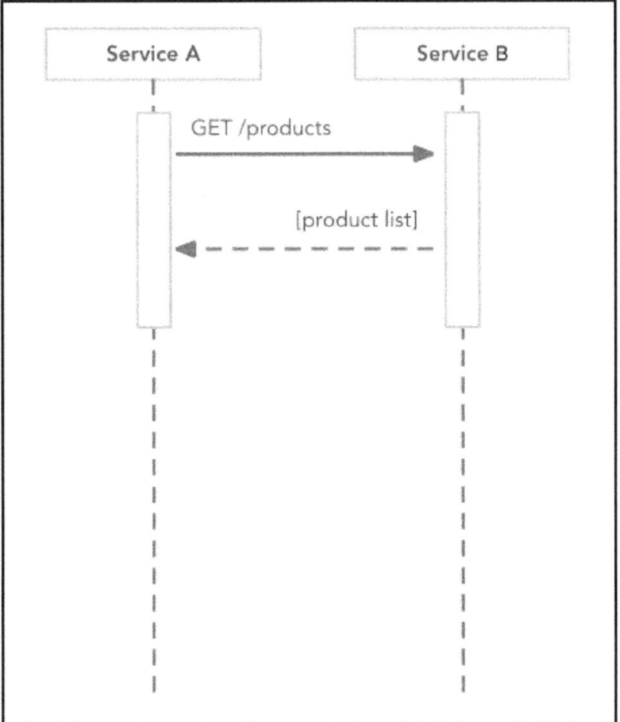

Asynchronous processing

With asynchronous processing, all the communication to the downstream application happens by leveraging a queue or a message broker as an intermediary. Rather than communicating directly with the downstream service, messages dispatch to a queue such as **AWS SQS/SNS**, **Google Cloud Pub/Sub**, or **NATS.io**. Because there is no processing performed at this layer, the only delay is the time it takes to deliver the message, which is very fast. Also, due to the design of these systems, acceptance or not of a message is the only situation you must implement. Retry and connection handling logic is delegated to either the message broker or the downstream system, as is the storage of messages for archive or replay:

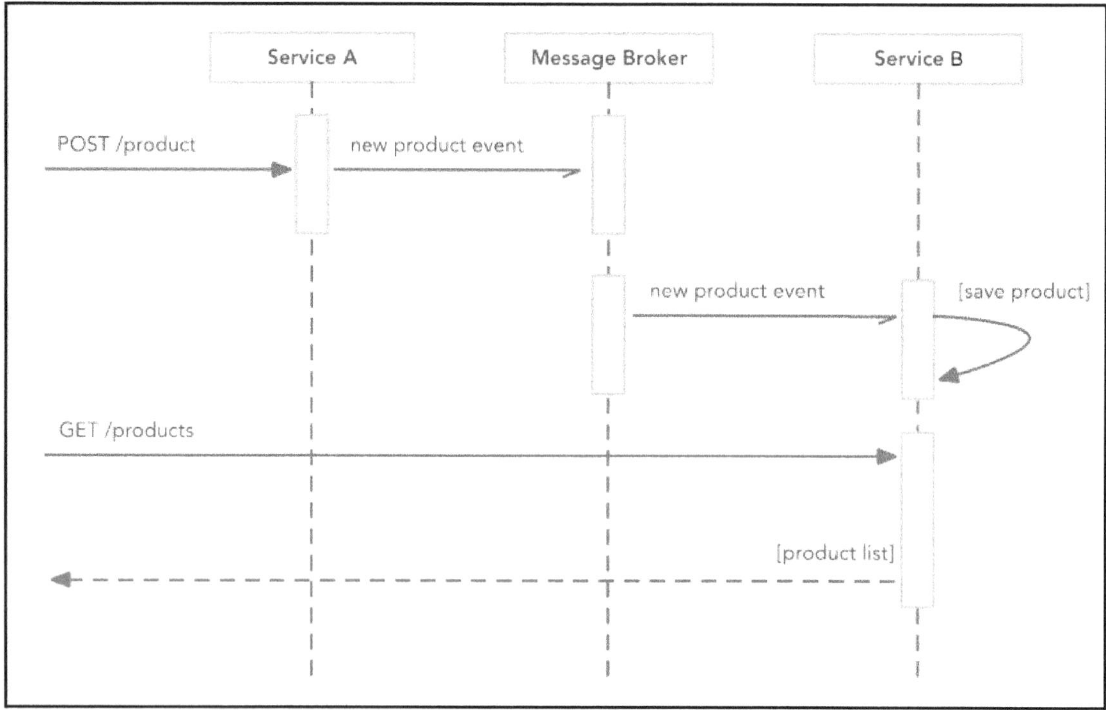

Types of asynchronous messages

Asynchronous processing often comes in two different forms, such as push and pull. The strategy that you implement is dependent upon your requirements, and often a single system implements both patterns. Let's take a look at the two different approaches.

Pull/queue messaging

The pull pattern is an excellent design where you may have a worker process running, for example, resizing images. The API would receive the request and then add this to a queue for background processing. The worker process or processes read from the queue, retrieve the messages one by one, perform the required work, and then delete the message from the queue. Often, there is also a queue commonly called a **dead letter queue**. Should the worker process fail for any reason, then the message would be added to the dead letter queue. The dead letter queue allows the messages to be re-processed in the case of an incremental failure or for debugging purposes. Let's take a look at the following diagram, which summarizes the whole process:

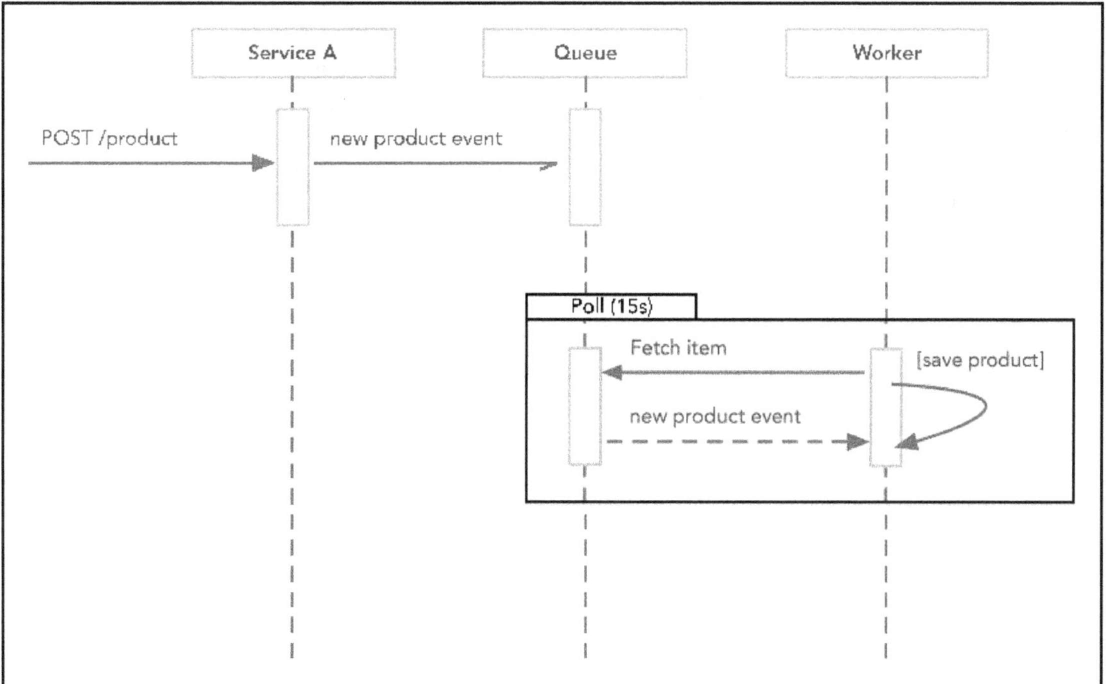

Implementing a queue-based service in Go is a relatively straightforward task. Let's walk through the example in the source code that accompanies this book. This example uses Redis for storing the messages. Redis is an incredibly fast data store, and, while it is nice to be able to leverage a cloud providers' queue, rather than managing our infrastructure, this is not always possible. However, even if we are using a cloud providers' queue, the pattern we are about to look at is easily replaceable with a different data store client. Consider the following listing from the example code in `queue/queue.go`:

```
// Message represents messages stored on the queue
type Message struct {
  ID      string `json:"id"`
  Name    string `json:"name"`
  Payload string `json:"payload"`
}

// Queue defines the interface for a message queue
type Queue interface {
  Add(messageName string, payload []byte) error
  AddMessage(message Message) error
  StartConsuming(size int, pollInterval time.Duration, callback
func(Message) error)
}
```

The first thing we are doing is defining a `Message` object that is used by the system and defines three simple parameters that are serializable to JSON. `ID` is never populated by the publisher directly. Instead, this is a calculated ID that is unique for every message. Should the consumer need a simple mechanism to determine whether a message has already been received and processed, then `ID` can be used. The interface for `Queue` defines three simple methods:

- `Add(messageName string, payload []byte) error`: `Add` is a convenience method to publish a new message. The sender only needs to provide the name of the message and a slice of byte.

- `AddMessage(message Message) error`: `AddMessage` performs the same function as `Add`, the only difference being that the caller needs to construct a `Message` type and pass this to the method. The implementation of `AddMessage` automatically generates the `ID` field on `Message struct` and overwrites any initial `ID` value.
- `StartConsuming(size int, pollInterval time.Duration, callback func(Message) error)`: `StartConsuming` allows a subscriber to retrieve messages from the queue. The first parameter size relates to the batch size, which is returned in any one connection. The `pollInterval` parameter determines how often the client checks for messages on the queue. The `callback` function is executed when messages return from the queue. It has a return parameter of `error`, which, when not `nil`, informs the client that processing has failed and the message should not be removed from the queue. One thing we need to note is that `StartConsuming` is not a blocking method; once it has registered the callback to the queue, it returns immediately.

The implementation in `queue/redis_queue.go` defines the `NewRedisQueue` function, which is a convenience function to create our queue. We are using the `github.com/adjust/rmq` library, which has an excellent implementation on top of Redis queues and, in line `27`, we are opening a connection to our Redis data store:

```
26 // NewRedisQueue creates a new RedisQueue
27 func NewRedisQueue(connectionString string, queueName string)
(*RedisQueue, error) {
28   connection := rmq.OpenConnection("my service", "tcp",
connectionString, 1)
29   taskQueue := connection.OpenQueue(queueName)
30
31   return &RedisQueue{Queue: taskQueue, name: queueName}, nil
32 }
```

Then, on line `29`, we need to open a connection to the queue that we are going to read and write from:

```
42 // AddMessage to the queue, generating a unique ID for the message
before dispatch
43 func (r *RedisQueue) AddMessage(message Message) error {
44   serialNumber, _ := rand.Int(rand.Reader, serialNumberLimit)
45   message.ID = strconv.Itoa(time.Now().Nanosecond()) +
serialNumber.String()
46
47   payloadBytes, err := json.Marshal(message)
48   if err != nil {
49     // handle error
```

```
50      return err
51    }
52
53    fmt.Println("Add event to queue:", string(payloadBytes))
54    if !r.Queue.PublishBytes(payloadBytes) {
55      return fmt.Errorf("unable to add message to the queue")
56    }
57
58    return nil
59 }
```

The `Add` method, which is the implementation of our interface's `Add` method, is merely a convenience method that creates a message from the given parameters and then calls the `AddMessage` function. The `AddMessage` function first generates an ID for the message. In this simple implementation, we are just generating a random number and appending it to the current time in nanoseconds, which should give us enough uniqueness without requiring a check to the queue. We then need to convert the message to its JSON representation as a slice of bytes before we finally publish the message to the queue on line 54.

The final part of our implementation is the method that consumes messages from the queue:

```
// StartConsuming consumes messages from the queue
func (r *RedisQueue) StartConsuming(size int, pollInterval time.Duration, callback func(Message) error) {
  r.callback = callback
  r.Queue.StartConsuming(size, pollInterval)
  r.Queue.AddConsumer("RedisQueue_"+r.name, r)
}

// Consume is the internal callback for the message queue
func (r *RedisQueue) Consume(delivery rmq.Delivery) {
  fmt.Println("Got event from queue:", delivery.Payload())

  message := Message{}

  if err := json.Unmarshal([]byte(delivery.Payload()), &message); err != nil {
    fmt.Println("Error consuming event, unable to deserialise event")
    // handle error
    delivery.Reject()
    return
  }

  if err := r.callback(message); err != nil {
    delivery.Reject()
```

```
83      return
84    }
85
86    delivery.Ack()
87 }
```

The `StartConsuming` method is only responsible for setting the callback to the queue instance; we then call the `StartConsuming` and `AddConsumer` methods, which are methods from the Redis package. On line 65, we set the callback consumer that the queue uses to `self` rather than the callback passed into the method. The delegate pattern assigned to an internal method allows us to abstract the implementation of the underlying queue from the implementing code base. When a new message is detected on the queue, the `Consume` method is called, passing an instance of `rmq.Delivery`, which is an interface defined in the `rmq` package:

```
type Delivery interface {
  Payload() string
  Ack() bool
  Reject() bool
  Push() bool
}
```

The first thing we need to do is unmarshal the message that is passed as a slice of byte into our `Message` structure. If this fails, then we call the `Reject` method on the `Delivery` interface, which pushes the message back onto the queue. Once we have the message in the format that our callback expects, we can then execute the `callback` function, which is passed to the `StartConsuming` method. The type of callback is as follows:

```
func(Message) error
```

It is the responsibility of the code that is implementing this method to return an error should the processing of the message fail. Returning an error allows our consuming code to call `delivery.Reject()`, which would leave the message in the queue for later processing. When the message processes successfully, we pass a `nil` error and the consumer calls `delivery.Ack()`, which acknowledges that the message has been successfully processed, and removes it from the queue. These operations are process safe; they should not be available to other consumers, so in the event that we have many workers reading a queue, we can ensure that they are all working from distinct lists.

Let's take a look at the implementation of a service that would write messages to the queue. If we take a look at the example code file, `queue/writer/main.go`, we can see that there is a very simple implementation. This is too simple an application for a production system and there is no message validation or security in the handler. However, this example is pared down to the bare minimum to highlight how messages are added to the queue:

```
func main() {
  q, err := queue.NewRedisQueue("redis:6379", "test_queue")
  if err != nil {
    log.Fatal(err)
  }

  http.HandleFunc("/", func(rw http.ResponseWriter, r
  *http.Request) {
    data, _ := ioutil.ReadAll(r.Body)
    err := q.Add("new.product", data)
    if err != nil {
      log.Println(err)
      rw.WriteHeader(http.StatusInternalServerError)
      return
    }
  })

  http.ListenAndServe(":8080", http.DefaultServeMux)
}
```

We create an instance of `RedisQueue` and pass it the location of our Redis server and the name of the queue to which we would like to write messages. We then have a very simple implementation of `http.Handler`; this function reads the body of the request as a slice of bytes and calls the `Add` method with the name of the message and the payload. We then check the outcome of this operation before returning and closing the connection.

The consumer implementation is even simpler, as this code implements a simple worker and does not implement an HTTP-based interface:

```
func main() {
  log.Println("Starting worker")

  q, err := queue.NewRedisQueue("redis:6379", "test_queue")
  if err != nil {
    log.Fatal(err)
  }

  q.StartConsuming(10, 100*time.Millisecond, func(message
queue.Message) error {
    log.Printf("Received message: %v, %v, %v\n", message.ID,
```

```
message.Name, message.Payload)

        return nil // successfully processed message
    })

    runtime.Goexit()
}
```

As in the client, we create an instance of our queue and then we call the `StartConsuming` method with our requested parameters and the `callback` function. The `callback` method executes for every message retrieved from the queue, and since we are returning batches of 10 potentially every 100 milliseconds, this method could be called in quick succession, and every execution runs in its own `goroutine`, so when writing the implementation, we need to consider this detail. If for example, we were processing the messages and then writing them to a database, then the number of connections to the database is not infinite. To determine an appropriate batch size, we need to conduct initial testing and follow this up with constant monitoring, in order to tweak the application for optimum performance. These settings should be implemented as parameters so that they are easily changed as the hardware scales.

Push messaging

Rather than using a queue, sometimes, you may want a service to act immediately on an event. Your service subscribes to receive messages from a broker such as NATS.io or SNS. When the broker receives a message, dispatched from another service, then the broker notifies all the registered services by making a call to the registered endpoint, sending it a copy of the message. The receiver will generally disconnect once the message has been received and assumes that the message processes correctly. This pattern allows the message broker extreme throughput. In the case of NATS.io, a single server instance can deliver millions of messages per second. Should the client be unable to process the message, then it must handle the logic to manage this failure. This logic could be to dispatch a notification to the broker, or again the message could be added to a dead letter queue for later replay. The following diagram showing the working of push messaging:

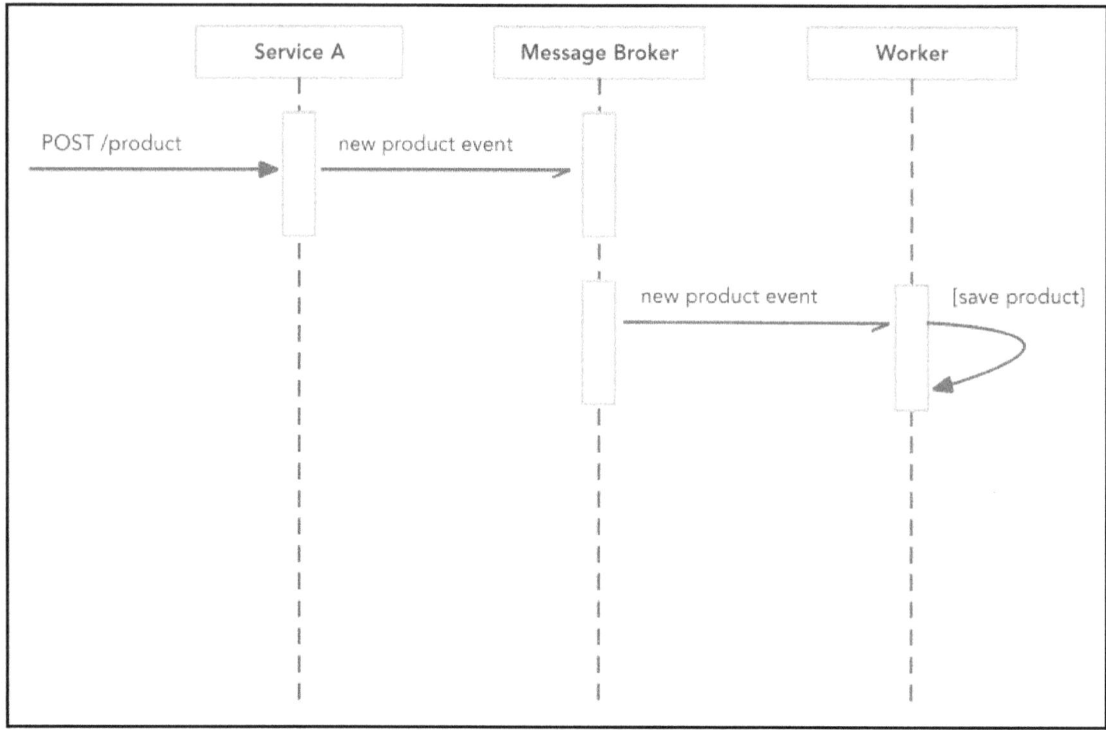

In this example, we are going to leverage the power of NATS.io to act as a message broker for our system. NATS is an incredibly lightweight application that is written in Go and provides astounding performance and stability. Looking at `push/writer/main.go`, we can see that there is not very much code we need to write in order to implement NATS.io:

```
func main() {
  var err error
  natsClient, err = nats.Connect("nats://" + *natsServer)
  if err != nil {
    log.Fatal(err)
  }
  defer natsClient.Close()

  http.DefaultServeMux.HandleFunc("/product", productsHandler)

  log.Println("Starting product write service on port 8080")
  log.Fatal(http.ListenAndServe(":8080", http.DefaultServeMux))
}
```

The first thing we need to do when starting our application is to connect to the NATS server by calling the `Connect` function on the `nats` package:

```
func Connect(url string, options ...Option) (*Conn,error)
```

The `url` parameter, which is defined as a string, requires a little clarification. While you can pass a single URL, such as `nats://server:port`, you can also pass a comma-separated list of servers. The reason for this is because of fault tolerance, NATS implements clustering. In our simple example, we only have a single instance; however, when running in production, you will have multiple instances for redundancy. We then define our `http.Handler` function and expose the `/product` endpoint:

```
37 func productsHandler(rw http.ResponseWriter, r *http.Request) {
38   if r.Method == "POST" {
39     insertProduct(rw, r)
40   }
41 }
42
43 func insertProduct(rw http.ResponseWriter, r *http.Request) {
44   log.Println("/insert handler called")
45
46   data, err := ioutil.ReadAll(r.Body)
47   if err != nil {
48     rw.WriteHeader(http.StatusBadRequest)
49     return
50   }
51   defer r.Body.Close()
52
53   natsClient.Publish("product.inserted", data)
54 }
```

The implementation of the handler is straightforward and we delegate the work to the `insertProduct` function. Again, in terms of implementation, this is brief to highlight the use of publishing a message; in production, there would be a higher level of implementation to manage security and validation.

On line 53, we call the `Publish` method on our client; the method has an incredibly simple signature with the subject and the payload:

```
func (nc *Conn) Publish(subjstring, data []byte)error
```

Concerning the subject, we need to consider that this is the same name that the subscriber is going to use and that it must be unique, otherwise it is possible that unintended recipients receive the messages, and this is an incredibly difficult error to track down. The fully configurable options for NATS are in the GoDoc at `https://godoc.org/github.com/nats-io/go-nats`, which is rather comprehensive.

Now we have seen how easy it is to publish messages to NATS, let's see how easy it is to consume them. If we take a look at the example code in `push/reader/main.go`, we can see that subscribing to messages is incredibly simple:

```
func main() {
  var err error
  natsClient, err = nats.Connect("nats://" + *natsServer)
  if err != nil {
    log.Fatal(err)
  }
  defer natsClient.Close()

  log.Println("Subscribing to events")
  natsClient.Subscribe("product.inserted", handleMessage)
}

func handleMessage(m *nats.Msg) {
  p := product{}
  err := json.Unmarshal(m.Data, &p)
  if err != nil {
    log.Println("Unable to unmarshal event object")
    return
  }

  log.Printf("Received message: %v, %#v", m.Subject, p)
}
```

Again, we make our connection to the NATS server, but, to start receiving events, we call the `Subscribe` method on the client:

```
func (nc *Conn) Subscribe(subjstring, cbMsgHandler) (*Subscription,error)
```

The `Subscribe` method will express interest in the given subject. The subject can have wildcards (partial: `*`, full: >). Messages will be delivered to the associated `MsgHandler`.

If no `MsgHandler` is given, the subscription is a synchronous subscription, and it can be polled via `Subscription.NextMsg()`.

Unlike in our queue example, we are not polling the NATS server. We are exposing an endpoint and registering that with NATS. When the NATS server receives a message, it attempts to forward that to all the registered endpoints. Using the implementation in the previous code sample, we obtain a copy of the message for every worker we have running on the system, which is not ideal. Rather than managing this ourselves, we can use a different method on the API, `QueueSubscribe`:

```
func (nc *Conn) QueueSubscribe(subj, queuestring, cbMsgHandler)
(*Subscription,error)
```

The `QueueSubscribe` function creates an asynchronous queue subscriber on the given subject. All subscribers with the same queue name form the queue group, and only one member of the group is selected to receive any given message asynchronously.

The signature resembles the `Subscribe` method, the only difference being we pass an additional parameter, which is the name of the queue or the unique cluster of subscribers who would like to register interest in the given subject.

Now that we have defined the two main types of asynchronous messaging and looked at the simple implementation of each, let's take a look at two common patterns that leverage this technique.

Command Query Responsibility Segregation (CQRS)

CQRS is an abbreviation for Command Query Responsibility Segregation, a term attributed to Greg Young. The concept is that you use a different model to update information than the model used for reading information. The two main reasons for implementing CQRS are when the storage of a model differs dramatically from the presentation of the model, and when the concepts behind this approach are that attempting to create a model that is optimized for storage and a model that is optimized for display might solve neither problem. For this reason, CQRS splits these models into a **Query** model used by the presentation logic, and a **Command** model that is used for storage and validation. The other benefit is when we would like to separate the load between reads and writes in high-performance applications. The CQRS pattern is not something that is hugely common and certainly should not be used everywhere as it does increase complexity; however, it is a very useful pattern to have in your arsenal.

Let's take a look at the following diagram:

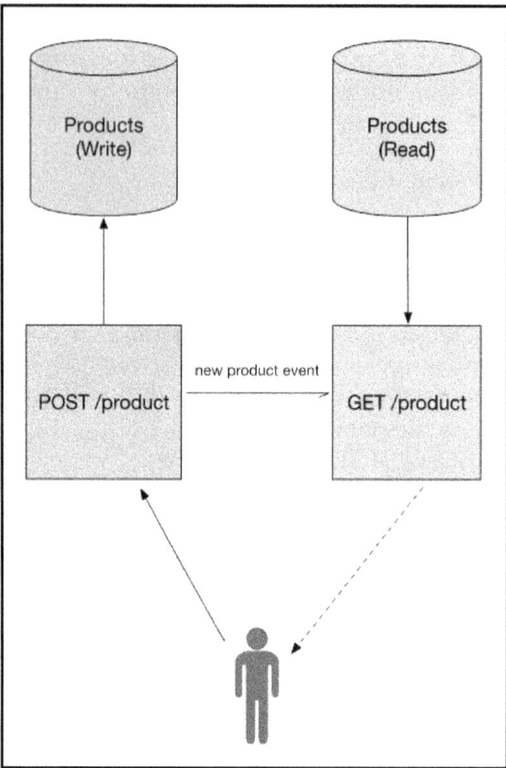

In our example code, we again were leveraging NATS.io to broker the messages. However, this need not be the case. It is a legitimate setup to have a single service that has two separate models for reading and writing. Instead of the complexity of a message broker, in-process communication could be used just as effectively.

Take a look at the example code at `cCQRS/product_writer/main.go`:

```
func init() {
  flag.Parse()

  schema = &memdb.DBSchema{
    Tables: map[string]*memdb.TableSchema{
      "product": &memdb.TableSchema{
        Name: "product",
        Indexes: map[string]*memdb.IndexSchema{
          "id": &memdb.IndexSchema{
            Name:    "id",
```

```
                Unique:  true,
                Indexer: &memdb.StringFieldIndex{Field: "SKU"},
            },
        },
    },
  },
}
...
  natsClient, err = nats.Connect("nats://" + *natsServer)
  if err != nil {
    log.Fatal(err)
  }
}
```

For simplicity, this example uses an in-memory database, `https://github.com/hashicorp/go-memdb`, written by HashiCorp, and the bulk of the setup is configuring this data store. We will be separating our data stores for read and write and the reader service does not implement any methods to return the products to the caller. Instead, this responsibility is delegated to a second service that is running a separate database and even a different data model:

```
func insertProduct(rw http.ResponseWriter, r *http.Request) {
  log.Println("/insert handler called")

  p := &product{}

  data, err := ioutil.ReadAll(r.Body)
  if err != nil {
    rw.WriteHeader(http.StatusBadRequest)
    return
  }
  defer r.Body.Close()

  err = json.Unmarshal(data, p)
  if err != nil {
    log.Println(err)
    rw.WriteHeader(http.StatusBadRequest)
    return
  }

  txn := db.Txn(true)
  if err := txn.Insert("product", p); err != nil {
    log.Println(err)
    rw.WriteHeader(http.StatusInternalServerError)
    return
  }
  txn.Commit()
```

```

  natsClient.Publish("product.inserted", data)
}
```

Our handler first writes the model to the database and then, like our push example, we are publishing a message to NATS containing the payload of the message.

Looking at the reader server at `CQRS/product-read/main.go`, again we are setting up our data store; however, the model is different from the read model:

- **Write model**:

```
type product struct {
   Name       string `json:"name"`
   SKU        string `json:"sku"`
   StockCount int    `json:"stock_count"`
}
```

- **Read model**:

```
type product struct {
  Name        string `json:"name"`
  Code        string `json:"code"`
  LastUpdated string `json:"last_updated"`
}
```

We are also defining an event structure that contains the details for our event received from NATS. In this instance, this structure mirrors the write model; however, this does not always need to be the case:

```
type productInsertedEvent struct {
  Name string `json:"name"`
  SKU  string `json:"sku"`
}
```

Upon receipt of a message, we first decode the payload into the expected type, `productInsertedEvent`, and then we convert this to our product model, that is stored in the database. Finally, we store the information in the database, creating our copy in a format that our consumers wish to receive:

```
func productMessage(m *nats.Msg) {
  pie := productInsertedEvent{}
  err := json.Unmarshal(m.Data, &pie)
  if err != nil {
    log.Println("Unable to unmarshal event object")
    return
  }
```

```

p := product{}.FromProductInsertedEvent(pie)

txn := db.Txn(true)
if err := txn.Insert("product", p); err != nil {
  log.Println(err)
  return
}
txn.Commit()

log.Println("Saved product: ", p)
}
```

When a user calls the `/products` endpoint, the data that they get back is that of the locally cached copy, not the master that is stored in a separate service. This process could cause issues with consistency, since the two copies of data are eventually consistent, and, when we implement the CQRS pattern, we need to consider this. If we were exposing the stock level, then it may not be desirable to have eventual consistency; however, we can make a design decision that, when this information is required, we sacrifice performance by making a synchronous call to the stock endpoint.

Domain-driven design

When implementing event-driven microservices, you need to have a good grasp of the way your system operates and the way data and interactions flow from one service to the next. A useful technique for modeling any complex system is domain-driven design.

When it comes to domain-driven design, there is Vernon Vaughn, whose two books, *Domain-Driven Design Distilled* and *Implementing Domain-Driven Design*, published by Addison-Wesley Professional, expand upon the seminal, and for some, there is a slightly difficult-to-read work by Eric Evans. For newcomers to DDD, I recommend starting with *Domain-Driven Design Distilled* and then moving to read *Implementing Domain-Driven Design*. Reading *Domain-Driven Design Distilled* first gives you a grounding of the terminology before you delve into what is a rather detailed book. DDD is most certainly an advanced topic and not something that can be covered comprehensively in one section of this book, nor do I profess to have the experience to write anything more detailed because DDD is a pattern that is learned by practice. DDD is also a tool for more complex, large systems with many stakeholders and many moving parts. Even if you are not working on such a system, the concepts of aggregation and isolation are compelling and applicable to most systems. If nothing else, keep reading to become more proficient at buzzword bingo in your next architecture meeting.

What is DDD?

To quote the words of Vaughn Vernon himself:

> *"DDD is a set of tools that assist you in designing and implementing software that delivers high value, both strategically and tactically. Your organization can't be the best at everything, so it had better choose carefully at what it must excel. The DDD strategic development tools help you and your team make the competitively best software design choices and integration decisions for your business."*
>
> *– Vaughn Vernon*

That is quite an introduction; however, I think it highlights the fact that DDD is a tool for designing software and not a software framework. In the dark days, a couple of decades ago, software architects and project managers would make the decisions for the design of a software system, often providing very detailed plans that were executed by the development teams. In my experience this was rarely an enjoyable way to work, nor did it produce good quality software or deliver on time. The agile revolution proposed a different way of working and, thankfully, has improved the situation. We also now regard ourselves as software engineers rather than developers. I do not believe that this shift is a fashion, but it is driven by the change in the role that we have seen. Your role as someone who creates software is now one of a designer, negotiator of features, architect, mediator, and you are also required to have a full understanding of the materials at your disposal, including the reactions to stress and strain. You now mirror the role of a traditional engineer rather than the assembly line worker role that software developers performed in the past.

Hopefully, that answers the question that may be in your head as to why you need to learn about DDD in a book about Go. Well, this book was never written to teach you the language; it was designed to show you how you can use it to build successful microservices.

I hear lots of noise surrounding DDD that it is a difficult technique, and admittedly, when I first read DDD, I felt the same way, with all this stuff about aggregates, ubiquitous language, domains, and subdomains. However, once I started to think about DDD to engineer separation and thought about many of the problems I have faced in the past with confused domain models, then it slowly began to sink in.

Technical debt

If you have ever worked on a monolithic application, you are aware of the coupling and dependency that occurs between objects. This is predominately in the data layer; however, you also often find code that is not implementing correctly and is tightly bound to another object. Problems arise when you want to change this system; a change in one area has an undesired impact in another, and only one if you are lucky. An enormous effort happens in refactoring the system before changes are made. Often, what happens is that the modification is shoehorned into the existing code base without refactoring, and, to be brutally honest, it would be kinder to the system to take it outside, around the back of the barn, and unload two shotgun shells in the back of its head.

Don't fool yourself that you will ever get the opportunity to do this; if you have ever worked on a system of any real age, your job is like Lenin's embalmers. You spend an enormous amount of effort to keep a dead body presentable when you should just dig a hole in the ground and drop it in. DDD can help with understanding the monolith and slowly decoupling it; it is also a tool to prevent the unruly monolith from ever occurring. Let's take a quick look at the technical anatomy.

Anatomy of DDD

The primary part of the strategic design in DDD is to apply a concept called **Bounded Contexts**. Bounded Contexts is a method of segregating your domain into models. Using a technique called **context mapping**, you can integrate multiple Bounded Contexts by defining both the team and technical relationships that exist between them.

The tactical design is where you refine the details of your domain model. In this phase, we learn how to aggregate entities and value objects together.

Strategic design

One of the phrases you will hear a lot when dealing with DDD is the term Bounded Contexts. A Bounded Context is a semantic contextual boundary in which the components inside each boundary have a specific meaning and does specific things. One of the most important of these Bounded Contexts is the **core domain**; this is the domain that distinguishes your organization competitively from all the others. We have already mentioned that you cannot do everything, and by concentrating on your core domain, this should be where you spend most of your time.

Tactical design

From the base of strategic design comes tactical design, to quote Vaughn Vernon again:

> *"Tactical design is like using a thin brush to paint the finer details of your domain model."*
>
> *– Vaughn Vernon*

At this stage in the design, we need to start thinking about **aggregates** and **domain events**. An aggregate is composed of entities and value objects. A value object models an immutable whole; it does not have a unique identity, and equivalence is determined by comparing the attributes encapsulated by the value types. Domain events are published by an aggregate and subscribed to by interested parties. This subscription could be from the same Bounded Contexts, or it may come from a different source.

Ubiquitous language

The term ubiquitous language in DDD refers to a core language that everyone on the team understands about the software under development. It is entirely possible that a component in a different context and developed by a different team has a different meaning for the same terminology. In fact, they are probably talking about different components from your model.

How you develop your ubiquitous language is an activity that the team will perform. You should not put too much emphasis onto using only nouns to describe your model; you should start to build up simple scenarios. Consider our example from `Chapter 4`, *Testing*, on testing where we used BDD for our functional and integration testing. These are your scenarios; the language in which you write them is your team's ubiquitous language. You should write these scenarios so that they are meaningful to your team and not attempt to write something that is meaningful for the entire department.

Bounded contexts

One of the main reasons for using a Bounded Context is that teams often do not know when to stop piling things into their software models. As the team adds more features, the model soon becomes difficult to manage and understand. Not only this, the language of the model starts to become blurred. When software becomes vast and convoluted with many unrelated interconnections, it starts to become what is known as a *big ball of mud*. The big ball of mud is probably far worse than your traditional monolith. Monoliths are not inherently evil just because they are monolithic; monoliths are bad because within them exists a place where good coding standards are long forgotten. The other problem with a Bounded Context that is too large and owned by too many people is that it starts to be difficult to describe it using a ubiquitous language.

Context mapping

When two Bounded Contexts in DDD need to integrate, the integration is known as context mapping. The importance of defining this context mapping is that a well-defined contract supports controlled changes over time. In the book *Domain-Driven Design Distilled,* Vaughn Vernon describes the following different kinds of mappings:

- **Partnership:** The partnership mapping exists when two teams are each responsible for a Bounded Context and have a dependent set of goals.
- **Shared kernel:** A shared kernel is defined by the intersection of two separate Bounded Contexts and exists when two teams share a small but common model.
- **Customer-supplier:** A customer-supplier describes a relationship between two Bounded Contexts and their respective teams. The supplier is the upstream context, and the customer is the downstream. The supplier must provide what the customer needs, and the two teams must plan together to meet their expectations. This is a very typical and practical relationship between the teams as long as the supplier still considers the customer's needs.
- **Conformist:** A conformist relationship exists when there are upstream and downstream teams and the upstream team has no motivation to support the specific needs of the downstream team. Rather than translate the upstream ubiquitous language to fit its own needs, the downstream team adopts the language of the upstream.
- **Anti-corruption layer:** This is the standard and recommended model when you are connecting two systems together. The downstream team builds a translation layer between its ubiquitous language and that of the upstream, thus isolating it from the upstream.

- **Open Host Service:** An Open Host Service defines a protocol or interface that gives access to your Bounded Contexts as a set of services. The services are offered via a well-documented API and are simple to consume.
- **Published language:** A published language is a well-documented information exchange language enabling easy consumption and translation. **XML Schema**, **JSON Schema**, and **RPC**-based frameworks such as **Protobufs** are frequently used.
- **Separate ways:** In this situation, there is no significant payoff through the consumption of various ubiquitous languages, and the team decides to produce their solution inside their Bounded Contexts.
- **Big ball of mud:** This should be pretty self-explanatory by now and not something a team should aim for; in fact, this is the very thing that DDD attempts to avoid.

Software

When we start working with DDD and event-oriented architectures in anger, we soon find that we need some help brokering our messages to ensure the at-least-once and at-most-once delivery that is required by the application. We could, of course, implement our strategy for this. However, there are many open source projects on the internet that handle this capability for us, and soon we find ourselves reaching out to leverage one of these.

Kafka

Kafka is a distributed streaming platform that allows you to publish and subscribe to streams of records. It lets you store streams of documents in a fault-tolerant way and process streams of records as they occur. It has been designed to be a fast and fault-tolerant system commonly running as a cluster of one or more servers to enable redundancy.

NATS.io

NATS.io is an open source messaging system written in Go, and it has the ability to perform two roles, such as at-most-once and at-least-once delivery. Lets look at what they mean:

- **At-most-once delivery**: In the basic mode, NATS can act as a Pub/Sub router, where listening clients can subscribe to message topics and have new messages pushed to them. If a message has no subscriber, then it is sent to `/dev/null` and is not stored internally in the system.
- **At-least-once delivery**: When a higher level of service and more stringent delivery guarantees are required, NATS can operate in at-least-once delivery mode. In this mode, NATS can no longer function as a standalone entity and needs to be backed by a storage device, which at present has support for file and in-memory. Now, there is no scaling and replication supported with NATS streaming, and this is where Kafka shines. However, we are not all building systems as big as Netflix, and the configuration and management of Kafka is a book in its own right. NATS can be understood very quickly.

AWS SNS/SQS

Amazon's **Simple Queue Service** (**SQS**) is a queuing service that allows a publisher to add messages to a queue, which can later be consumed by clients. A message is read and then removed from the queue, making it no longer available to other readers.

There are two different types of SQS, such as the standard mode, which allows maximum throughput at the expense that a message may be delivered more than once; and SQS FIFO, which ensures that messages are only ever delivered once and in the order in which they are received. However, FIFO queues are subject to vastly reduced throughput, and therefore their use must be carefully considered.

Amazon's **Simple Notification Service** (**SNS**) is a service for coordinating and managing the delivery of queues of messages. SNS stands for Simple Notification Service; you configure a topic that you can publish messages to and then subscribers can register for notifications. SNS can deliver messages to the following different protocols:

- HTTP(S)
- Email
- Email-JSON
- SMS
- AWS Lambda
- SQS

You may wonder why you would want to add a message to a queue when you can just push a message to the recipient. One of the problems with SNS is that it can only deliver over HTTP to services that are publicly accessible. If your internal workers are not connected to the public internet (and after reading `Chapter 8`, *Security*, I hope that they are not), a pull-based approach may be your only option. Reading from a queue is also potentially a better option for managing large streams of messages. You do not need to worry about the availability of SQS (most of the time), and you do not need to implement an HTTP interface for a simple application worker that can poll a queue.

Google Cloud Pub/Sub

Google Cloud Pub/Sub is very like AWS SNS in that it is a messaging middleware, allowing the creation of topics with publishers and subscribers. At the time of writing, there is no formal product on Google Cloud such as SQS. However, it would be trivial to implement something using one of the many data storage options you have available.

Summary

In this chapter, we have looked at some of the main patterns for decoupling microservices using events. We have also had an introduction to a modern design methodology for building distributed systems—domain-driven design. With the correct tools and upfront design, building highly scalable and maintainable systems should not be too challenging, and you now have all the information you need to do this with Go. In the final chapter, we are going to look at automated building and deployment of your code, finalizing the information you need to be a successful microservices practitioner.

10
Continuous Delivery

We have covered a lot so far, including how to build resilient systems and how to keep them secure, but now we need to look at how to replace all the manual steps in our process and introduce continuous delivery.

In this chapter, we will discuss the following concepts:

- Continuous delivery
- Container orchestration
- Immutable infrastructure
- Terraform
- An example application

What is continuous delivery?

Continuous delivery is the process of building and deploying code, well, continuously. The aim is that we move code from development to production as efficiently and effectively as possible.

In a traditional or waterfall workflow, releases revolve around the completion of a major feature or update. It is not untypical for large enterprises to release once a quarter. When we look at the reason for this strategy, risk and effort are often cited. There is a risk to releasing as confidence in the software is weak; there is effort involved in releasing because there needs to be a mostly manual process involved in quality assurance and the operational aspects of releasing the software. One part of this is something that we have covered in `Chapter 5`, *Common Patterns*, which is the concern with quality, and the possible absence of a satisfactory test suite or possibly the ability to run this automatically. The second element involves the physical deployment and post-deployment testing process. We have not covered this aspect much in this book so far; we touched on it when we looked at Docker in `Chapter 4`, *Testing*.

If you could reduce the risk and effort involved in deploying code, would you do it more frequently? How about every time you complete a minor feature, or every time a bug is fixed, several times a day even? I would encourage you to do just that, and in this chapter, we will look at all the things we need to know and build on all the things we have previously learned to deliver continuously.

Manual deployment

Manual deployment is at best problematic; even if you have an amazing team, things can and will go wrong. The larger the group, the more distributed the knowledge and the greater the need for comprehensive documentation. In a small team, the resources are constrained, and the time it takes for deployment can be a distraction from building great code. You could also end up with a weak link; do you suspend deployment when the person who usually carries out the process is sick or on holiday?

These are the problems with manual deployment:

- Issues can arise with the ordering and timing of the various deployment steps
- The documentation needs to be comprehensive and always up to date
- There is a significant reliance on manual testing
- There are application servers with different states

As a system grows in complexity, there are more moving parts, and the steps required to deploy the code increase with it. Since the steps to deploy need to be carried out in a set order, the process can quickly become a burden. Consider deploying an update to an application: the application and its dependencies install on all instances of the application servers. Often, a database schema needs to be updated, and there needs to be a clean switch over between the old and the new application. Even if you are leveraging the power of Docker, this process can be fraught with disaster. As the complexity of the application grows, so does the required documentation to deploy the application, and this is often a weak link. Documentation takes time to update and maintain. In my personal experience, this is the first area that suffers when deadlines are approaching.

Once the application code is deployed, we need to test the function of the application. If the application is manually deployed, it is often assumed that the application is also manually tested. A tester would need to run through a test plan (assuming there is a test plan) to check that the system is in a functioning state. If the system is not functioning, then either the process would need to be reversed to roll back to a previous state, or a decision would need to be made to hotfix the application and again run through the standard build-and-deploy cycle. When this process falls into a planned release, there is a little more safety as the whole team is around for the release. However, what happens when this process takes place in the middle of the night as a result of an incident? At best, what happens is that the fix is deployed without updating any of the documentation or processes. At worst, the application ends up in a worse state than before the hotfix of the application code was attempted

Out-of-hours incidents are also often carried out by first-line response, which is usually the infrastructure team. I assume that if you are not running Continuous Deployment, then you will also not be following the practice of developer on call. Also, what about the time it takes to deploy? What is the financial cost of the entire team taking time out to babysit a deployment? What about the motivational and productivity costs of this process? Have you ever felt the stress due to the uncertainty of deploying application code into production?

Continuous delivery removes these risks and problems.

The benefits of continuous delivery

The concept of continuous delivery is that you plan for these problems and do the up-front work required to solve them. Automation of all the steps involved allows consistency of operation and is a self-documenting process. No longer do you need specialized human knowledge, and the additional benefit of the removal of the human is that the quality improves due to the automation of the process. Once we have the automation and have improved the quality and speed of our deployments, we can then level this up and start to deploy continuously. The benefits of continuous delivery are as follows:

- The releases are smaller and less complicated
- The differences between the master and feature branches are smaller
- There are fewer areas to monitor post deployment
- The rollbacks are potentially easier
- They deliver business value sooner

We start to deploy our code in smaller chunks, no longer after waiting for the completion of a major feature, but potentially after every commit. The primary benefit of this is that the differences between the master and the feature branches are smaller and less time is spent merging code between branches. Smaller changes also create fewer areas to monitor post deployment, and because of this, should something go wrong, it is easier to roll back the changes to a known working state. Most important of all, it gives you the capability to deliver business value sooner; whether this is in the form of a bug or a new feature, the capability is ready for your customers to use far earlier than would be available in a waterfall model.

Aspects of continuous delivery

There area number of aspects of continuous delivery, most of which are essential to the success of the process. In this section, we will look at what these aspects are before we look at how we can implement them to build our own pipeline.

These are the important aspects of continuous delivery:

- Reproducibility and easy setup
- Artifact storage
- Automation of tests
- Automation of integration tests
- Infrastructure as code
- Security scanning

- Static code analysis
- Smoke testing
- End-to-end testing
- Monitoring—tracking deployments in metrics

Reproducibility and consistency

I have little doubt that, at some point in your career, you will have seen this meme:

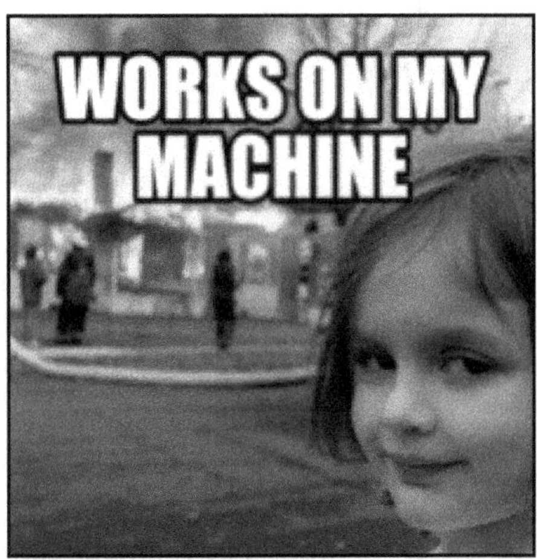

If you have not, don't worry, I am confident you are going to encounter it at some point. Why is this meme so popular? Could it be because there is a heavy element of truth in it? I certainly know that I have been there, and many of you have too, I am sure. If we are to deliver continuously, then we need to care about consistency and reproducibility.

Reproducibility is the ability of the entire analysis of an experiment or study to be duplicated, either by the same researcher or by someone else working independently. *Works on my machine* is not acceptable. If we are to deliver continuously, then we need to codify our build process and make sure that our dependencies for software and other elements are either minimized or managed.

The other thing that is important is the consistency of our builds. We cannot spend time fixing broken builds or manually deploying software, so we must treat them with the same regard that we treat our production code. If the build breaks, we need to stop the line and fix it immediately, understand why the build broke, and if necessary, introduce new safeguards or processes so that it does not occur again.

Artifact storage

When we implement any form of **Continuous Integration** (**CI**), we produce various artifacts because of the build process. The artifacts can range from binaries to the output of tests. We need to consider how we are going to store this data; thankfully, cloud computing has many answers to this problem. One solution is cloud storage, such as AWS S3, which is available in abundance, and at a small cost. Many of the software-as-a-service CI providers such as Travis and CircleCI also offer this capability built into the system; so, for us to leverage it, there is very little we need to do. We can also leverage the same storage if, for example, we are using Jenkins. The existence of the cloud means we rarely need to worry about the management of CI artifacts anymore.

Automation of tests

Test automation is essential, and to ensure the integrity of the built application, we must run our unit tests on the CI platform. Test automation forces us to consider easy and reproducible setup, as well as any dependencies that need minimizing, and the fact that we should only be checking the behavior and integrity of the code. In this step, we avoid integration tests. The tests should run without anything but the `go test` command.

Automation of integration tests

Of course, we do need to verify the integration between our code and any other dependencies, such as a database or downstream service. It is easy to misconfigure something, especially when database statements are involved. The level of integration tests should be far lower than the coverage of the unit tests, and again, we need to be able to run these tests in a reproducible environment. Docker is an excellent ally in this situation; we can leverage the capability of Docker to run in multiple environments. This enables us to configure and debug our integration tests on our local environment before executing them on the build server. In the same way that unit tests are a gate to a successful build, so are integration tests; failure of these tests should never result in a deployment.

Infrastructure as code

When we automate our build and deploy the process, this step is essential; ideally, we do not want to be deploying code to a dirty environment because this raises the risk of pollution, such as an incorrectly vendored dependency. However, we also need to be able to rebuild the environment, if necessary, and this should be possible without enacting any of the problems we introduced earlier.

Security scanning

If possible, security scanning should be integrated into the pipeline; we need to be catching bugs early and often. Regardless of whether your service is external facing or not, scanning it can ensure that there is a limited attack vector for an attacker to misuse. We have looked at fuzzing, and the time it can take to perform this task is quite considerable and possibly not suitable for inclusion inside a pipeline. However, it is possible to include various aspects of security scanning into the pipeline without slowing down deployments.

Static code analysis

Static code analysis is an incredibly effective tool to combat bugs and vulnerabilities in your applications, and developers often run tools such as **govet** and **gofmt** as part of their IDE. When the source is saved, the linter runs and identifies issues in the source code. It is important to run these applications inside the pipeline as well because we cannot always guarantee that the change has come from an IDE that has it configured in this way. In addition to the time-saving linters, we can also run static code analysis to detect problems with SQL statements and code quality. These additional tools are often not included in the IDE's save workflow, and therefore, it is imperative to run them on CI to detect any problems that may have slipped through the net.

Smoke tests

Smoke tests are our way of determining whether a deployment has gone successfully. We run a test, which can range from a simple curl to a more complex codified test, to check various integration points within the running application.

End-to-end tests

End-to-end (**E2E**) tests are a complete check on the running system and typically follow the user flow, testing various parts. Often, these tests are global to the application, not local to the service, and are automated using BDD-based tools such as Cucumber. Determining whether you run E2E tests as a gate to deployment or a parallel process that is either triggered by a deployment or set as a continually running process is dependent upon your company's appetite for risk. If you are confident that your unit, integration, and smoke tests have adequate coverage to give you peace of mind or that the service in question is not essential to the core user journey, then you may decide to run these in parallel. If, however, the functionality in question is part of your core journey, then you may choose to run these tests sequentially as a gateway to deployment on a staging environment. Even when E2E tests run as a gateway, if any configuration changes are made, such as the promotion of staging to production, it is advisable to again run the E2E tests before declaring a deployment successful.

Monitoring

Post deployment, we should not rely on our users to inform us when something has gone wrong, which is why we need application monitoring linked to an automated notification system such as **PagerDuty**. When a threshold of errors has been exceeded, the monitor triggers and alerts you to the problem; this gives you the opportunity to roll back the last deployment or to fix the issue.

Continuous delivery process

So far, we have talked about the problems to be aware of with continuous delivery and why they are so important to understand. We have also looked at the constituent parts of a successful continuous delivery system, but how can we implement such a process for our application, and what does Go provide that helps us with this? Now let's look at the process:

- Build
- Test
- Package
- Integration test
- Benchmark test
- Security test

- Provision production
- Smoke test
- Monitor

Overview

The build process is mainly a focus for developers to get things up and running on their local machine, but my recommendation is that we need to be thinking about cross-platform and cross-system builds from the beginning. What I mean by cross-system builds is that even if we are developing on a Mac, we may not be building a release product for a Mac. In fact, this behavior is quite common. We need our releases built by a third party and preferentially in a clean-room environment that is not going to be affected by pollution from other builds.

Every feature should have a branch and every branch should have a build. Every time your application code is pushed to the source repository, you should trigger the build, even if this code is going nowhere near production. It is good practice never to leave a build in a broken state, and that includes branch builds. You should deal with the issues as and when they occur; delaying this action risks your ability to deploy, and while you may not plan to deploy to production until the end of the sprint, you must consider unforeseen issues that can occur, such as the requirement to change the configuration or hotfix a bug. If the build process is in a broken state, then you will not be able to deal with the immediate issues, and you risk delaying a planned deployment.

The other important aspect, other than automatically triggering a build whenever you push to a branch, is to run a nightly build. Nightly builds for branches should be rebased with the master branch before building and testing. The reason for this step is to give you early warning about potential merge conflicts. We want to catch these earlier rather than later; addressing a failed nightly build should be the first task of the day.

We talked about Docker earlier on in `Chapter 4`, *Testing*, and we should bring Docker into our build process. Docker, through its immutability for a container, gives us the clean room environment required to ensure reproducibility. Because we start from scratch with every build, we cannot rely on a pre-existing state, which causes differences between the development environment and the built environment. Environmental pollution may seem like a trivial thing, but the amount of time I have wasted over my career debugging a broken build because one application was using a dependency installed on a machine and another used a different version is immeasurable.

What is container orchestration?

Simply, container orchestration is the process of running one or more instances of an application. Think of the common understanding of an orchestra: a group of musicians who work together to play a piece of music. The containers in your application are like the musicians in the orchestra. You may have specialist containers, of which there are low numbers of instances, such as the percussionists; or you may have many instances, such as the strings section. In an orchestra, the conductor keeps everything in time and ensures that the relevant musicians are playing the right music at the right time. In the world of containers, we have a scheduler; the scheduler is responsible for ensuring that the correct number of containers are running at any one time and that these containers are distributed correctly across the nodes in the cluster to ensure high availability. The scheduler, like a conductor, is also responsible for ensuring that the right instruments play at the right time. In addition to ensuring a constant suite of applications is constantly running, the scheduler also can start a container at a particular time or based on a particular condition to run ad hoc jobs. This capability is similar to what would be performed by **cron** on a Linux-based system.

Options for container orchestration

Thankfully, today there are many applications that provide an orchestration function. These are broken into two categories: **managed**, including PaaS solutions such as AWS ECS; and **unmanaged**, including open source schedulers such as Kubenetes, which need management of both servers and the scheduler application. Unfortunately, there is no one-size-fits-all solution. The option you choose is dependent on the scale you require and how complex your application is. If you are a start-up or just starting to break out into the world of microservices, then solutions at the more managed end of the spectrum, such as **Elastic Beanstalk**, will more than suffice. If you are planning a large-scale migration, then you might be better looking at a fully fledged scheduler. One thing I am confident about is that by containerizing your applications using Docker, you have this flexibility. Even if you are planning a large-scale migration, then start simple and work up to the complexity. We will examine how the concepts of orchestration and infrastructure as code enable us to complete this. We should never ignore the upfront design and long-term thinking, but we should not let this stop us from moving fast. Just like code, infrastructure can be refactored and upgraded; the important concepts for doing so are patterns and strong foundations.

What is immutable infrastructure?

Immutability is the inability to be changed. We have already looked at Docker and how a Docker container is an immutable instance of an image. However, what about the hardware that the Docker server runs on? Immutable infrastructure gives us the same benefits—we have a known state and that state is consistent across our estate. Traditionally, the software would be upgraded on an application server, but this process was often problematic. The software update process would sometimes not go to plan, leaving the operator with the arduous task of trying to roll it back. We would also experience situations where the application servers would be in different states, requiring different processes to upgrade each of them. The update process may be okay if you only have two application servers, but what if you have 200 of them? The cognitive load becomes so much to bear that the administration is distributed across a team or multiple teams, and then we need to start to maintain documentation to upgrade each of the applications. When we were dealing with bare metal servers, there was often no other way to deal with this; the time it would take to provision a machine was measured in days. With the virtualization, this time improved as it gave us the ability to create a base image, which contained a partial config, and we could then provision new instances in tens of minutes. With the cloud, the level of abstraction became one layer greater; no longer did we even need to worry about the virtualization layer, as we had the capability to spin up compute resources in seconds. So, the cloud solved the process of the hardware, but what about the process of provisioning the applications? Do we still need to write the documentation and keep it up to date? As it happens, we do not. Tooling has been created to allow us to codify our infrastructure and application provisioning. The code becomes the documentation, and because it is code, we can version it using standard version control systems, such as Git. There are many tools to choose from, such as Chef, Puppet, Ansible, and Terraform; however, in this chapter, we will take a look at Terraform because, in my opinion, besides being the most modern of the tools and the easiest to use, it embodies all of the principles of immutability.

Terraform

Terraform (`https://terraform.io`) is an application by HashiCorp (`https://hashicorp.com`) that enables the provisioning of infrastructure for several applications and cloud providers. It allows you to write codified infrastructure using the HCL language format. It enables the concepts of reproducibility and consistency that we have discussed, and that are essential for continuous deployment.

Terraform as an application is a powerful tool and is a bigger topic than this book can cover; however, we will look at the basics of how it works to understand our demo application.

We will split our infrastructure into multiple chunks, with the infrastructure code owned by each microservice located in the source code repository.

In this section, we will look closely at the shared infrastructure and services to get a deeper understanding of the Terraform concepts. Let's take a look at the example code in the following GitHub repository:

`https://github.com/building-microservices-with-go/chapter11-services-main`

The shared infrastructure contains the following components:

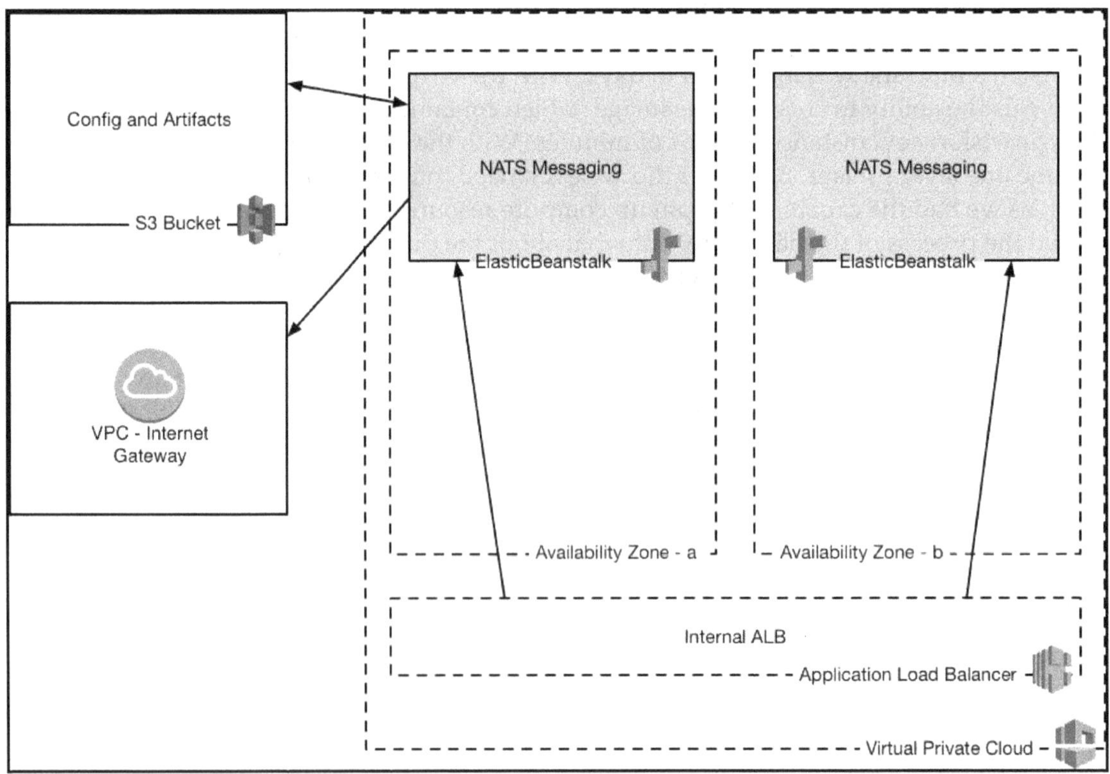

Let's discuss a few components in detail:

- **VPC**: This is the virtual private cloud. It allows all of the applications connected to it to communicate without needing to go over the public internet.

- **S3 bucket**: This is the remote storage for config and artifacts.
- **Elastic Beanstalk**: This is the Elastic Beanstalk application that will run the NATS.io messaging system. We can split this over two availability zones, which are the equivalent to a data center; hosting applications in multiple zones gives us redundancy in the instance that the zone suffers an outage.
- **Internal ALB:** To communicate with our NATS.io server, when we add other applications to our VPC, we need to use an internal **application load balancer** (**ALB**). An internal ALB has the same features as an external load balancer, but it is only accessible to applications that are attached to the VPC. Connections from the public internet are not allowed.
- **Internet gateway:** If we need our application to be able to make outbound calls to other internet services, then we need to attach an internet gateway. For security, a VPC has no outbound connections by default.

Now that we understand the components that we need to create, let's take a look at the Terraform configuration that can create them.

Providers

Terraform is broken up into providers. A provider is responsible for understanding the API interactions and exposing the resources for the chosen platform. In the first section, we will look at the provider configuration for AWS. In the following code, the `provider` block allows you to configure Terraform with your credentials and set an AWS region:

```
provider "aws" {
    access_key = "XXXXXXXXXXX"
    secret_key = "XXXXXXXXXXX"
    region = "us-west-1"
}
```

Blocks in Terraform typically follow the previous pattern. HCL is not JSON; however, it is interoperable with JSON. The design of HCL is to find that balance between machine-and human-readable formats. In this particular provider, we can configure some different arguments; however, as a bare minimum, we must set up your `access_key`, `secret_key`, and `region`. These are explained as follows:

- `access_key`: This is the AWS access key. This is a required argument; however, it may also be provided by setting the `AWS_ACCESS_KEY_ID` environment variable.

- `secret_key`: This is the AWS secret key. This is a required argument; however, it may also be provided by setting the `AWS_SECRET_ACCESS_KEY` environment variable.
- `region`: This is the AWS region. This is a required argument; however, it may also be provided by setting the `AWS_DEFAULT_REGION` environment variable.

All of the required variables can be replaced with environment variables; we do not want to commit our AWS secrets to GitHub, because if they leak, we will most likely find that someone has kindly spun up lots of expensive resources to mine bitcoin (`http://www.securityweek.com/how-hackers-target-cloud-services-bitcoin-profit`).

If we use environment variables, we can then securely inject these into our CI service where they are available for the job. Looking at our provider block, `provider.tf`, we can see that it does not contain any of the settings:

```
provider "aws" { }
```

Also, in this file, you will notice that there is a block by the name of `terraform`. This configuration block allows us to store the Terraform state in an S3 bucket:

```
terraform {
  backend "s3" {
    bucket = "nicjackson-terraform-state"
    key    = "chapter11-main.tfstate"
    region = "eu-west-1"
  }
}
```

The state is what the `terraform` block uses to understand the resources that have been created for a module. Every time you change your configuration and run either of the Terraform plans, Terraform will check the state files for differences to understand what it needs to delete, update, or create. A special note on remote state is that, again, it should never be checked into Git. The remote state contains information about your infrastructure, including potentially secret information, not something you would ever want to leak. For this reason, we can use the remote state, rather than keep the state on our local disk; Terraform saves the state files to a remote backend such as S3. We can even implement locking with certain backends to ensure that only one run of the configuration takes place at any one time. In our config, we are using the AWS S3 backend, which has the following attributes:

- `bucket`: This is the name of the S3 bucket that stores the state. S3 buckets are globally named and are not namespaced to your user account. So, this value must not only be unique to you, but specific to AWS.

- `key`: This is the key of the bucket object that holds the state. This is unique to the bucket. You can use a bucket for multiple Terraform configs as long as this key is unique.
- `region`: This is the region for the S3 bucket.

Terraform config entry point

The main entry point for our application is the `terraform.tf` file. There is no stipulation on this filename; Terraform is graph-based. It recurses through all files that end in `.tf` in our directory and builds up a dependency graph. It does this to understand the order to create resources.

If we look at this file, we see that it is made up of modules. Modules are a way for Terraform to create reusable sections of infrastructure code or just to logically separate things for readability. They are very similar to the concepts of packages in Go:

```
module "vpc" {
  source = "./vpc"

  namespace = "bog-chapter11"
}

module "s3" {
  source = "./s3"

  application_name = "chapter11"
}

module "nats" {
  source = "./nats"

  application_name        = "nats"
  application_description = "Nats.io server"
  application_environment = "dev"

  deployment_bucket    = "${module.s3.deployment_bucket}"
  deployment_bucket_id = "${module.s3.deployment_bucket_id}"

  application_version = "1.1"
  docker_image        = "nats"
  docker_tag          = "latest"

  elb_scheme   = "internal"
  health_check = "/varz"
```

```
  vpc_id  = "${module.vpc.id}"
  subnets = ["${module.vpc.subnets}"]
}
```

Let's take a look at the VPC module in greater depth.

VPC module

The VPC module creates our private network inside AWS; we do not want to or need to expose the NATS server to the outside world, so we can create a private network that only allows the resources attached to that network to access it, as shown in the following code:

```
module "vpc" {
  source = "./vpc"

  namespace = "bog-chapter11"
}
```

The `source` attribute is the location of the module; Terraform supports the following sources:

- Local file paths
- GitHub
- Bitbucket
- Generic Git and Mercurial repositories
- HTTP URLs
- S3 buckets

Following the `source` attribute, we can configure custom attributes, which correspond to the variables in the module. Variables are required placeholders for a module; when they are not present, Terraform complains when we try to run it.

The `vpc/variables.tf` file contains the following content:

```
variable "namespace" {
  description = "The namespace for our module, will be prefixed to all
resources."
}

variable "vpc_cidr_block" {
  description = "The top-level CIDR block for the VPC."
  default     = "10.1.0.0/16"
}
```

```
variable "cidr_blocks" {
  description = "The CIDR blocks to create the workstations in."
  default     = ["10.1.1.0/24", "10.1.2.0/24"]
}
```

The configuration for a variable is very much like that of the provider, and it follows the following syntax:

```
variable "[name]" {
  [config]
}
```

A variable has three possible configuration options:

- `type`: This is an optional attribute that sets the type of the variable. The valid values are `string`, `list`, and `map`. If no value is given, then the type is assumed to be `string`.
- `default`: This is an optional attribute to set the default value for the variable.
- `description`: This is an optional attribute to assign a human-friendly description for the variable. The primary purpose of this attribute is for documentation of your Terraform configuration.

Variables can be explicitly declared inside a `terraform.tfvars` file like the one in the root of our repository:

```
namespace = "chapter10-bog"
```

We can also set an environment variable by prefixing `TF_VAR_` to the name of the variable:

```
export TF_VAR_namespace=chapter10-bog
```

Alternatively, we can include the variable in the command when we run the `terraform` command:

```
terraform plan -var namespace=chapter10-bog
```

We are configuring the namespace of the application and the IP address block allocated to the network. If we look at the file that contains the VPC blocks, we can see how this is used.

The `vpc/vpc.tf` file contains the following content:

```
# Create a VPC to launch our instances into
resource "aws_vpc" "default" {
  cidr_block           = "${var.vpc_cidr_block}"
  enable_dns_hostnames = true
```

```
  tags {
    "Name" = "${var.namespace}"
  }
}
```

A `resource` block is a Terraform syntax that defines a resource in AWS and has the following syntax:

```
resource "[resource_type]" "[resource_id]" {
    [config]
}
```

Resources in Terraform map to the objects needed for the API calls in the AWS SDK. If you look at the `cidr_block` attribute, you will see that we are referencing the variable using the Terraform interpolation syntax:

```
cidr_block = "${var.vpc_cidr_block}"
```

Interpolation syntax is a metaprogramming language inside of Terraform. It allows you to manipulate variables and the output from resources and is defined using the `${[interpolation]}` syntax. We are using the variables collection, which is prefixed by `var` and references the `vpc_cidr_block` variable. When Terraform runs `${var.vpc_cidr_block}`, it will be replaced with the `10.1.0.0/16` value from our variable's file.

Creating a VPC that has external internet access in AWS consists of four parts:

- `aws_vpc`: This is a private network for our instances.
- `aws_internet_gateway`: This is a gateway attached to our VPC to allow internet access.
- `aws_route`: This is the routing table entry to map to the gateway.
- `aws_subnet`: This is a subnet that our instances launch into—we create one subnet for each availability zone.

This complexity is not because of Terraform but AWS. The other cloud providers have very similar complexity, and unfortunately, it is unavoidable. It feels daunting at first; however, there are some amazing resources out there.

The next part of the VPC setup is to configure the internet gateway:

```
# Create an internet gateway to give our subnet access to the outside world
resource "aws_internet_gateway" "default" {
  vpc_id = "${aws_vpc.default.id}"

  tags {
    "Name" = "${var.namespace}"
  }
}
```

Again, we have a similar format as the `aws_vpc` block; however, in this block, we need to set the `vpc_id` block, which needs to refer to the VPC setup created in the previous block. We can again use the Terraform interpolation syntax to find this reference even though it has not yet been created. The `aws_vpc.default.id` reference has the following form, which is common across all resources in Terraform:

```
[resource].[name].[attribute]
```

When we reference another block in Terraform, it also tells the dependency graph that the referenced block needs to be created before this block. In this way, Terraform is capable of organizing which resources can be set up in parallel and those that need to have an exact order. We do not need to declare the order ourselves; when the graph is created, it automatically builds this for us.

The next block sets up the routing table for the VPC, enabling outbound access to the public internet:

```
# Grant the VPC Internet access on its main route table
resource "aws_route" "internet_access" {
  route_table_id         = "${aws_vpc.default.main_route_table_id}"
  destination_cidr_block = "0.0.0.0/0"
  gateway_id             = "${aws_internet_gateway.default.id}"
}
```

Let's take a look at the attributes in this block in a little more detail:

- `route_table_id`: This is the reference to the routing table we would like to create a new reference for. We can obtain this from the `main_route_table_id` output attribute from `aws_vpc`.
- `destination_cidr_block`: This is the IP range of the instances that will be connected to the VPC that can send traffic to the gateway. We are using the block `0.0.0.0/0`, which allows all the connected instances. If required, we could only allow external access to certain IP ranges.
- `gateway_id`: This is a reference to the gateway block we previously created.

The next block introduces a new concept for us: data sources. Data sources allow data to be fetched or computed from information stored outside Terraform or stored in a separate Terraform configuration. A data source may look up for information in AWS. For example, you can query a list of existing EC2 instances that may exist in your account. You can also query other providers. For instance, you might have a DNS entry in CloudFlare that you would like the details for, or even the address of a load balancer in a different cloud provider, such as Google or Azure.

We will use data sources to retrieve the lists of availability zones in AWS. When we create the VPC, we need to create a subnet in each availability zone. Because we are only configuring the region, we have not set the availability zones for that region. We could explicitly configure these in the variables section; however, that makes our config more brittle. The best way, whenever possible, is to use data blocks:

```
# Grab the list of availability zones
data "aws_availability_zones" "available" {}
```

The configuration is quite simple and again follows a common syntax:

```
data [resource] "[name]"
```

We will make use of this information in the final part of the VPC setup, which is to configure the subnets; this also introduces another new Terraform feature, `count`:

```
# Create a subnet to launch our instances into
resource "aws_subnet" "default" {
  count                   = "${length(var.cidr_blocks)}"
  vpc_id                  = "${aws_vpc.default.id}"
  availability_zone       =
"${data.aws_availability_zones.available.names[count.index]}"
  cidr_block              = "${var.cidr_blocks[count.index]}"
  map_public_ip_on_launch = true

  tags {
    "Name" = "${var.namespace}"
  }
}
```

Let's look closely at the `count` attribute. A `count` attribute is a special attribute that, when set, creates *n* instances of the resource. The value of our attribute also expands on the interpolation syntax that we examined earlier to introduce the `length` function:

```
# cidr_blocks = ["10.1.1.0/24", 10.1.2.0/24"]
${length(var.cidr_blocks)}
```

`cidr_blocks` is a Terraform list. In Go, this would be a slice, and `length` will return the number of elements inside a list. For comparison, let's look at how we would write this in Go:

```
cidrBlocks := []string {"10.1.1.0/24", "10.1.2.0/24"}
elements := len(cidrBlocks)
```

Interpolation syntax in Terraform is an amazing feature, allowing you to manipulate variables with many built-in functions. The documentation for the interpolation syntax can be found at the following location:

`https://www.terraform.io/docs/configuration/interpolation.html`

We also have the ability to use conditional statements. One of the best features of the `count` function is that if you set it to `0`, Terraform omits the creation of a resource; as an example, it would allow us to write something like the following:

```
resource "aws_instance" "web" {
  count = "${var.env == "production" ? 1 : 0}"
}
```

The syntax for conditionals uses the ternary operation, which is present in many languages:

```
CONDITION ? TRUEVAL : FALSEVAL
```

When we use `count` in Terraform, it also provides us with an index, which we can use to obtain the correct element from a list. Consider how we are using this in the `availability_zone` attribute:

```
availability_zone =
"${data.aws_availability_zones.available.names[count.index]}"
```

`count.index` will provide us with a zero-based index, and because `data.aws_availability_zones.available.names` returns a list, we can use to access list like a slice. Let's take a look at the remaining attributes on our `aws_subnet`:

- `vpc_id`: This is the ID of the VPC that we created in an earlier block and we would like to attach the the subnet.
- `availability_zone`: This is the name of the availability zone for the subnet.
- `cidr_block`: This is the IP range of addresses that will be given to an instance when we launch it in this particular VPC and availability zone.

- `map_public_ip_on_launch`: Whether we should attach a public IP address to the instance when it is created, this is an optional parameter, and determines whether your instance should also have a public IP address in addition to the private one that is allocated from the `cidr_block` attribute.

Output variables

When we are building modules in Terraform, we often need to reference attributes from other modules. There is a clean separation between modules, which means that they cannot directly access another module resources. For example, in this module, we are creating a VPC, and later on, we would like to create an EC2 instance that is attached to this VPC. We could not use the syntax as shown in the upcoming code.

The `module2/terraform.tf` file contains the following content:

```
resource "aws_instance" "web" {
# ...
    vpc_id = "${aws_vpc.default.id}"
}
```

The previous example would result in an error because we are trying to reference a variable that does not exist in this module, even though it does exist in your global Terraform config. Consider these to be like Go packages. If we had the two following Go packages which contained non-exported variables. Have a look at the following code snippet for package `a`:

```
package a

var notExported = "Some Value"
```

Refer to the following code snippet for package `b`:

```
package b

func doSomething() {
    // invalid reference
    if a.notExported == "Some Value {
        //...
    }
}
```

In Go, we could, of course, have the variable exported by capitalizing the name of the `notExported` variable to `NotExported`. To achieve the same in Terraform, we use output variables:

```
output "id" {
  value = "${aws_vpc.default.id}"
}

output "subnets" {
  value = ["${aws_subnet.default.*.id}"]
}

output "subnet_names" {
  value = ["${aws_subnet.default.*.arn}"]
}
```

The syntax should be starting to get familiar to you now:

```
output "[name]" {
    value = "..."
}
```

We can then use the output of one module to be the input of another—here's an example found in the `terraform.tf` file:

```
module "nats" {
  source = "./nats"

  application_name        = "nats"
  application_description = "Nats.io server"
  application_environment = "dev"

  deployment_bucket    = "${module.s3.deployment_bucket}"
  deployment_bucket_id = "${module.s3.deployment_bucket_id}"

  application_version = "1.1"
  docker_image        = "nats"
  docker_tag          = "latest"

  elb_scheme   = "internal"
  health_check = "/varz"

  vpc_id  = "${module.vpc.id}"
  subnets = ["${module.vpc.subnets}"]
}
```

The vpc_id attribute is referencing an output from the vpc module:

```
vpc_id   = "${module.vpc.id}"
```

The syntax for the preceding statement is as follows:

```
module.[module name].[output variable]
```

In addition to allowing us to keep our code dry and clean, output variables and module references allow Terraform to build its dependency graph. In this instance, Terraform knows that because there is a reference to the vpc module from the nats module, it needs to create the vpc module resources before the nats module. This might feel like a lot of information, and it is. I did not say infrastructure as code was easy, but by the time we get to the end of this example, it will start to become clear. Applying these concepts to create other resources becomes quite straightforward, with the only complexity being how the resource works, not the Terraform configuration that is needed to create it.

Creating the infrastructure

To run Terraform and to create our infrastructure, we must first set some environment variables:

```
$ export AWS_SECRET_ID=[your aws secret id]
$ export AWS_SECRET_ACCESS_KEY=[your aws access key]
$ export AWS_DEFAULT_REGION=[aws region to create resource]
```

We then need to initialize Terraform to reference the modules and remote data store. We normally only need to perform this step whenever we first clone the repository, or if we make changes to the modules:

```
$ terraform init
```

The next step is to run a plan; we use the plan command in Terraform to understand which resources are created, updated, or deleted by the apply command. It will also syntax check our config without creating any resources:

```
$ terraform plan -out=main.terraform
```

The -out argument saves the plan to the main.terraform file. This is an optional step, but if we run apply with the output from the plan, we can ensure that nothing changes from when we inspected and approved the output of the plan command. To create the infrastructure, we can then run the apply command:

```
$ terraform apply main.terraform
```

The first argument to the `apply` command is the `plan` output, which we created in the previous step. Terraform now creates your resources in AWS. This can take anything from a few seconds to 30 minutes, depending upon the type of resource you are creating. Once the creation is complete, Terraform writes the output variables, which we defined in the `output.tf` file, to `stdout`.

We have only covered one of the modules in our main infrastructure project. I recommend that you read through the remaining modules and familiarize yourself with both the Terraform code and the AWS resources it is creating. Excellent documentation is available on the Terraform website (`https://terraform.io`) and the AWS website.

Example application

Our sample application is a simple distributed system consisting of three services. The three main services, product, search, and authentication, have a dependency on a database that they use to store their state. For simplicity, we are using MySQL; however, in a real production environment, you would want to choose the most appropriate data store for your use case. The three services are connected via the messaging system for which we are using NATS.io, which is a provider-agnostic system that we looked at in `Chapter 9`, *Event-Driven Architecture*:

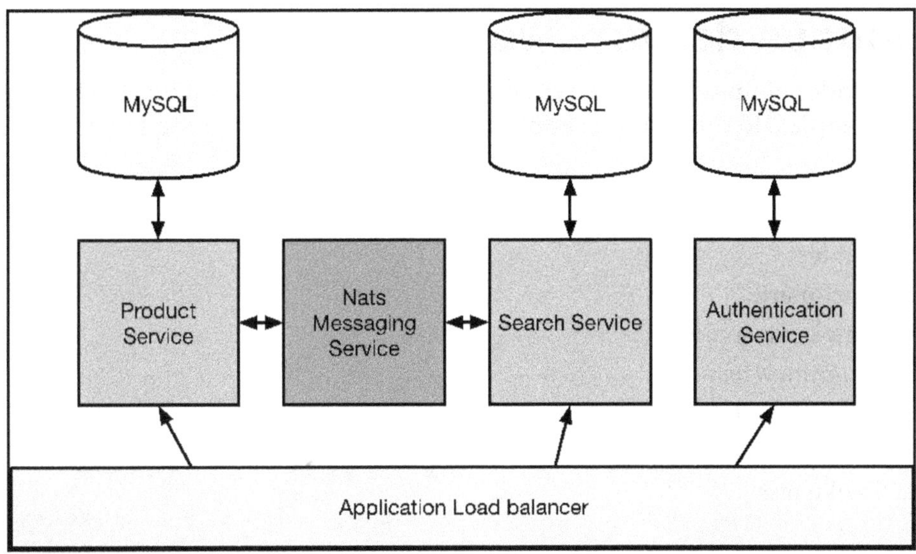

To provision this system, we have broken down the infrastructure and source code into four separate repositories:

- **Shared infrastructure and services** (`https://github.com/building-microservices-with-go/chapter11-services-main`)
- **Authentication service** (`https://github.com/building-microservices-with-go/chapter11-services-auth`)
- **Product service** (`https://github.com/building-microservices-with-go/chapter11-services-product`)
- **Search service** (`https://github.com/building-microservices-with-go/chapter11-services-search`)

The individual repositories enable us to separate our application in such a way that we only build and deploy the components that change. The shared infrastructure repository contains Terraform configuration to create a shared network and components to create the NATS.io server. The authentication service creates a JWT-based authentication microservice and contains separate Terraform configuration to deploy the service to Elastic Beanstalk. The product service and the search service repositories also each contain a microservice and Terraform infrastructure configuration. All the services are configured to build and deploy using Circle CI.

Continuous delivery workflow

For the remainder of this chapter, we concentrate on the search service as the build pipeline is the most complex. In our example application, we have the following steps to build a pipeline:

1. Compile application
2. Unit test
3. Benchmark
4. Static code analysis
5. Integration test
6. Build Docker image
7. Deploy application
8. Smoke test

Many of these steps are independent and can run in parallel, so when we compose the pipeline, it looks like the following diagram:

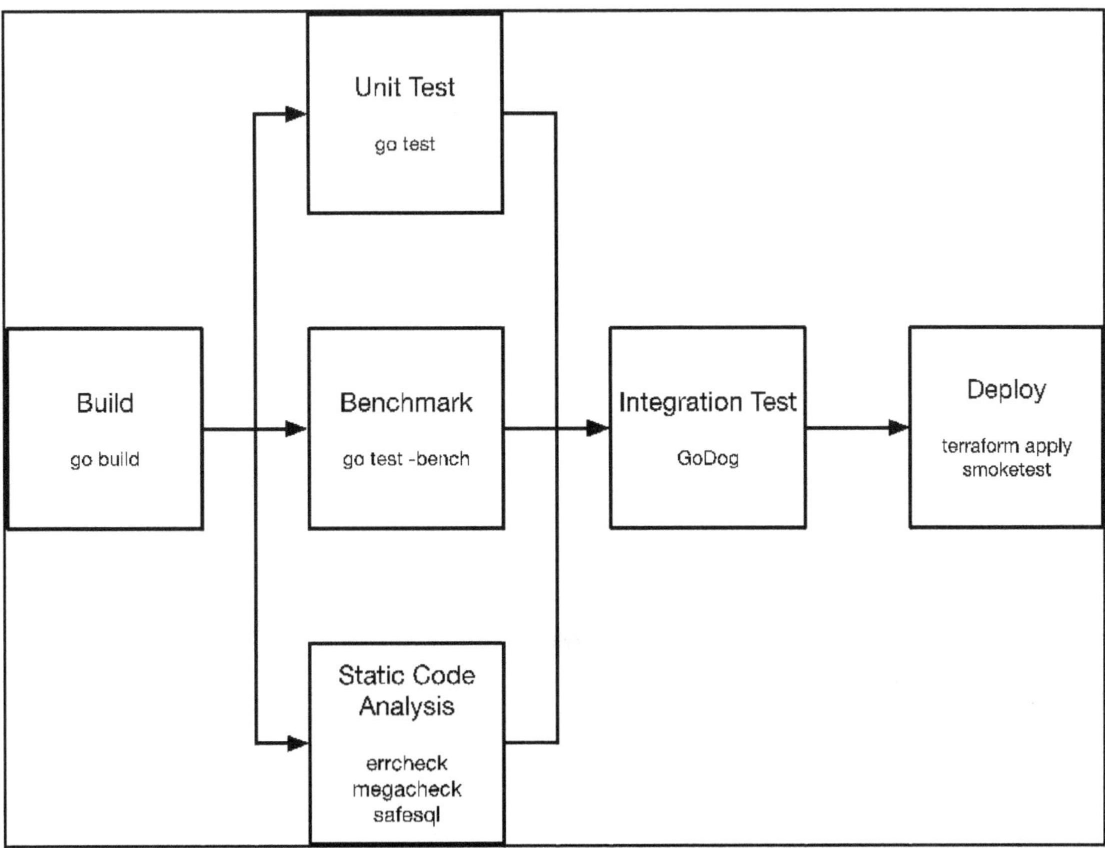

Take a look at the example code at `https://github.com/building-microservices-with-go/chapter11-services-auth`. We are building this application with Circle CI; however, the concepts apply to whatever platform you use. If we look at the `circleci/config.yml` file, we see that we are first setting up the configuration for the process, which includes choosing the version of the Docker container within which the build executes and installs some initial dependencies. We then compose the jobs that are performed in the workflow and the various steps for each of the jobs:

```
defaults: &defaults
  docker:
    # CircleCI Go images available at:
https://hub.docker.com/r/circleci/golang/
```

```
    - image: circleci/golang:1.8

  working_directory: /go/src/github.com/building-microservices-with-
go/chapter11-services-search

  environment:
    TEST_RESULTS: /tmp/test-results

version: 2
jobs:
  build:
    <<: *defaults

    steps:
      - checkout

      - run:
          name: Install dependencies
          command: |
            go get github.com/Masterminds/glide
            glide up
      - run:
          name: Build application for Linux
          command: make build_linux
      - persist_to_workspace:
          root: /go/src/github.com/building-microservices-with-go/
          paths:
            - chapter11-services-search
# ...
workflows:
  version: 2
  build_test_and_deploy:
    jobs:
      - build
      - unit_test:
          requires:
            - build
      - benchmark:
          requires:
            - build
      - staticcheck:
          requires:
            - build
      - integration_test:
          requires:
            - build
            - unit_test
            - benchmark
```

```
            - staticcheck
      - deploy:
          requires:
            - integration_test
```

Finally, we will compose these jobs into a workflow or a pipeline. This workflow defines the relationship between the steps as there are obvious dependencies.

To isolate dependencies in our configuration and to ensure that the commands for building and testing are consistent across various processes, the commands have been placed into the Makefile in the root of the repository:

```
start_stack:
    docker-compose up -d

circleintegration:
    docker build -t circletemp -f ./IntegrationDockerfile .
    docker-compose up -d
    docker run -network chapter11servicessearch_default -w
/go/src/github.com/building-microservices-with-go/chapter11-services-
search/features -e "MYSQL_CONNECTION=root:password@tcp(mysql:3306)/kittens"
circletemp godog ./
    docker-compose stop
    docker-compose rm -f

integration: start_stack
    cd features &&
MYSQL_CONNECTION="root:password@tcp(${DOCKER_IP}:3306)/kittens" godog ./
    docker-compose stop
    docker-compose rm -f

unit:
    go test -v -race $(shell go list ./... | grep -v /vendor/)

staticcheck:
    staticcheck $(shell go list ./... | grep -v /vendor/)

safesql:
    safesql github.com/building-microservices-with-go/chapter11-services-
search

benchmark:
    go test -bench=. github.com/building-microservices-with-go/chapter11-
services-search/handlers

build_linux:
    CGO_ENABLED=0 GOOS=linux go build -o ./search .
```

```
build_docker:
    docker build -t buildingmicroserviceswithgo/search .

run: start_stack
    go run main.go
    docker-compose stop

test: unit benchmark integration
```

Build

Let's take a closer look at the build process. Inside the build job configuration, we have three steps. The first is to check out the repository. The jobs themselves are broken up into steps, and the first notable one of these is to install the dependencies. Glide is our package manager for the repository, and we need this to be installed to fetch updates to our vendored packages. We also need a `go-junit-report` utility package. This application allows us to convert the Go test output into JUnit format, which Circle CI requires for presenting certain dashboard information. We then execute `glide up` to fetch any updates. In this example, I have checked in the `vendor` folder to the repository; however, I am not pinning the packages to a version. You should set a minimum package version rather than an exact package version. Updating your packages frequently allows you to take advantage of regular releases in the open source community. You do, of course, run the risk that there will be a breaking change in a package and that change may break the build, but as mentioned earlier, it is better to catch this as soon as possible rather than deal with the problem when you are under pressure to release.

Because we are building for production, we need to create a Linux binary, which is why we are setting the `GOOS=linux` environment variable before running the build. Setting the environment is redundant when we are running the build on Circle CI as we are already running in a Linux-based Docker container; however, to enable cross-platform builds from our developer machines, if they are not Linux-based, it is useful to have a common command.

Once we have built our application, we need to persist the workspace so that the other jobs can use this. In Circle CI, we use the special step, `persist_to_workspace`; however, this capability is common to pipeline-based workflows:

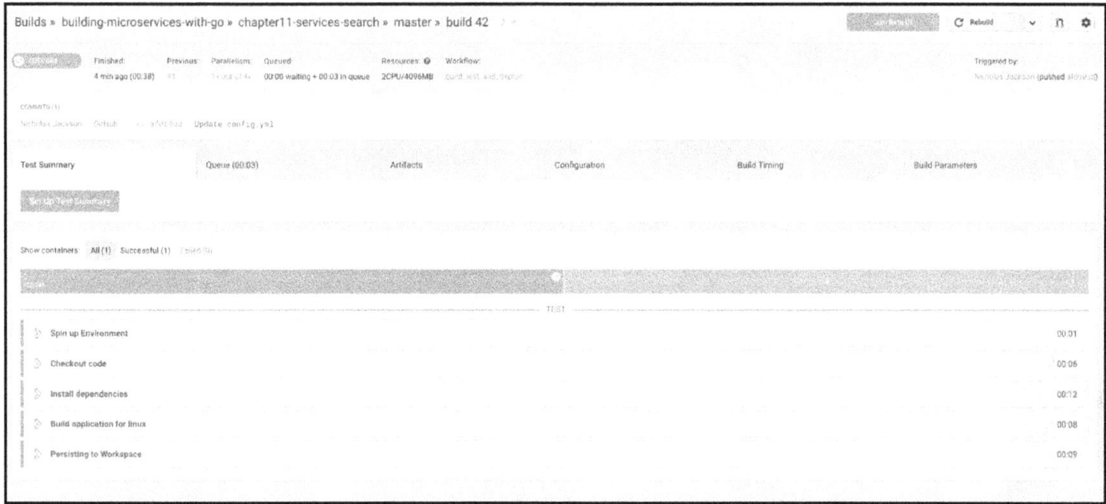

Testing

We also mentioned the fact that we need consistency and that, if we are deploying continuously, we need to have a good solid testing suite that replaces almost all our manual testing. I am not saying there is no place for manual testing because there is always a use for exploratory testing, but when we are deploying continuously, we need to automate all of this. Even if you are adding manual testing into your process, it will be most likely running as an asynchronous process complimentary to your build pipeline, not as a gate to it.

The testing section of the configuration runs our unit tests, as we saw in `Chapter 4`, *Testing*. With the following configuration, we first need to attach the workspace that we created in the build step. The reason for this is that we do not need to check out the repository again:

```
unit_test:
    <<: *defaults
    steps:
      - attach_workspace:
          at: /go/src/github.com/building-microservices-with-go
      - run: mkdir -p $TEST_RESULTS
      - run:
          name: Install dependencies
```

```
            command:  go get github.com/jstemmer/go-junit-report
        - run:
            name: Run unit tests
            command: |
              trap "go-junit-report <${TEST_RESULTS}/go-test.out >
${TEST_RESULTS}/go-test-report.xml" EXIT
              make unit | tee ${TEST_RESULTS}/go-test.out

        - store_test_results:
            path: /tmp/test-results
```

The second thing we need to do is to install the dependencies. Circle CI requires the output of the tests to be in JUnit format for presentation. To enable this, we can fetch the `go-junit-report` package, which can take the output of our tests and convert them into JUnit format.

To run the tests, we have to do something slightly different. If we just ran our unit tests and piped them into the `go-junit-report` command, then we would lose the output. Reading the command in reverse order, we run our unit tests and output `make unit | tee ${TEST_RESULTS}/go-test.out`; the `tee` command takes the input piped to it and writes to both the output file specified as well as to the `stdout` file. We can then use `trap`, which executes a command when an exit code is matched from another command. In our instance, if the unit tests exit with a status code `0` (normal condition), then we execute the `go-junit-report` command. Finally, we write our test results for Circle CI to be able to interpret them using the `store_test_results` step.

Benchmarking

Benchmarking is an important feature for our CI pipeline; we need to understand when the performance of our application degrades. To do this, we are going to both run our benchmark tests and use the handy **benchcmp** tool, which compares two runs of tests. The standard version of `benchcmp` only outputs the difference between two test runs. While this is fine for comparison, it does not give us the ability to fail our CI job should this difference be within a certain threshold. To enable this ability, I have forked the `benchcmp` tool and added `flag-tollerance=[FLOAT]`. If any of the benchmarks change within the given tolerance, then benchcmp exits with status code `1`, allowing us to fail the job and investigate why this change has taken place. For this to work, we need to keep the previous benchmark data available for comparison, so we can use the caching feature to store the last run data.

Static code analysis

Static code analysis is a fast and efficient way to check for any problems in our source code automatically. In our example, we will run two different static code analysis tools. The first is **megacheck** by Dominik Honnef, which examines the code for common problems such as misuse of the standard library and concurrency issues.

The second is **SafeSQL** from the Stripe team. SafeSQL runs through our code and looks for uses of the SQL package. It then examines the ones looking for vulnerabilities such as incorrectly constructed queries, which may be open to SQL injection.

Lastly, we will be checking our code, including the tests for unhandled errors. For example, you have the following function:

```
func DoSomething() (*Object, error)
```

When invoking a method like this, the error object can be thrown away and not handled:

```
obj, _ := DoSomething()
```

Unhandled errors are more often found in tests rather than the main body of code; however, even in tests, this could introduce a bug due to unhandled behavior.
Now, `errcheck` runs through the code looking for instances like this, reports an error when it finds one, and fails the build:

```
staticcheck:
    <<: *defaults

    steps:
      - attach_workspace:
          at: /go/src/github.com/building-microservices-with-go

      - run:
          name: Install dependencies
          command: |
            go get honnef.co/go/tools/cmd/staticcheck
            go get github.com/stripe/safesql

      - run:
          name: Static language checks
          command: make staticcheck

      - run:
          name: Safe SQL checks
          command: make safesql

        - run:
```

```
            name: Check for unhandled errors
            command: make errcheck
```

`staticcheck` invokes the `megacheck` linter, which runs `staticcheck`, a static code analysis tool that helps to detect bugs; GoSimple, which identifies areas of the source code that should be improved by re-writing in a simpler way; and `unused`, which identifies unused constants, types, and functions. The first checker is designed to spot bugs; however, the remaining three are concerned with your application life cycle management.

Clean code is essential to bug-free code; the easier and the simpler your code, the lower the likelihood that you have logic bugs. Why? Because the code is easier to understand, and since you spend more of your time reading code than writing it, it makes sense to optimize for readability. Static code analysis should not be a replacement for the code review. However, these tools allow you to focus on logic flaws rather than semantics. Integrating this into your continuous integration pipeline acts as a gatekeeper to the sanity of your code base. The checks run incredibly quickly and, in my humble opinion, are an essential step (`https://github.com/dominikh/go-tools/tree/master/cmd/megacheck`).

SafeSQL from the Stripe team is a static code analysis tool that protects against SQL injections. It attempts to find problems with the use of the `database/sql` package (`https://github.com/stripe/safesql`).

Integration tests

Then there are integration tests. In this example, we are again using GoDog BDD; however, when we are running on Circle CI, we need to modify our setup a little because of the way that Circle CI deals with security for Docker. The first steps are again to attach the workspace, including the binary that we built in a previous step (in the *Build* section); then we can get the dependencies, which are only the GoDog application. The `setup_remote_docker` command requests a Docker instance from Circle CI. The current build is running in a Docker container; however, because of the security configuration, we cannot access the Docker host, which is currently running the current build:

```
circleintegration:
    docker build -t circletemp -f ./IntegrationDockerfile .
    docker-compose up -d
    docker run -network chapter11servicessearch_default -w
/go/src/github.com/building-microservices-with-go/chapter11-services-
search/features -e "MYSQL_CONNECTION=root:password@tcp(mysql:3306)/kittens"
circletemp godog ./
    docker-compose stop
    docker-compose rm -f
```

The section of the Makefile for running on Circle CI is quite a bit more complex than when we run it on our local machine. We need this modification because we need to copy the source code and install the `godog` command to a container, which will be running on the same network as the stack we start with Docker Compose. When we are running locally, this is not necessary because we have the capability to connect to the network. This access is forbidden on Circle CI and most likely other shared continuous integration environments:

```
FROM golang:1.8

COPY . /go/src/github.com/building-microservices-with-go/chapter11-
services-search
RUN go get github.com/DATA-DOG/godog/cmd/godog
```

We build our temporary container, which contains the current directory and adds the `godog` dependency. We can then start the stack as normal by running `docker-compose up` and then the `godog` command.

Integration tests on continuous delivery are an essential gate before we deploy to production. We also want to be able to test our Docker image to ensure that the startup process is functioning correctly and that we have tested all our assets. When we looked at integration tests in `Chapter 4`, *Testing*, we were only running the application, which is fine for our development process—it gives us the happy medium of quality and speed. When it comes to building our production images, however, this compromise is not acceptable, and therefore we need to make some modifications to the development process to ensure that we include the production image in our test plan.

Deployment

Since we have all our application code build, tested and packaged, it is time to think about deploying it into production. We need to start thinking about our infrastructure as immutable; that is, we will not make changes to the infrastructure but replace it instead. The levels at which this occurs can be many. For example, we have our container scheduler, which only runs the containers. When we deploy an update to our application binary, we are replacing a container on the scheduler, not refreshing the application in it. Containers give us one level of immutability; the other is the scheduler itself. To operate successful continuous delivery, the setup of this facet also needs to be automated. We need to think of our infrastructure as code.

For our application, we are splitting the infrastructure up into separate parts. We have the main infrastructure repository, which creates the VPC; the S3 buckets used by deployments, and an Elastic Beanstalk instance for our messaging platform, NATS.io.

We also have Terraform config for each of the services. We could create one massive Terraform config because Terraform replaces or destroys infrastructure that has changed; however, there are several reasons why we would not want this. The first is that we want to be able to break down our infrastructure code into small parts in the same way we break up our application code; the second is due to the way Terraform works. To ensure the consistency of the state, we can only run a single operation against the infrastructure code at any one time. Terraform obtains a lock when it runs to ensure that you cannot run it multiple times at once. If we consider a situation where there are many microservices and these services are being continuously deployed, then having a single deployment that is single-threaded becomes a terrible thing. When we decompose the infrastructure configuration and localize it with each service, then this is no longer a problem. One problem with this distributed configuration is that we still need a method of accessing resource information in the master repository. In our case, we are creating the main VPC in this repository, and we need the details to be able to connect our microservices to it. Thankfully, Terraform manages rather pleasantly using the concept of remote state:

```
terraform {
  backend "s3" {
    bucket = "nicjackson-terraform-state"
    key    = "chapter11-main.tfstate"
    region = "eu-west-1"
  }
}
```

We can configure our master Terraform config to use remote state, which we can then access from the search Terraform config using the `remote_state` data element:

```
data "terraform_remote_state" "main" {
  backend = "s3"

  config {
    bucket = "nicjackson-terraform-state"
    key    = "chapter11-main.tfstate"
    region = "eu-west-1"
  }
}
```

When all the previous steps in the build process complete, we deploy this to AWS automatically. This way we always deploy every time a new instance of the master branch builds.

Smoke tests

Smoke testing the application post deployment is an essential step in continuous delivery. We need to ensure that the application is functioning correctly and that nothing has gone wrong in the build and deployment steps. In our example, we are simply checking that we can reach the health endpoint. However, a smoke test can be as simple or as complex as required. Many organizations run more detail checks, which confirm that the core integration to the deployed system is correct and functioning. The smoke tests are conducted as either a codified test reusing many of the steps in the GoDog integration tests, or a specialized test. In our example, we are simply checking the health endpoint for the `search` service:

```
- run:
          name: Smoke test
          command: |
            cd terraform
            curl $(terraform output search_alb)/health
```

In our application, we can run this test because the endpoint is public. When an endpoint is not public, testing becomes more complicated, and we need to check the integration by calling through a public endpoint.

One of the considerations for E2E testing is that you need to be careful of polluting the data inside the production database. A complimentary or even alternative approach is to ensure that your system has extensive logging and monitoring. We can set up dashboards and alerts, which actively check for user errors. When an issue occurs post deploy, we can investigate the problem, and if necessary, rollback to a previous version of the build with a known good state.

Monitoring/alerting

When the application is running, we need to be sure of the health and status of the application. Monitoring is an incredibly important facet of the continuous deployment life cycle. If we are deploying automatically, we need to understand how our application is performing and how this differs from the previous release. We have seen how we can use StatsD to emit data about our service to a backend such as Prometheus, or a managed application such as Datadog. Should our recent deploy exhibit anomalous behavior, we are alerted, and from there we can act to help identify the source of the problem, intermittently rolling back if necessary or modifying our alerts because our server may just be doing more work:

```
# Create a new Datadog timeboard
resource "datadog_timeboard" "search" {
  title       = "Search service Timeboard (created via Terraform)"
  description = "created using the Datadog provider in Terraform"
  read_only   = true

  graph {
    title = "Authentication"
    viz   = "timeseries"

    request {
      q    = "sum:chapter11.auth.jwt.badrequest{*}"
      type = "bars"

      style {
        palette = "warm"
      }
    }

    request {
      q    = "sum:chapter11.auth.jwt.success{*}"
      type = "bars"
    }
  }

  graph {
    title = "Health Check"
    viz   = "timeseries"

    request {
      q    = "sum:chapter11.auth.health.success{*}"
      type = "bars"
    }
  }
}
```

Again, using the concepts of infrastructure as code, we can provision these monitors at build time using Terraform. While errors are useful for monitoring, it is also important to not forget timing data. An error tells you that something is going wrong; however, with the clever use of timing information in the service, we can learn that something is about to go wrong.

Complete workflow

Assuming all is functioning well, we should have a successful build, and the UI in our build environment should show all steps passing. Remember our warning from the beginning of this chapter—when your build fails, you need to make it your primary objective to fix it; you never know when you are going to need it:

Diagram showing the complete workflow

Summary

In this chapter, we have learned that it need not be an arduous task to set up Continuous Integration and Deployment for your application, and in fact, it is essential to the health and success of your application. We have built on all the concepts covered in the previous chapters, and while the final example is somewhat simple, it has all the constituent parts for you to build into your applications to ensure that you spend your time developing new features and not fixing production issues or wasting time repetitively and riskily deploying application code. Like all aspects of development, we should practice and test this process. Before releasing continuous delivery to your production workflow, you need to ensure that you can deal with problems such as hotfixing and rolling back a release. This activity should be completed across teams and, depending on your process for out-of-hours support, should also involve any support staff. A well-practiced and functioning deployment process gives you the confidence that when an issue occurs, and it most likely will, you can comfortably deal with it.

I hope that by working through this book, you now have a greater understanding of most of the things you need to build microservices with Go successfully. The one thing I cannot teach is the experience that you need to gain for yourself by getting out there and performing. I wish you luck on this journey, and the one thing that I have learned from my career is that you never regret putting in the time and effort to learn these techniques. I am sure you will be hugely successful.

Index

D

E

F

G

H

N

O

P

Q

R

S

T

U

V

W

X

www.ingramcontent.com/pod-product-compliance
Lightning Source LLC
Chambersburg PA
CBHW062053050326
40690CB00016B/3079
9781786468666